Cather and Opera

DAVID MCKAY POWELL

Cather and Opera

Louisiana State University Press

Baton Rouge

Published by Louisiana State University Press
lsupress.org

Manufactured in the United States of America
First printing

DESIGNER: Mandy McDonald Scallan
TYPEFACE: Adobe Caslon Pro

Cover image: Willa Cather as Electra, ca. 1894. Philip L. and Helen Cather
Southwick Collection (MS 77). Archives and Special Collections, University of
Nebraska–Lincoln Libraries.

Library of Congress Cataloging-in-Publication Data

Names: Powell, David McKay, author.
Title: Cather and opera / David McKay Powell.
Description: Baton Rouge : Louisiana State University Press, [2022] |
    Includes bibliographical references and index.
Identifiers: LCCN 2021047181 (print) | LCCN 2021047182 (ebook) | ISBN
    978-0-8071-7711-2 (cloth) | ISBN 978-0-8071-7779-2 (pdf) | ISBN
    978-0-8071-7780-8 (epub)
Subjects: LCSH: Cather, Willa, 1873–1947—Criticism and interpretation. |
    Opera in literature. | Music and literature.
Classification: LCC PS3505.A87 Z776 2022 (print) | LCC PS3505.A87 (ebook)
    | DDC 813/.52—dc23/eng/20211006
LC record available at https://lccn.loc.gov/2021047181
LC ebook record available at https://lccn.loc.gov/2021047182

For Presley,
who likes to write and sing

CONTENTS

Cather and Opera

✾

CATHER AND OPERA

Serpolette: You horrid old miser—who then, am I?
Gaspard: Why only Serpolette, the mischief-maker of the village—
a peasant's daughter, that is all!
—*The Chimes of Normandy*, the first opera Cather
saw performed on stage, December 1888

*J*t is a truth universally acknowledged that a frontier town in possession of the basic needs of survival must be in want of an opera house. While "opera" tends to conjure grand auditoria in large coastal cities attended by nobs and swells, such is only a fraction of the history of American opera, especially during the late nineteenth century. Rather, opera was frequently a small-town event, performed by traveling troupes who performed in English for frontier folk for fifty cents a head. It was an event where "half a dozen times during each winter [. . .] a traveling stock company settled down at the local hotel and thrilled and entertained" a local population eager for culture.[1] The performances themselves were a mix of variety shows, plays, and opera, both light opera and scaled-down grand opera: *The Bohemian Girl, The Mikado, Martha.*[2] As the nation had expanded rapidly westward, towns that had been mining camps and trading posts only last year swelled in wealth and ambition to become micropolises; entrepreneurs and immigrants brought their families and the accompanying need for education and entertainment. In short order, this meant funding for cultural events performed live: lecture series, plays, and musical theater. While in many locations the venues remained modest—city halls, library parlors, barns, tents—about as often as not the local movers and shakers invested in opera houses, not only convenient loci for community gatherings, but important symbols of sophistication.

Opened in 1885, the Red Cloud Opera House in Nebraska is much like its peer institutions in form and function. As with most of the thousands of opera houses listed in Julius Cahn's *Official Theatrical Guide*—the standard directory of performance venues in the rail era, published annually from 1896 to 1910—it occupies space on a downtown thoroughfare and boasts a self-consciously City Beautiful–movement façade. An indication of its pragmatic frontier small-town roots, its ground floor was once shared by a hardware store and a grocery. The performance hall itself is on the second floor, accessed by double doors from the sidewalk. It has no fixed seating, but chairs could be added to accommodate well over five hundred people for a performance, or removed to allow for dancing or basketball.[3] And, like the hundreds of other opera houses that had sprung up across the country in the late nineteenth century, it was meant, in part, to serve as a beacon of civilization for a far-flung community. Just as Red Cloud, with a population of around a thousand residents in 1885, needed to assert itself as something more than a hub for sod-housed farmers, so were opera houses serving a similar purpose in places like Woonsocket, South Dakota and Arkadelphia, Arkansas.

It was there that Willa Cather, age fifteen and five years resident in Nebraska, attended *The Chimes of Normandy*, an opéra-comique by Robert Planquette, translated into English, as was typical of frontier light opera of the time. The opera, originally *Les cloches de Corneville*, had been first performed in Paris in 1877 and ran for four hundred consecutive performances,[4] elevating Planquette from an overlooked composer of café-comiques to an internationally recognized figure, if only briefly. It is a comedy situated, like so many light operas, on the unknown origins of its characters—including a girl named Serpolette, considered a misfit—and the events that unravel their identities, leading, inevitably, to a few happy surprises, inheritances, and nuptials. Though popular in its day, having already migrated to New York by the end of 1877,[5] it remains a footnote in opera history, warranting only one brief mention in Grout and Williams's ironically named *Short History of Opera* (the "short" history is more than one thousand pages),[6] and is seldom, if ever, performed today. Even so, we might count it as an improbable catalyst of some of the finest American fiction ever written—one might imagine the character of Serpolette, a peasant girl mischief maker, one who stood out from the crowd and had unknown potential, capturing a young Cather's imagination.

In the course of her fiction, Cather mentions forty-seven operas. Assuming a typical opera takes around three hours to perform, that's 141 hours of opera, nearly a week straight. All but three of her twelve novels reference opera, and roughly half of her short fiction makes mention of it. Despite a dearth of musical education—she'd been an indifferent piano student in her youth—surprisingly astute writing about opera was evident in some of her earliest writings, at least as early as her 1895 review of the Metropolitan Opera's *Falstaff* performance in Chicago, and continued throughout her career as a critic. She counted at least one opera star among her close friends, and Edith Lewis, her closest companion throughout adulthood, recounted that the two of them "went constantly to the opera," even in their early days in New York, before Cather's success, "when the future seemed so uncertain."[7] Opera was important to Cather's life, and it might serve to tell us much about her artistic outlook; it is more important than a biographical sidebar. Essential characteristics of opera, from the lightest light opera to the weightiest Wagner, informed her early artistic sensibilities, her "Kingdom of Art," and she built upon—and struggled with—these sensibilities her entire career. Opera is a self-consciously emotional medium housed in a self-consciously sophisticated cultural environment. Likewise, Cather's work tends simultaneously to exploit both the primitive and the refined. Both Cather's work and opera can be critical conundrums.

Despite the many books devoted to the subject, or perhaps as an illustration, Cather's artistic bent can be difficult to pin down. Books have been devoted to her romanticism and her modernism; she clearly utilized the techniques of realism throughout her work, though critics, for good reason, typically refrain from labeling her a Realist, and her primitivism remains an interpretive default. "What was she like when she left Nebraska [in 1896]?" wondered Bernice Slote before responding that Cather "was primarily a romantic and a primitive." "That she was eventually to be called a classicist, a Jamesian sophisticate, and the reserved stylist of the novel démeublé, may be one of the great jokes of literary criticism,"[8] Slote continues, because behind all of the apparent worldliness of Cather's mature writings is the "fundamentally primitivistic position—historical, cultural, human" at which Cather had arrived in her youth. And yet she *was* a classicist and a Jamesian sophisticate and a reserved stylist, as well—those are not assessments easily dismissed given that she knew classical literature well and followed its forms, followed James's example in her early career, and intentionally restrained herself from florid writing. The difficulty doesn't end there. She was a writer of and for the people, but she also decried popular trends and was not beholden to commercial dicta as to what was and was not popular. According to John Flannigan, she "retained a strong populist streak in her musical tastes that enabled her to enjoy, without embarrassment or irony, art, be it great or modest," and, to Slote, "she chose action and power; emotion, sympathy, and life. She rejected whatever was effete, over-refined, or delicate. She rejected, too, whatever was hard and intellectually inhuman."[9] Yet she was anything but a populist in her attitudes toward the artistic tastes of the American middle class with their "grinning, stupid faces"[10] and dime-store novels. She alienated Americans by placing their tastes well below those of French readers.[11] Yet she wrote popular literature, built an editorial career on understanding popular tastes, and "couldn't take Gertrude Stein or Ezra Pound seriously, wouldn't go to see an O'Neill play, and probably could not have been dragged to hear Schönberg."[12] She was not avant-garde and declared herself to be a creature of the world pre-1922.[13] But she did unorthodox things with form and character in her novels, and in her private life was anything but a keeper of the status quo. She is difficult to pin down because she was implicitly, even self-consciously, contradictory. It is appropriate that Cather chose a line from Whitman to be the title of her second novel, O Pioneers!—Cather was a diversity within herself, like Whitman's view of America as a field of grass, undifferentiated at a distance, a carpet of green, but upon closer inspection a wealth of individualisms. If Cather sometimes contradicts herself, very well then, she contradicts herself; she is large and contains multitudes. She is simultaneously an urban sophisticate and a dirt-handed frontier girl; a breaker of social norms and a champion of tradition. She is not an oxymoron, but rather in the fashion of a koan renders the impossible into simple being. Perhaps Booth Tarkington, reviewing S. S. McClure's autobiography, which was ghost-written by Cather, stumbled on the most apt characterization of Cather's work: "It's as simple as a country church—or a Greek statue."[14] This is Cather writ brief: an accessible, deceptive, simple complexity.

These apparent contradictions are important for understanding the force of Cather's work. While Cather's fiction is some of the most deliberately written and artistically aware in the American literary tradition, an instinctive and experienced understanding of brute emotional life always undergirds it. Though she wrote from the heart, two decades in publishing trained her with a publisher's eye for readership. There is a persistent balance in Cather between the primitive and the proper, the purchaser and professor: For every artist's salon and well-kept country garden, a frontier winter; and for every plow silhouetted against a setting sun, an order of art. Always there is a need for a rawness born from natural emotion more than hard intellectual irony. "We have stood the awfulness of French realism very patiently," she wrote in 1894, "but we must draw the line at the Russian. French anguish isn't so bad after all, it's such a self-satisfied, intentional, stagey kind of anguish." The anguish of the northern people, however, "is such a dumb, brutal, helpless sort of suffering. When the French lover commits suicide he does it artistically and dramatically with a fan in his pocket, a neat epigram on his lips and a rose in his button-hole. The northern man does it in an awful disgusting manner like Ibsen's Lövborg,"[15] who, in *Hedda Gabler,* dies of an accidental gunshot wound in the gut while in visiting a whorehouse. People die, often gruesomely, she tells us, but a simple recounting of this fact isn't art. Cather was not a realist; she wrote of a real world that she knew first-hand, but only insofar as she might extract from it transcendent meaning and beauty. Instead, she preferred the French iteration of beauty with its artistic and dramatic reality. One need only look at Violetta's choking death in *Traviata*—a brutally predictable end with emotional truth— to know what she means.

Opera, at least from Strauss backward, tends to offer the same shameless commitment to aesthetic over literal truth. Perhaps more than any other artistic form, opera exploits the need for emotional rawness. Classicists from Monteverdi to Mozart composed delicate intricacies, but only to deal with plots that expose eros and thanatos. Verdi wrote the most memorable melodies in opera, but ironically, covering shocking plots of quasi-incestuous revenge and tubercular courtesans. Verismo composers like Bizet and Mascagni never ignored that real world drama only functioned in relation to the balance between sacred and profane. Puccini tested the limits of vocal dynamism to give voice to the screaming soul. And Wagner, Cather's primary operatic focus, understood the world in fundamentally archetypal terms, disregarding centuries of compositional caution to reveal the world as people didn't quite know that they knew it. Cather wrote, nominally, about farmers and plows, parlors and conversation, singers coming to know their song, but always with an artistic restraint that masked the primal truths of existence that gave otherwise routine events a universal relatability.

Consider the rattlesnake scene in *My Ántonia.* Jim and Ántonia, both young, are out to dig up a prairie dog hole to see if the holes go deep enough to reach the water table or whether the prairie dogs "lapped up the dew in the early morning, like the rabbits."[16] Upon examining a burrow, Ántonia screams, shouts in her native language, Bohemian, and runs, leaving Jim to see "not merely a big snake" but a "circus monstrosity."[17] The snake coils to spring at Jim, who strikes it with a shovel. A battle ensues, with the monster "all about [his] feet [. . .] in wavy loops," Jim "pound[ing] his ugly head flat." The battle done, they examine the snake. It is old. It "must have been there when white men first came, left on from buffalo and Indian times." Jim, who writes of himself ironically as a "dragon-slayer,"[18] thinks that the snake "seemed like the ancient, eldest Evil." This event is a petty excitement, no more than a child narrowly stepping out of oncoming traffic or one almost missing the last step on a staircase. But it is writ large, and in archetypal tones. A boy and girl in the wild, seeking a primal knowledge of the natural world, encounter a vicious serpent. He battles the serpent with a shovel, the first tool of human civilization, and overcomes, realizing that the enemy, the "eldest Evil" is something from a world long before the two of them. He relishes his savage, confrontational self, and in his capacity as "dragon-slayer" it is hard for one acquainted with opera not to hear Siegfried overcoming Fafner in dragon form. It is a fundamentally operatic novel scene.

In the introduction to his book *Shakespeare & Opera*, the irrepressibly clever Gary Schmidgall wonders, "Is there an art form that receives more satirical or downright derisive publicity than opera?" He goes on to note one commentator who leveled accusations of "sensational [. . .] barrenness covered by sentimentality [with] plenty of bogus characterization [among] a poverty of meaning."[19] He is actually quoting George Bernard Shaw's assessment of Shakespeare, but doing so to make the point that opera, like Shakespeare, is easy to read as ridiculous. Rephrased from a more complimentary standpoint was W. H. Auden: "No good opera plot can be sensible, for people do not sing when they are feeling sensible."[20] The source of this raillery lies in the fact that opera is lacking in shame; it allows—encourages—emotional states to run wild, something very much at odds with social rules. It is the primitive run free, even when packaged and prepared by the most acutely trained performers on earth.

Cather was not herself a musician. She was unmotivated in her piano studies as a child. Her mother, Jennie (Viriginia) Cather had hired a German man named Albert Schindelmeisser to teach her, but Cather never offered a willingness to learn the instrument in any real way.[21] As James Woodress notes, "harmony, counterpoint, the technical mastery of an instrument, held no attraction for her. Music to her was an emotional release, not an intellectual exercise." Schindelmeisser attempted to convince Jennie to stop wasting money on lessons, but Cather's mother resisted because Willa "was getting a lot out of listening to him play and talking to him about his musical life in the old country."[22] No doubt, those conversations about the old country paid dividends throughout Cather's career, not only in her persistent focus on immigrant populations, but also as her stories are peppered with characters, immigrant and domestic, who remain attached to their upbringing through music: Aunt Georgiana in "A Wagner Matinée," Mr. Shimerda in *My Ántonia*, Godfrey St. Peter's youth in France in *The Professor's House*, Clement Sebastian in *Lucy Gayheart*. Schindelmeisser himself became the model for one of Cather's most interesting minor characters, A. Wunsch from *The Song of the Lark*. Wunsch is a wandering, German-born drunk, once a musician of some note, who teaches music lessons in Moonstone, Colorado, the home of protagonist Thea Kronborg. Unlike Cather, Thea is an obsessive practitioner of the piano—she is a pupil Wunsch would never want to give up. He demands that she practice four hours a day, and she complies with minimal grumbling. "She went after it like a terrier after rats," her mother remembers.[23] Wunsch is not a taskmaster but a teacher, and Thea thrives under his guidance. He demands devotion to craft, but only to students who deserve the fruits of the labor. "He's a good teacher," Thea's mother tells a family friend. "It's good for us he does drink. He'd never be in a little place like this if he didn't have some weakness."[24] In the ruthless pragmatism of the frontier, Thea's mother recognizes that Wunsch's misfortune is Moonstone's boon.

His relentless demands for practice will pay off, but not as anticipated. Thea will go on to great success not as a pianist but as a soprano and becomes Cather's greatest musical artist, both in accomplishment and in terms of Cather's theories as to what makes a great artist great. She is one of the "artists [who] profit by exile,"[25] the one who has "the fewer friends [. . .] the better."[26] Cather believed that the artist's journey was one done alone. Thea neglects meaningful human connection and personal indulgence of any sort to reach artistic heights. Cather would adopt the edict of Wunsch for her artist characters and herself: the true artist would be devoted to art above all else. Cather, of course, was a prodigy of story rather than song, and she never herself pursued a musical education beyond the bit of youthful training and what her keen insight and audience experience would allow her. Though John Flannigan has made a cogent case, based on passages from later commentary and fiction, for her intuitive understanding of music to have reached a high level, her technical knowledge of music never developed. Later in life, she attended a symphonic performance in the company of H. L. Mencken, who was left befuddled by her taste; Cather had preferred a suite from Ravel's ballet *Daphnis and Chloe,* a "very cheap piece of trash," according to Mencken, to the evening's main event, the New York première of Mahler's Symphony no. 9. "I had always thought of Cather as a musician," he recalled, "but she told me she really knew very little about music."[27] She could never have analyzed a score or coached an ingénue, but that doesn't mean that she lacked a principal and profound knowledge of what made music work, and, as importantly, what made an artist great.

Aside from her fruitless piano studies, her youth would have been peppered with the classical music tradition. Across the frontier, people gathered in homes and public places around pianos and parlor organs with opera scores on the racks. Immigrants from Germany, Bohemia, and Italy brought native knowledge of the form not only from the grand houses of Milan and Paris, but also from the hundreds of smaller venues that had scattered across small cities across the continent. Aunt Georgiana in "A Wagner Matinée" knew a cowpoke from Bayreuth who sang from *Meistersinger*[28]—he would have lived in Bayreuth before it was *Wagner's* Bayreuth.

It might be difficult for contemporary readers of Cather to understand the extent to which classical music would have permeated the frontier world. Recorded music was at its dawn. Professional performances were regularly attended, but not an everyday occurrence. What music one had was typically the music that one performed or heard performed by friends and family, and that music would have been based in the classical tradition and before twentieth century distinctions between "high" and "low" culture severed how we perceive art and entertainment, meaning that a person playing a selection from Gluck would be considered no more highbrow than one playing the latest waltz. "The kind of music that was fundamental to Cather's cultural life—music of the opera house and concert hall—is not so fundamental to the experience of readers today," notes Philip Kennicott. "Things that she took for granted—the cultural context of nineteenth-century composers, for instance—can't be taken for granted anymore."[29] While we might presume that an educated reader of today would know a bit of Mozart, Verdi, and Wagner and the basic playbook of the *Ring* or *Faust,* we'd best not be so presumptuous as to *Les Huguenots* or *Mignon;* we certainly should not assume familiarity with composers such as

Robert Planquette or Reginald de Koven or with fallen titles by still-canonical composers like Massenet's *Hériodiade*. Consider this: The famous Bugs Bunny short "What's Opera, Doc?," featuring a pastiche of opera, particularly Wagner, would be a de novo introduction to *Tannhäuser* or *Der Fliegende Holländer* for most viewers today, but it wouldn't have been for audiences when it premiered in 1957—at least not for the grandparents in the crowd, who would likely have grown up hearing the music of Venusberg picked out on parlor uprights.

Cather's audience's presumed familiarity is important. As Kennicott notes, "Cather drops musical references with great fluency, and these references function as a kind of shorthand and counterpoint within her fiction."[30] Wunch's favorite opera is Gluck's *Orpheus and Eurydice,* and "if he believes Gluck's opera 'the most beautiful opera ever made'" then he must be "a purist and a classicist and more than a bit crusty." This is how Cather and her readers would have interpreted the operatic clue. "That the character of Aunt Georgiana, the prairie exile who hears Wagner again for the first time in decades in the short story 'A Wagner Matinee' knew the composer's early works [even having saved a copy of *Der Fliegende Holländer*] from her days as an apprentice musician tells us that she is extraordinary," because it tells us that she must have taken to Wagner in the 1860s, well before Walter Damrosch declared Wagnermania in the United States. This information "tells us immediately that she was an adventurous musician, perhaps a firebrand of the avant garde." That such character clues appear in much of Cather's work does not tell us that Cather prided herself as a matron of obscurity, testing her readers' intellect to determine their worthiness; rather, she was communicating using mutually intelligible reference points. Such were Cather's youthful environs, and she would quickly encounter greater familiarity with opera as she grew.

Post–Red Cloud, Cather enrolled at the University of Nebraska in Lincoln, originally intending to study science and become a physician. Famously, Cather changed course after an English professor, Ebenezer Hunt, submitted an essay of hers on Thomas Carlyle to the *Nebraska State Journal,* unbeknownst to Cather herself. The essay was published, Cather was flattered, and water found its own level: "Up to that time," she recalled, "I had planned to specialize in science; I thought I would like to study medicine. But what youthful vanity can be unaffected by the sight of itself in print!"[31] Cather approached her formal studies with varying levels of academic vigor, but her true education came from her role as a journalist and theater critic, contributing material to five publications, including the *Journal,* Lincoln's largest paper, and the *Hesperian,* the University's student paper. By 1896, the year she left Nebraska to edit the *Home Monthly* in Pittsburgh, she had published nearly half a million words of artistic criticism and commentary.[32]

Of course, most of her theatrical criticism during this period was aimed at local productions and traveling troupes. She hadn't yet experienced opera performed by a major company. Cather's music education received an important boon during her senior year of college, when Dr. Julius Tyndale, a middle-aged bachelor and doctor whom Cather had befriended, financed a trip for her to see opera in Chicago with her friend Mary Jones, a librarian at the university. The Metropolitan Opera of New York was presenting five operas in Chicago over the course of three weeks. She saw all five: Verdi's *Falstaff, Otello,* and *Aida;* Meyerbeer's *Les Huguenots;* and Gounod's *Romeo et Juliette.* Prior to this, the only grand opera Cather had seen was *Il Trovatore* performed by a traveling company and *Cavalleria Rusticana* performed as an oratorio, both underwhelming performances. The Met performances, however, were opera in its fullest form. As Woodress notes, "she was carried away by *Falstaff,* Verdi's final masterpiece, and felt privileged to have heard only the fourth American performance of that new work."[33] She gushed over the "French baritone Victor Maurel, who had created the role in the French, British, and American premières," who could "both sing and act," and whose "performance was not only a great operatic triumph but was also a faithful tribute to Shakespeare." *Falstaff,* Verdi's final work and the last complete opera in his Shakespearean corpus after *Macbeth* and *Otello* (he had begun a *Re Lear* before his death, but never finished it),[34] she believed was "an absolutely new creation," a bold declaration given she was evaluating the great composer's swan song and that she'd also heard, in the same week, "Nellie Melba, Lillian Nordica, and Jean de Reszke," performing other operas. Cather's evaluation of *Falstaff* has preceded well over a century of critical analysis that agrees that the opera was one of the composer's best works. Her instinctive appreciation of the music demonstrates that Cather needed less formal training to understand great opera and great performance. The production stuck with Cather firmly enough that it would appear forty years later in her novel *Lucy Gayheart.*

If Cather's technical knowledge of music remained undeveloped, her understanding of the operatic milieu certainly grew over time, and she makes note of snippets of operatic history frequently in her fiction. The title character of

"Uncle Valentine" recollects, "Do you remember how we used to play the Ring to each other hours on end, long ago, when Damrosch first brought the German opera over?"[35] In "Coming, Aphrodite!," Don Hedger hears "the tempestuous, over-lapping phrases of Signor Puccini, then comparatively new in the world, but already so popular that even Hedger recognized his unmistakable gusts of breath."[36] "The Diamond Mine" makes reference to "a charming bit from Massenet's 'Manon,' then little known in this country."[37] In *The Song of the Lark,* Theodore Thomas, both a character and the actual conductor of the Chicago Symphony Orchestra, thinks of having been "awakened by two voices, by two women who sang in New York in 1851,—Jenny Lind and Henrietta Sontag."[38] Cather acclimated herself sufficiently to the opera world to effortlessly reference key moments in opera history—Damrosch promoting Wagner, the advents of Puccini and *Manon,* who performed in New York in 1851 who might have inspired Maestro Thomas, not to mention knowing Thomas's name in the first place. Beyond the potential intertextual relevance of any of these references (they are intentional, after all), these and many others demonstrate Cather's thorough familiarity with how opera had entered America from its east-coast ascendance in the early to mid-1800s forward.

Edith Lewis, with whom Cather cohabitated from 1906 on, remembered that the two of them "went constantly to the opera" when they first resided in New York City. This was during "one of the great periods of opera in New York. Nordica and the de Reszkes, Melba and Calvé were still singing. [. . .] From 1905 on our old programmes continually list such names as Sembrich, Farrar, Chaliapin, Plancon, Destinn, Renaud, Mary Garden, Caruso, Amato, Homer, and Tetrazzini. Toscanini, not then half so famous, but at the height of his powers, was conducting two or three times a week at the Metropolitan. But the most thrilling, to us, of all the new stars that came up over the horizon was Olive Fremstad. We heard her nearly every time she sang."[39] It's interesting that Lewis, as would Cather, focuses on the performers rather than on what was performed. To do so suggests a meaningful saturation with the content of the operas themselves so that one cares as much about *how* a particular iteration was performed as with *what* was actually being performed. Lewis's mention of Fremstad is particularly important, as Fremstad would remain a close friend of Cather's throughout the 1910s and would become a model for Cather's idea of the artist; Fremstad embodied many of the high Parnassian ideals of art that Cather had developed in her apprentice writings.

While Cather would likely have seen Fremstad on stage many times beforehand, her first personal encounter came in the course of writing the article "Three American Singers," published in *McClure's Magazine* in December 1913.[40] The article focused on Fremstad, Louise Homer, and Geraldine Farrar, all singers at the top of the operatic game in New York. It is clear that Cather was most enamored of Fremstad. The section on Homer is the briefest, around a thousand words long, noting that Homer was an excellent mother to her five children in addition to being an excellent singer; her Brangäne was "one of the most beautiful and satisfying things" and "certainly improved upon the German tradition."[41] Farrar's section, around three thousand words, notes Farrar's ability to captivate even a baseball audience. She was a celebrity engaging opera on the cusp of the jazz age, embodying the "mining-camp ideal" of easy and early success, something for which Farrar was not apologetic. She was a nondomestic "darling of fortune" who "would rather live ten years thick than twenty thin."[42] "Why should I want to string it out twenty, thirty years?" she asked. "I want to give it out all in a lump. I want to go hard while I'm at it!" There are moments in Cather's writing on Farrar where one notes a Catherian severity in terms of an artist's devotion to craft—"she does not believe that, for an artist, anything can be very real or very important except art" and that "there is nothing in the world so ugly that it can not be made beautiful in art; and that there is nothing in the world so beautiful that it can not be made banal by a stupid or prudish artist"[43]—but, generally speaking, Cather is not entirely won over by the glamor of Farrar. Fremstad's portion is well over four thousand words, and far more analytically dense. Whereas Cather used Homer and Farrar as foils of one another—wife and mother versus flapper—Cather authors a *Künstlerroman* in brief for Fremstad, complete with her upbringing, her ambition, her artistic isolation, and her theories of performance.

Cather recounts Fremstad's youth as a Swedish immigrant in Minnesota. Her father, a physician and occasional revivalist preacher, was so insistent that she excel at the piano that their "easy-going American neighbors" thought the girl should be taken away: "She spent hours every day at the piano. Her wrists still show the mark of early strain. After each music lesson she had to take home a report from her teacher, stating how well she had known her exercises. If the report was not satisfactory, her father punished her—not by argumentative methods."[44] Nevertheless, Fremstad valued this push toward strenuous and consistent work, noting that she still thanked her father for her work ethic, "the most valuable thing in the world." "And there are very few people," she continued in a line worthy of Thea Kronborg, "indeed who know what real work is." Unlike Farrar and Homer, Fremstad's ascent was not a smooth progression to the top. Cather references a reviewer for the *New York Sun* who, in a brutal comment on Fremstad's 1905 debut in a soprano role, wrote that "Olive Fremstad awoke from the dream that she was a dramatic soprano."[45] Fremstad was undeterred. The same reviewer six years later would praise her as having "such an outpouring of dramatic eloquence that she fairly lifted her associates above themselves." Fremstad had earned her fame through years of hard work, from her youth onward. In Cather's phrasing, she was a "worker, not a dreamer."[46] Cather wrote to Elizabeth Shepley Sargent that "if one could write all that that battered Swede makes one know, that would be worth while. Lord, but she is like the women on the Divide! The suspicious, defiant, far-seeing pioneer eyes."[47] This becomes one of the unlikely intersections of Cather's frontier experience and the travails of art. The frontier could be brutal and isolating, offering truths only accessible by experience. Likewise, hard work for an artist can never be fully satisfying because the hard work that goes into producing art lifts the artist to a level the audience can never reach. Quoting Fremstad: "'We are born alone, we make our way alone, we die alone.' She believes that the artist's quest is pursued alone, and that the highest rewards are, for the most part, enjoyed alone. She is not confident that much of a singer's best work ever crosses the footlights to the people who sit beyond. She says: 'My work is only for serious people. If you ever really find anything in art, it is so subtle and so beautiful that—well, you need never be afraid any one will take it away from you, for the chances are nobody will ever know you've got it.'"[48] This philosophy by which artistic competence only serves to separate the artist from the audience is one that will be repeated in Cather's fiction in characters such as Kitty Ayrshire, Harvey Merrick, and, most importantly, Thea Kronborg.

It isn't surprising that Cather viewed opera just as much a dramatic medium as a musical one. The operatic war cry *"prima la musica e poi le parole"* ("first the music and then the words," from Salieri's opera of that title) would have gone against her basic attraction to the form, the opportunity for grand emotional gesture that stems from a total work of art: music, narrative, poetry, production, and acting. When Richard Giannone claims that "in opera it is the music, not the libretto, which carries the higher excitement,"[49] he's referring not to the primacy of music but to the need for music to bring the total force of art together; Cather, at least in her earlier career, needed the confluence of elements endemic of opera. In the words of Catherine Clément, "she commit[ted] the sacrilege of listening to the words, reading the libretti, following the twisted, tangled plots." "An opera whose words I do not know, draws me in and attracts me," she continues, "but, when I know the words, the passions, what is at stake, then opera wraps me totally in a world of fantastic clarity, of matchless life. The music is then revealed in all its richness."[50] As Thea says, "I think oratorio is a great chance for bluffers."[51] Oratorio, performed as concert rather than staged, music without action, allows for insincerity. Consider how Cather treats Fremstad's performance of Kundry's kiss, one of the more difficult acts to perform in Wagner's *Parsifal.* In it, Kundry, typically reclined, offers to kiss Parsifal, claiming that the kiss will grant him understanding. The music during this moment lingers, and depending on the conductor's whims could endure longer than would be convincing for the kiss. Cather wonders, "How is the singer to manage the mere element of duration without making the caress either formal or ridiculous?" Fremstad, a dramatic artist as much as a singer,

> bends over the youth to give him this kiss with perfect self-confidence, almost indifference; she has never failed to vanquish her knight. But, as her face comes near to his, her indolence changes into something less negative; she is moved by a sort of tenderness, powerful because it is corporeal and sincere. Her right arm is about the boy; with her left hand she lifts her flowing hair and holds it before her face and his, like a scarf. Behind this she kisses him. The inclination of her head, every line of her body, contribute to the poetry of the moment. In Mme. Fremstad's performance of the part this is always a great moment;—it might so easily be a great stupidity.[52]

In the course of her article on Homer, Farrar, and Fremstad, Cather makes little mention of musical technique, but she devotes this longish paragraph to the acting ability of Fremstad. This is not to claim that Cather neglected music in writing about opera, but rather that she had an intuitive sense of *die Gesamtkeit,* the totality of artistic effect upon which Wagner based his own dramatic theories. This is what sets opera apart from other forms of music. "The opera composer," writes Wallace Dace, "must also possess that rare attribute, histrionic imagination, which is required of all artists who dream of expressing themselves on the stage, whether playwright, opera composer or ballet choreographer." This "histrionic imagination" is what separates composers like Mozart, Verdi, and Bizet from those who write purely for the concert hall or the church.[53]

Cather's relationship with Fremstad burned brightly during the 1910s. After the *McClure's* interview, they remained friendly and in contact. Fremstad visited Cather in the hospital (the result of an infection from a hairpin scratch) in the winter of 1914[54] and nursed her through a bout of bronchitis as late as 1918.[55] In the summer of 1914, Cather visited Fremstad in Maine, marveling at her vitality: "She fished as if she had no other means of getting food; cleaned all the fish, swam like a walrus, rowed, tramped, cooked, watered her garden. I was not much more than an audience—very little help, but it was the grandest show of human vigor and grace I've ever watched. I feel as if I'd lived for a long while with the wife of the Dying Gladiator in her husky prime, in deep German forests."[56] A 1915 letter to Ferris Greenslet mentions "a glorious day with [Fremstad] in Nebraska," who had a "dirty rumpled book which had once been 'The Song of the Lark,' and which she said had 'not been read but eaten'"— Fremstad had loved the novel, claiming it had the "right 'stimmung.'"[57] One gets the sense, however, that Cather's fascination with opera peaked sometime around then, around the time she'd published *Ántonia* and was writing *One of Ours*. She'd written much about opera in her apprentice years and in her first novels, but, while opera continues to appear in her work afterward, it does so less frequently. Later in life, "her preference shifted from the dramatic and symphonic to the more intimate, lyrical forms, from the elaborate to the simple [. . .] chamber music and recitals interested her more than did the opera."[58] Cather knew opera from a young age. It fed her understanding of art and the relationship between artistic understanding and raw human experience during her key developmental years. But she began to move away from the form sometime after *The Song of the Lark* and her friendship with Fremstad.

Why?

John Flannigan notes "the apparent contradiction between the youthful seriousness of her 1896 manifesto—'In the kingdom of art there is no God, but one God'—and the mature wistfulness of 'Art is too terribly human to be very "great."'"[59] Over the course of her career, Cather's timbre in writing about art changed. "The cultural chasm between these two artistic credos" is perhaps not as great as it might seem, observes Flannigan, and her youthful enthusiasm and mature sobriety are views from the same standpoint. Cather certainly became reflective of her artistic credos later in her career. In "A Chance Meeting," she claims that "it is scarcely exaggeration to say that if one is not a little mad about Balzac at twenty, one will never live; and if at forty one can still take Rastignac and Lucien de Rubempré at Balzac's own estimate, one has lived in vain."[60] Balzac—whom she likens to Flaubert, Stendhal, Mérimée, Hardy, Conrad, Brahms, Franck, Dickens, and Scott in their emotional heft along with their ability to be both popular and artistically sound—"has a strong appeal for the great multitudes of humanity who have no feeling for any form of art, and who read him only in poor translations. This is overwhelming evidence of the vital force in him, which no rough handling can diminish."[61] This "vital force" was at the heart of Cather's developing attitudes toward art, and her later work, which tends to the meditative and frequently pessimistic, represents a later coming to terms with the inapproachability of transcendent ideals. Things that have the vital force have a romantic core. But romantic ideals possess a driving force only until one lives long enough to realize those ideals die in the presence of reality.

Slote sums up Cather's youthful attitude toward creativity in terms of the emergent realism of art simply not being *grand* enough: "The world is diminished, but she gives a reason. It is lessened by our failure to aspire and in 'these days of pigmies' no one seemed to be attempting greatness in literature, the 'Wagnerian flashes and thunders and tempests of Carlyle and the lofty repose and magnificent tranquility of Emerson.'"[62] In "The Novel Démeublé," Cather ties Balzac directly to Wagner, claiming that "Balzac tried out the value of literalness in the novel, tried it out to the uttermost, as Wagner did the value of scenic literalness in the music drama";[63] but here she is not asserting a literalness of realism, but one that represented a "passion of discovery, with the inflamed zest of an unexampled curiosity." Or Cather at her most droll: "Can one imagine anything more terrible than the story of *Romeo and Juliet* rewritten in prose by D. H. Lawrence?" Love in youth, represented in heady Shakespearean verse, could only be corrupted by Lawrence's explicit sexual realism. In the course of her career, Cather used tools of realism—literalness—to frame ethereal concerns. In later writings like *The Professor's House* or *Not Under Forty,* tinged with reactionary unease at the progression of culture but persistently defending the ambitious, emotionally-oriented art of her youth, she evinces a need to come to terms with a world that has not met her youthful ideals. But this does not mean that a failure of those ideals meant an evacuation from them. One doesn't give up the ideals of youth; one disguises them. Cather moved away from opera because opera represented a "wild thing" for her, and she had tamed somewhat.

Music is a wild thing for Cather, part of a nexus of wild things—literature, music, humanity—that represent artistic understanding. Just as Nils says of Clara in "The Bohemian Girl" that "you can't tame a wild thing; you can only chain it,"[64] so would Valentine in "Uncle Valentine" claim that songs are "too wild. . . . No, you can't catch them."[65] Opera is music at its wildest, and Cather, waning, no longer saw herself as part of that wildness. This tension between youthful artistic idealism and mature realism was one she'd anticipated for years, quoting Helena von Doenhoff in 1894: "'to always want to sing[,] to be always young and in love, to keep up the enthusiasm, to sustain the ecstasy, that is what is means to be a singer. Of course Tavary and I are no more sixteen, but,' as she gave her satin slipper an impatient toss, 'art does not come at sixteen.'"[66] Or in *My Ántonia:* "In the course of twenty crowded years one parts with many illusions."[67] It's worth noting that Cather's penultimate novel, *Lucy Gayheart,* is also a sustained exploration of the singer's craft and progress. Though it is primarily focused on Schubert's song cycle *Die Winterreise,* it makes mention of ten operas, and Lucy's awakening to artistic sophistication comes upon a performance of *Lohengrin* (Thea's great awakening, incidentally, came upon hearing songs over opera is meaningful and "her gentle mocking, [of Lucy's] starry-eyed intoxication at a performance of *Lohengrin* at the Auditorium can be read as a parody, albeit a fond one, of her own youthful tendency to go weak-kneed in the presence of art, great or not so great."[68] From a instrumental music, Antonín Dvořák's "New World" symphony). But the emphasis on more staid art perspective of age and experience, Cather still understood and smiled upon, but no longer experienced, the youthful invigoration that opera can give.

In her speech at the presentation of the 1933 Pulitzer Prizes, where Cather, a ten-year inductee, was chosen to speak on behalf of literature, she likened the novel form to the Tarnhelm of the *Ring* in its "amazing elasticity and variety": "this lightly woven net of words has the power of transformation, can present a giant, a dragon, a mouse or a worm."[69] She still, at that late point in her career, had opera in mind and found herself compelled to explain her own art in operatic terms. Though she'd drifted away from opera compared to her earlier efforts, she never quite could separate opera and literature. For her, the two remain sister disciplines. According to Giannone, "Willa Cather will call Sarah Bernhardt's acting musical and she will remind a musician that 'singing is idealized speech.'" "One need not know the vocabulary of a foreign play," he claims, "to respond to it. [According to Cather,] 'great actors can overcome the obstacle of speaking in a foreign tongue—[. . .] we can feel the fire and pathos of Bernhardt's French, or the majesty of Salvini's Italian.'"[70] Art, executed well, is universal. In 1936, facing accusations that her writing ignored real world concerns in favor of aesthetics, she published a letter in *Commonweal* defending the notion of escapism. "The world has a habit of being in a bad way from time to time, and art has never contributed anything to help matters—except escape," she posits. "Hundreds of years ago, before European civilization had touched this continent, the Indian women in the old rock-perched pueblos of the Southwest were painting geometrical patterns on the jars in which they carried water up from the streams. Why did they take the trouble?" She proceeds to note the immense existential pressures under which the makers of these jars must have lived, pressures well above the modern mode, the real threat of starvation year in and out, and yet "they often shaped their graceful cooking pots when they had nothing to cook in them. Anyone who looks over a collection of pre-historic Indian pottery dug up from old burial-mounds knows at once that the potters experimented with form and color to gratify something that had no concern with food and shelter. The major arts (poetry, painting, architecture, sculpture, music) have a pedigree all their own. They did not come into being as a means of increasing the game supply or promoting tribal security. They sprang from an unaccountable predilection of the one unaccountable thing in man."[71] That one thing is an appreciation of beauty, and it is the one thing that binds every human community. It is unaccountable because it provides nothing tangible to prolong our lives or increase our comfort, and yet we are compelled to it even in our dying moments—just ask Aida, Isolde, or Tosca.

❧

CHAPTER 2

WAGNER AND CHURCH CHOIRS

Opera in America in Cather's Time

Who would have expected this here?
—Stenciled on the curtain of a log cabin theater in Staunton, Virginia,
during the American Revolutionary War

At the beginning of *Overtones of Opera in American Literature*, Carmen Skaggs notes that opera and America share a birthday: the year 1607 saw both the foundation of the first permanent English settlement in North America at Jamestown, Virginia, as well as the performance of the first fully developed opera ever performed, Claudio Monteverdi's *L'Orfeo*, in Mantua.[1] This coincidence is convenient and cleverly noted, but not without complication. We might ask, "What is America's real birthday?" The first people are estimated to have crossed to the continent thirty thousand or so years ago. The first Europeans were represented by Leif Erikson, who set foot in North America a few decades before William the Conqueror laid claim to Britain. Then Columbus, then Cortes, then the lost colony of Roanoke, and eventually Jamestown—not to mention 1776. So, yes, in a way 1607 is the beginning of the permanent anglophone experience in the Americas that would eventually lead to the United States itself. But it's not the only way to look at it.

The origination of opera is even more complicated, if chronologically more succinct. While 1607 saw the performance of *L'Orfeo* in the Mantuan court, Jacopo Peri's *Euridice* from 1600 is the oldest opera score still in existence, and Peri's *Dafne*, now lost, was a chamber opera generally thought to originate the form. It was performed at the home of Jacopo Corsi "with great applause" among a group of Renaissance Humanists known as the Camerata Fiorentina in 1597. "This," noted Charles Burney in 1804, "seems the true æra when the *opera*, or drama, *wholly set to Music*, and in which the dialogue was neither sung in measure, nor declaimed without Music, but *recited* in simple musical tones, which amounted not to singing, and yet was different from speech, should be dated."[2] Burney's identification of 1597 as *the* date has, despite the long-windedness in which its explanation was couched, endured. But Burney's need to identify the date and explain exactly what was meant by the term "opera" suggests a debate that continues. The Camerata, in fact, was self-consciously working toward a pure form of drama based on the belief, now partially discredited, that the Hellenistic world had combined dramatic text with music. If the Greeks did it, shouldn't the Renaissance Italians do so as well? But if their form was opera, why wasn't the Greeks' or any earlier form of music-drama? Defining what opera *is* is tricky given that people have combined words and music for dramatic purposes for likely as long as we've had drama itself.

The marriage of music and drama on its own doesn't necessarily constitute opera, but then, what does? When does *chantefable* or *Singspiel* or ballad opera or *zarzuela* (popular music-drama forms from French-, German-, English-, and Spanish-language traditions) cross a line and become opera? What about the ancient Greek plays that incorporated music and upon which Renaissance opera was supposedly based, or a harp-handed scop rhythmically rumbling through *Beowulf*? Once one's asked about the difference between a "musical" and an "opera," it's not long before an old saw comes out: Opera is when all lines are sung and musicals are when music is interspersed with dialogue— meaning, of course, that *Les Misérables* is an opera and *Die Zauberflöte* is a musical. We begin to wonder if a film with music is simply an all-recitative opera. Or, considering that all human speech abides by instinctive tides of rhythm and tempo to express emotion and that our gestures and habits of dress are performative, perhaps all human society is opera.

Perhaps.

Opera, like American culture in the mid- to late 1800s, Whitman's America, was expansive and defied definition. It's as difficult to pin down exactly what is an opera and when opera began as it is to do the same for America. They might share a birthday, but, more so, they have a mutual resistance to classification. Was a performance wherein an upright piano was ferried into a ballroom to provide accompaniment for two people performing an opera centered on a love triangle *opera* in the same sense as what was happening in newly built three-thousand-seat auditoria in New York or Chicago? Yes, arguably more so. It was certainly more intimate, like the form's Florentine origin, and more dedicated to popular entertainment, as the form would grow to be in the eighteenth and nineteenth centuries.

Precisely when opera became part of the American cultural landscape can likewise be difficult to determine. Ballad operas, plays in which dialogue was interspersed with popular melodies, were the order of the day at the beginning, and the first of these performed in America was Colley Cibber's *Flora*, performed in Charleston, South Carolina, in 1735. Fifteen years later, *The Beggar's Opera* came to New York, and sixty-one and sixty-two years later, respectively, opera first appeared in New Orleans and Boston.[3] The first American attempt at serious opera was a reworked version of Thomas Arne's *Alfred* (from which the anthem "Rule, Britannia" remains a popular expression of British patriotism), performed at the College of Philadelphia in 1757.[4] These early expressions of opera, if cruder than what would come, were nonetheless popular: More than one thousand were performed in the United States between 1785 and 1815.[5] What might be less controversially identified as the advent of opera in America is the Garcia family's performance of *Il Barbiere di Siviglia* in New York at the Park Theatre on November 29, 1825—the first opera in America that was indisputably of the Florentine lineage.[6]

Opera, like America, endured a series of identity crises in its early years. Among other things, it was never quite sure what to call itself. Elise Kirk catalogs the struggle, noting that it was alternately referred to as "pasticcio, burletta, dramatic fable, farce, extravaganza, opera-ballet, comic masque, interlude, afterpiece, and olla podrida (hodgepodge). It was common to see a music theater piece advertised as 'tragi-comi-pastoral farcical opera' or a 'histori-tragi-comi-ballad opera.'"[7] And, like any new cultural force, it encountered opposition from the establishment. Just as Italian opera's introduction in England was met with Alexander Pope calling it a "harlot form" full of "affected airs," and Jonathan Swift claiming that "Italian music [. . .] is wholly unsuitable to our northern climate, and the genius of the people whereby we are over-run with Italian effeminacy and Italian nonsense,"[8] so was the Garcias' performance of *Barbiere* interrupted by the venerable legal scholar Chancellor James Kent standing and shouting "it's an insult to human nature!" before storming out.[9] But if the old guard expressed unease with the foreignness—both national and artistic—of opera, popular audiences tended to accept and financially support the form as part of a growing national theater movement that included opera and various forms of musical theater, spoken drama, and performative lecture series, so much so that by 1905, Julius Cahn's *Theatrical Guide* would boast "an absolutely correct, national managers' directory of thirty-five hundred" venues nationwide. Musical theater would serve multiple purposes across the nation: bringing a veneer of cosmopolitan cultural heft to the back country, creating a common body of cultural referents to unite a rapidly expanding nation, and allowing for cultural distinction among the various immigrant groups of America. This latter function was one reason that New Orleans became an early capital of American opera; once the Louisiana Purchase was made broadly known, "Creole disdain for the barbarous Americans fueled a concerted effort to maintain cultural distinctiveness," including by way of French opera.[10]

Edifices dedicated to theater began to appear in the early to mid-1700s in regional capitals like Charleston, Williamsburg, and New York. These were typically "small wooden affairs, customarily painted red" to advertise their purpose. Within decades, the popularity of theater in America allowed for the construction of more permanent buildings, often financed by theater troupes to use as bases of operations for their cross-country tours. Among these was the Southwark in Philadelphia, built in 1766, the first American theatrical structure to be dubbed an "opera house."[11] These early theaters were "crude and uncomfortable places" with neither adequate ventilation to cool in the summer nor a manner of heating that was both effective and safe. Attempts to light and heat theaters were fraught with the peril of conflagration. Between 1797 and 1897, there were at least 1,100 theater fires in America and Europe, and insurance companies typically refused to insure theaters on actuarial grounds. Apart from being dimly lit and uncomfortably cold or hot, eighteenth- and early nineteenth-century theaters also lacked toilets, despite typically serving both food and drinks during performances, and the sale of spirited beverages to boost the bottom line invited rambunctiousness frequently enough that many theaters hired private police forces to maintain order.[12] If the performances were bringing civilization to the masses, the venues in which the performances took place certainly were not.

Many of these problems are inherent in scale; the larger the theater, the more difficult it would be to manage lighting and temperature, or the dining and hygienic needs of the audience. But most opera wasn't performed in the scaled-up venues. Most of the nation's three thousand–plus theaters were modest and scattered across the emerging small towns of Middle America. The distinction between the small town and big city venues was not lost on the urban sophisticates, themselves perpetually engaged in a battle to prove their own legitimacy relative to their European counterparts. In line with the "view that only 'grand' opera was opera at all," an editor of *Musical America* quipped, "I do not call them opera houses in Elmira and Wilmington. [. . .] We make a distinction between opera houses and opera houses." Given that the small town theaters could hardly support year-round professional theater, they were often used for a variety of other civic functions, exacerbating the divide between urban and rustic venues. Theodore Dreiser, novelist nemesis of small-town milieux, set his 1915 novel *The Genius* in the fictional hamlet of Alexandria, Illinois, which boasted, along with a streetcar line and a public square, "a theatre—or, rather, an opera house, so-called (why no one might say, for no opera was ever performed there)."[13] While it's true that opera was seldom the sole reason for being among village opera houses, often "kept busy with dances, bazaars, temperance lectures, high-school bands, basketball games, and elocution contests," it was not typical that such facilities *never* had opera performed. In the late nineteenth century, there were dozens—if not hundreds—of traveling opera companies at work at any given moment, and while not every small town could boast that its opera house would host one of these companies any particular week or month, it was important that the opera house be waiting, available, whenever the company came to town to bring a scaled-down *Norma* or the latest Offenbach.

Even if showing opera was not the primary function of most small opera houses, the term "opera" was nevertheless innate in the aspirationalism of the edifice. As John Dizikes notes, "calling it an opera house *was* the point. Carved in stone, lettered in brass or iron, painted on a wooden surface, the words *opera house* were a lifeline to the great world beyond the plains or the mountains, a part of the tradition which stretched from San Cassiano to San Francisco." Town leaders often took great care in the design of their opera houses to ensure that theirs was distinctive, asserting its importance in the untamed, uncultured expanse of America. Accordingly, the nation's opera houses boasted a great diversity of architectural styles:

In Buena Vista, Virginia, it was Queen Anne, with a rounded corner tower and twin gables over the front; in Elizabeth City, North Carolina, Richardsonian Romanesque, three stories elaborately plastered. Natchez, Mississippi represented Greek Revival; Sesser Illinois, California Mission style. The opera house in Cheyenne, brick faced with stone, "combined several styles of architecture," while that in Leesburg, Virginia, resolutely defied categorization, as did the one in Ray, North Dakota, its façade a metal false front stamped to simulate rusticated stone blocks. Four windows ran across the second story, each with a pediment with rosettes and Corinthian brackets.[14]

The opera house was a symbol of what a town *could* be, just as opera itself, as an art form, can symbolize a transcendent unity of art, even if the actual event of opera often falls short of those aspirations. Willa Cather recognized all of this—the problems and potential in the form and the way in which it was addressed in both small towns and metropolitan hubs—and she often exploited the narrative potential of the complexities of opera and its execution in American culture.

Cather wrote often of opera in a small town context, going beyond well-worn city-opera tropes of coattails and pearls and demonstrating the growing pains of, and unexpected cultural diversity among, the frontier country. Her portrayal of small-venue opera went hand-in-glove with Cather's attempt to reconcile higher art with the popular mind. In a way, the frontier *was* opera, "not," in John Flannigan's terms, "an effete 'eastern' entertainment incorporating a distorted vision of the world" but rather an environment that "echoes all human conduct under intense emotional pressure."[15] Marilyn Arnold observes "prairie-born characters who yearn for the advantages of the East's more civilized lifestyle" despite that they have the "more vital, if cruder, West in their blood."[16] The emotional lawlessness of opera and the gunmetal toughness of the frontier complemented one another in that both defied convention with utter self-assurance. They each represented a creative nexus of theory and praxis. The rough edges of the borderlands not only didn't hinder artistic accomplishment, it gave art a self-possession that the Old World could not. In 1913, Cather published an article on the Metropolitan School of Ballet Dancing, which had recently opened, supplying the opera, for the first time, with home-grown dancers. Cather wrote that these local dancers "made better dancers than European women, because they were stronger, better nourished, had better figures, and were not afraid to make mistakes as they learned."[17] For Cather, art forms like ballet and opera stood to benefit from the fresh air of the prairie because it combined both the "intellection coming from European culture" with the vitality of humanity finding itself anew. As James Woodress notes, "Cather's roots in the soil of Webster County [, Nebraska,] were deep and well-watered; her knowledge and use of Old World culture was substantial and pervading. The warp and woof of her work is native American, but threads of European culture are woven into the fabric."[18]

Cather was not, however, unaware of the shortcomings of rusticated high art, and her frequent references to opera among the plains folk can also demonstrate ambivalence about the quality of cultural attainment in a small-town setting. On the one hand, common people were engaging with Handel and Gluck with a casualness that seems mostly alien today; on the other, Cather frequently laments an apparent shortfall in their understanding of the possibilities of artistic attainment. In "The Joy of Nelly Deane," for instance, Cather writes of a Christmas Eve performance of Handel's oratorio *Esther,* which has "cost [the performers] three months of hard practice" and attracted "country folk for miles about [who had] come in through a deep snow, [. . .] their teams and wagons [standing] in a long row at the hitch-bars on each side of the church door." Cather notes that despite the best efforts of the tenor to "eclipse her in his dolorous solos about the rivers of Babylon," the crowd is there to hear the phenom Nelly sing the title role.[19] While this scene shows us a Catherian frontier in which farmers will travel hours through the snow to spend an entire evening listening to Handel in a country church—not to mention that they have an apparently innate appreciation for true vocal talent such as Nelly's versus the ersatz strainings of the tenor—Cather shortly thereafter undermines the inborn sophistication of the prairie by having Nelly confide that she's "going to live in Chicago, and take singing lessons, and go to operas, and do all those nice things"—nice things that can't be done, at least not properly, on the prairie.[20] This was an environment that Cather would later describe in relation to Fremstad's upbringing as a "new, crude country where there was neither artistic stimulus nor discriminating taste."[21] And yet the backwaters couldn't have been entirely "crude," as we see in *O Pioneers!,* in which a choir rehearses Rossini's *Petite Messe Solenelle,*[22] or in *My Ántonia,* when Mrs. Harling spends her Saturdays performing *Martha, Norma,* and *Rigoletto* for the locals ("every Saturday night was like a party"),[23] or in *The Song of the Lark* when Thea, a Colorado girl of Swedish extraction, sings songs from Italian operas with Mexican immigrants.[24]

The frontier wasn't perhaps as polished as the city, but the cultural offerings, Cather frequently reminds us, sometimes in spite of herself, were every bit as rich. At the least, Cather recognized a legitimate appreciation among country folk for great art. In a 1916 letter to Dorothy Canfield Fisher, Cather explained why she felt that Thea Kronborg had to be a singer, noting that people from Red Cloud traveled as far as Kansas City to hear singers like Geraldine Farrar, Mary Garden, Adelina Patti, Jenny Lind, and Maria Malibran. "It's half art and half natural phenomenon," she wrote; "it's personal, concrete, a living woman, a living voice there before them." In Red Cloud, she claims, "they truly love, as they say 'the voice.' It fills them with pleasure and content." This is why Thea had to be a singer—it was "for them, not because I happen to go to the Opera a great deal. I wasn't trying to put something over on Red Cloud. I was writing it from their point of view." According to Cather, plains people appreciated the "concrete" and "living" qualities of singers and were willing to travel 250 miles to hear the great ones.[25]

Part of Cather's conflict in portraying culture on the Divide was no doubt to do with her own mixed feelings. Had she been exposed to a vibrant, if unpolished, cultural curriculum in Red Cloud, or had her education been stunted by the lack of quality relative to the city? Were her later artistic accomplishments and the artistic world she inhabited as a successful writer a refined and amplified version of Nebraska, or had a rural upbringing poisoned the well, forcing her to reimagine the prairie as a place of truer art? In an interview with *Good Housekeeping* in 1931, Cather reflected on how she'd created Mr. Shimerda from *My Ántonia* as more of an artist than perhaps he should have been: "I had just heard Bernhardt, and the magic of her voice was still in my ears—and so I made my old man a violinist—a good violinist, who had once played an obligato with a great singer, when she came to the little theatre in which he was first violin in the orchestra. I made that a frill for him [. . .] and did not realize that old Shimerda, just as he was, was good enough for anybody. He was not a violinist. He was just a fiddler—and not even a very good fiddler. He did not need to be. He was enough just as he was."[26] Cather apparently maintained a sort of insecurity with regard to the legitimacy of frontier art well into her life; she was in her early forties when she began writing *Ántonia* and well-established as both a writer and an editor, and yet she still felt the need to puff up the abilities of a character like Shimerda to make art on the frontier worthy of notice. In her essay "My First Novels (There Were Two)," she remembered the comment of one critic's "very general opinion": "I simply don't care a damn what happens in Nebraska, no matter who writes about it"; part of Cather carried the need to prove that the prairie was a place of unexpected artistic virtue, and, hence, worth "caring a damn."[27] Sometimes, for instance with Mrs. Harling or the Mexican immigrants, Cather settled into an attitude that allowed for characters to be perhaps technically inferior but more genuine in their art. For instance, in an interview with the *Lincoln Sunday Star* in 1921, she asserted that "the old-fashioned farmer's wife is nearer to the type of the true artist and the prima donna than is the culture enthusiast."[28] Untutored appreciation is purer than self-aware appreciation. But just as often Cather put small-town artistic fare under a magnifying glass at noonday, scorching it mercilessly.

Cather's attitude toward towns like Moonstone and Black Hawk were as complicated and conflicted as would have been their historical models. On one hand, they could represent a triumph of art making itself felt in unlikely places; on the other, they could exemplify middle-American banality. But this is not to say that Cather blindly admired urban cultural hubs. Her antipathy toward general artistic or intellectual flimsiness extended beyond the small town. In 1924, she cautioned an interviewer with the *New York Times* not to "confuse reading with culture or art [. . .] not in this country, at any rate." Confronted with book sales figures as evidence that Americans were becoming a particularly cultured people, she acknowledged a "vast amount of writing and reading" among Americans and that Americans might have advanced in the practical arts of architecture and bridge building: "but literary art, painting, sculpture, no. We haven't yet acquired the good sense of discrimination possessed by the French, for instance." This dig at American sensibilities relative to the French resulted in a great deal of bad press for Cather. The French, she claimed, "have a great purity of tradition; they all but murder originality, and yet they worship it. The taste of the nation is represented by the Academy; it is a corrective rod which the young artist ever dreads. He revolts against it, but he cannot free himself from it. He cannot pull the wool over the eyes of the academy by saying his is a new movement, an original movement, a breaking away from the old. His work is judged on its merits, and if it isn't good, he gets spanked." But in the United States, "every little glimmer of color calls itself art; every youth that misuses a brush calls himself an artist, and an adoring group of admirers flatter and gush over him. It's rather pathetic."[29] In this statement she is emphatically not referencing a stultifying rural sensibility, but rather national, and particularly urban, America: Americans "want a book which will fill up commuting boredom every morning and evening; they want a book to read mornings after breakfast when the maid takes care of the apartment housework; they want a book to keep in the automobile while they're waiting for tardy friends or relatives; they want fillers-in, in a word, something to take off the edge of boredom and empty leisure." "Empty leisure," "commuting boredom," and maids cleaning apartments clearly are not evocative of frontier Nebraska.

Much earlier, in 1894, she leveled accusations of insufficient sophistication against American audiences of light opera: "Light opera," she lamented, "in any form is popular in America and is becoming more so every year." She contrasted American taste for light opera with the Germans, who were "built for heavy music." The Germans, she claimed, enjoyed just as much a "prima donna [. . .] as old as the 'hills' and as uncomely as those withered dames Hans Holbein drew." They would "not only forgive her [for her appearance], but in their artistic enthusiasm and naïve simplicity they will fancy her an Aphrodite rising from the waves" if her musical skill were sufficient. Americans, however, "prefer action to music" and are, accordingly, less choosey as to the gravity of sound. They need beauty and magnetism—or at least "such an elusive and fascinating sort of homeliness that she can make the public believe it is beauty." Though Cather claimed that American preferences were "not a depravity of taste" but "merely a temperamental difference," the propensity toward light opera sidelined appreciation of both voice and action to the benefit of beauty: "Either she [the singer] must possess the genuine article like Lillian Russell and Della Fox and Pauline Hall, or like Marie Tempest she must" seem to be beautiful. "This is not a repetition of the adoration of the chappies; it is an indisputable fact, and perhaps it is not a fact to be proud of. No woman who did not possess unusual physical charms has ever succeeded in light opera. The result of this is that the American stage is always crowded with women who can neither act or sing and who do not even make an honest endeavor to do either."[30] She had weighed French culture and German musical appreciation against their American counterparts and found her homeland wanting.

If Cather sometimes went to war with American tastes, those prevalent in both small towns and urban centers, she always did so with a measure of internal conflict. Late in her career, she wrote in *Lucy Gayheart* of the quaintness of the Haverford, Nebraska, opera house. "The theatre in every little Western town was then called an opera house," she notes of the theater, full of folding chairs where Lucy had had her commencement exercises years before. But regardless of its modesty, by the end of a performance by a traveling troupe, Lucy has been taken with the prima donna, a woman "slender and graceful, but far from young. She sang so well that Lucy wondered how she had ever drifted into a little road company like this one." The performance is an epiphany for Lucy. She wonders why "singing this humdrum music to humdrum people, [. . .] was [. . .] worth [her] while? This poor little singer had lost everything: youth, good looks, position, the high notes of her voice. And yet she sang so well! Lucy wanted to be up there on the stage with her, helping her to do it. A wild kind of excitement flared up in her. She felt she must run away tonight, by any train, back to a world that strove after excellence—the world out of which this woman must have fallen."[31] Like Thea before her, Lucy fears the artistic vacuum of the small town and chooses to flee to another world. In "A Wagner Matinée," Cather follows the same idea but in inverse order. In this story, Aunt Georgiana has left a life of culture in Boston to settle on the plains, resulting in "dullness" and "silence" for thirty years. It's only when she returns to Boston as an old woman, broken by prairie life, that she can reengage with the beauty of opera. After the story's publication, Cather found herself compelled to protest in a letter to Will Owen Jones that her story did not portray Nebraska in a negative light,[32] but the message was nevertheless indisputable: Boston was culture, Nebraska was an absence of culture.

On a few occasions, Cather paid homage to the Andrews Opera Company, one of the most successful traveling opera companies of the period, and whose *Chimes of Normandy* in Red Cloud was the first opera Cather saw. The performance initiated Cather's lifelong fascination with opera, and she never forgot the troupe itself, mentioning them in *The Song of the Lark* and as late as a 1929 letter to Harvey E. Newbranch. Cautiously, she noted that "they usually had a good voice or two among them, a small orchestra and a painstaking conductor, who was also the pianist"; and with characteristic reserve, "What good luck for a country child to hear those tuneful old operas sung by people who were doing their best: *The Bohemian Girl, The Chimes of Normandy, Martha, The Mikado*. Nothing takes hold of a child like living people."[33] Those "living people" "doing their best"—a perhaps uncomfortably condescending way to put it—is a fair representation of Cather's small-town opera experience.

The Andrews troupe was rare—if not unique—in that it was fully a product of the frontier rather than imported from the coast or from Europe; it was a troupe built on the talent and sweat of a single Midwestern family. It began as a vocal group in 1875, later adding a brass band before becoming a full-fledged opera company by 1884; they performed for twenty-five years in total, at least fifteen devoted to opera performed in English. When Cather wrote of a traveling troupe coming to town to entertain "half a dozen times during each winter," she was remembering Andrews and its ilk, the troupe driving into town with all six horses bedecked with plumes, pulling a blaring bandwagon, the youths of the Andrews clan running alongside to hand out notices of the upcoming performances. Earlier in their history, the Andrews performed light opera, *Pinafore* and *The Doctor of Alcantara;* later they matured into *Faust, Cavalleria,* and *Carmen.* They, like countless other traveling opera companies, represented the apparent dissonance between high culture and common folk that can be prevalent in Cather's writing. They "were not above appearing in any town that would give them a two-hundred-dollar guarantee, and their seat prices never went above a dollar top." The Andrews played a major role in bringing opera to the Midwest, "producing grand opera in English for those whose opportunities to see and hear any form of entertainment, good or bad, were extremely meager. To countless people living in a new, rough country just emerging from its frontier beginnings they took entertainment and conveyed the sense of beauty and inspiration that comes from hearing great music."[34] In the words of John Dizikes, it was "by means of these small troupes that a national American audience was created [before radio and records]. The Alice Oates Opera Company, the Solomon Opera Company, the Comley-Barton Opera Company, the Emily Melville Comic Opera Company, the Castle Square Light Opera Company—these went wherever railroads would take them after the Civil War. And then there were the regional companies. The Pike Opera Company played in and around San Francisco. The Chicago Church Choir Opera Company covered the Middle West. The Bennett and Moulton Opera Company limited itself to New England."[35] The American journalist and novelist Vincent Sheean recalled once hearing a mezzo-soprano named Elaine de Sellem perform *Carmen* with such a troupe: "I have never heard of this artist since, but I thought she was wonderful and I went back again." Despite the apparent general lack of quality in the performance, with "these small, traveling companies with their shabby stage settings and their sketchy orchestras, their powerless conductors and their general bad taste," Sheean noted, "you could get to know the works performed and imagine for yourself, if you had that kind of imagination, what they might be under other circumstances."[36]

As Cather noted with the singer in *Lucy Gayheart* and Sheean with de Sellem, it was a difficult life to work for a traveling opera company, both physically and emotionally: "Many older performers had no future. Young and ambitious ones had to avoid the trap of carelessness and cynicism. Reputations weren't made in Salt Lake City."[37] Ticket prices were kept cheap, which was good for the propagation of culture, but bad for the finances of the companies and performers. The Grand Italian Opera Company would perform up to three operas in a single evening (much abridged, of course) for only fifty cents.[38] One can imagine how hard it would be for a performer to escape such an arrangement either by financial ascendancy or by artistic reputation, especially considering the tools they often had to work with. Composers and directors would frequently have to double as actors, artists, or dancers. The actor Sol Smith recalled one musician-actor "who frequently played two or three parts in one play, and after being killed in the last scene [of *Pizarro*] was obliged to fall far enough off the stage to play slow music as the curtain descended." At the premiere of Reginald De Koven's *Robin Hood,* one of the most popular operas in Cather's day, the tenor was forced to sing in his *Trovatore* costume, and the "dresses of all the principals had seen service in 'Martha,' 'The Bohemian Girl' and other operas."[39]

These companies also had to negotiate the cultural context in which they found themselves, particularly regarding language barriers. Performing in English, as promoted by those such as Caroline Richings of the Richings Grand Opera Company, was a way to reach out to a primarily anglophone audience, or at least an audience that shared English as a common language more than any other, but certainly there were opera purists in places of power that would have not taken seriously an opera aspirant who'd trained on translated libretti. Among these was German-born financier and philanthropist Otto Hermann Kahn, "a staunch defender of the nexus between the original language and the music." Among other reasons, Kahn noted that "not only did the United States lack a state-sanctioned official language, but it was a country of immigrants, and these very same immigrants were counted on to fill the top tiers of the opera house. They would cringe at hearing Aïda invoked as 'Heavenly' rather than 'Celeste' or Lohengrin's 'Lieber' swan addressed as 'Beloved.'"[40] How could even the most talented and ambitious young performer be taken seriously in New York if their resume was singing *The Fallen Girl* (*La Traviata*) in Wyoming?

In addition to professional, financial, and artistic challenges faced by performers, the world in which these companies operated could be unmannerly at the least and dangerous at worst. As Ann Satterthwaite describes the scene, "audiences in the pit and balconies hissed, screamed, corrected actors, and flirted with one another as prostitutes and dandies mingled in the upper balconies. Such rowdy participatory theater was generally deemed unsuitable for 'ladies.' To combat this behavior, as late as 1896 in Lexington, Kentucky, a city ordinance declared it 'unlawful for any person in any public place of amusement to stamp their feet, make cat calls, whistle, hiss, halloo, or make any other noisy demonstrations except clapping of the hands.'"[41] John Dizikes records a dust-up at an opera performance in Bozeman, Montana, in 1871. A traveling group of Italian singers were performing at the Bozeman opera hall, which was above a saloon. Some locals had stolen a stack of business cards, which looked enough like tickets to fool the Italians, who read little English. "When the fraud was discovered, a 'general breakup' ensued. 'Several pistols were drawn, and some of the congregation went downstairs like a demoralized whiskey barrel—head first.'"[42] This is hardly the pinkies-out reputation one might associate with opera. Worth noting, as well, is that wealthy operagoers in New York often didn't behave much better. Tired of the rude indifference and chatter coming from the boxes, the *Musical Courier* in 1884 threatened to publish the names of those who disrupted performances with conversation. A year and a half after, *Harper's* published a piece "urging that the philistines who treated the opera house as their private salon repair to 'the congenial circles of miners and Indian reservations upon the frontier,' an allusion to the West, where so many recent fortunes had been made. In a reversal of class typology, it was the ill-behaved, well-born, well-heeled, and stubbornly middlebrow box holders who were shown up by the well-behaved, modestly born, middle-class, and highbrow ticket holders."[43]

Cather seldom seemed to note that sort of philistinism in city opera, though she was, of course, thoroughly familiar with the opera experience beyond the frontier. When she left Red Cloud, she traded its five-hundred-seat opera house for the Funke and Lansing Theaters in Lincoln (1,200 and 1,800 seats, respectively). There, she was able occasionally to see nationally and internationally prominent performers and ensembles, as well as to be exposed to the accompanying frippery: "Discouraged Bohemian farmers like Mr. Shimerda may have been blowing their brains out on the bleak, lonely prairie of Webster County, but in Lancaster County there were people in top hats and tails eating oysters shipped in from the East in blocks of ice and sipping French champagne at their after-theater parties."[44] Her connections in Lincoln allowed her to have her first exposure to grand opera on her 1895 trip to see the Met's company perform in Chicago. The city of Chicago, founded in 1833, had grown to a population of 28,000 by 1850, the first time opera was performed there. By 1885, the city hosted its Chicago Grand Opera Festival, with ticket prices ranging from one dollar to twelve dollars. Elise Kirk describes Chicago's growth as an American opera hub: "Although not a cultural rival of the East Coast, the City of Big Shoulders was beginning to occupy a prominent position in the world of opera. Chicago saw Bellini's *La Sonnambula* staged by a touring company in 1850, and fifteen years later the city could boast an opera house larger than La Scala. With the opening of the four-thousand-seat Auditorium Theater in 1889, Chicago housed the nation's first cultural center." In its inaugural season, the Auditorium "witnessed Wagner's complete *Ring* during its Metropolitan Opera tour and Verdi's *Otello* (1887) before it appeared in Paris." The Polish tenor Jean De Reszke and the American soprano Emma Eames made their debuts there. "Thus, by the opening of the new century, Chicagoans could hear opera of a quality comparable to any in the country."[45] By the time of Cather's first visit, Midwestern Chicago was the peer of any other American opera city. Clearly, it left an impression, as this is where both Thea Kronborg and Lucy Gayheart, Cather's two novel singer-heroines, go to grow into their craft.

Settling in Pittsburgh in the summer of 1896, Cather found herself living full-time in a larger city with the cultural offerings that go along with such environs. During her time in Pittsburgh, Cather sent drama reviews back to the *Journal,* first reviewing Massenet's oratorio *Eve.*[46] In Pittsburgh, she had her first opportunity to hear Wagner performed. Despite the fact that "all the singers had colds, 'which beset every singer who ventures into this foggy river atmosphere'" and that "Herr Kraus, who sang Lohengrin, had to stop in the middle of an aria for a coughing seizure, and 'poor Frau Venus on her couch coughed until Tannhäuser's head which rested on her knee shook as if he had the palsy,'"[47] she nonetheless decided that "Wagner is perhaps not so effective as elsewhere, we are all so used to the noise of the iron mills."[48] Even so, every year Walter Damrosch would bring a company to Pittsburgh to perform Wagner for a week, and it was this exposure that led her to a lifelong fascination with the composer.

She moved to New York in 1906, near the crest of the American Wagner craze. A few decades before, New York had remained the principal situs of Italian opera in the United States, bolstered by the "old family" Knickerbockersupported Academy of Music: "There the Knickerbocracy had contrived to maintain a last foothold, for the eighteen boxes at the Academy were passed from father to son by Old Guard families like Livingston, Cutting, Bayard, Duer, Beekman, Schermerhorn, Schuyler, and Barlow."[49] Gilded Age new wealth families such as the Goulds, Morgans, Roosevelts, Vanderbilts, and Whitneys were cut out of the old guard Academy and opted to build their own opera house: the Metropolitan. The Met, featuring 122 boxes and costing $1,732,478.71 to build, represented a break from exclusionary grand opera, not only allowing wealthy industrial families access to premier opera, but emphasizing price-conscious ticketing practices that would allow nonwealthy people access to opera as well (today, Met ticket prices remain notably less than those of most major venues). To compete with the better-established Academy, the Met hired Leopold Damrosch in 1884. Whereas the Met's inaugural season had featured only two German operas, both in Italian translation, Damrosch had proposed a season of German-language opera. The directors of the Met, believing that their success relied on "Damrosch or nothing," assented and gambled that German opera would elevate the venue above the Academy.[50] Their bet paid off massively. By 1886, the Academy had failed, its impresario, James Henry Mapleson, walking away from the institution saying, "I cannot fight Wall Street." The Academy was used for various means—from theater to labor rallies—for a few decades before it and its neighboring structure, Tammany Hall, were demolished, with great historical irony, to build the Consolidated Edison Company Building.[51]

Until the outbreak of World War I, Wagner reigned supreme in American opera. Elise Kirk wonders why the "love affair" with Wagner and posits a temperamental cause: "He promulgated a new kind of visionary morality in what was to Americans a familiar format—the melodrama. His operas were, in essence, the final cry of waning nineteenth-century melodrama—provocative, spiritual, and uplifting." She notes a "Yankee push" in his work and claims that "women especially were drawn to him, both through the passion of his music and the courage of his heroines." She further notes that Wagner's music was new music and that America self-consciously thought of itself as a new world: "Wagner seemed to inspire ambitious Americans who felt they were following a genuine cultural hero. The younger generation especially, wrote a critic in 1882, 'thinks and feels and sees with Wagner by instinct and not by effort.' For Americans, Richard Wagner's 'Music for the Future' was also the music of the present."[52] Jed Rasula notes Wagner's rise in America "despite widespread resistance to his music in Europe," citing a variety of evidence: "an all-Wagner concert was given in Boston to great acclaim as early as 1853. [. . .] Walt Whitman, with characteristic good cheer, said of the music, 'it makes my old bones sweeter.' In Philadelphia, the Centennial Exposition of 1876 [. . .] had a Wagner soundtrack for its opening ceremony. [. . .] Wagner concerts dominated the summer music program at Brighton Beach, on the east side of Coney Island, mingling 'Wagner and clam fritters, Wagner and soft-shell crabs, Wagner and fish chowder, Wagner and bathing-suits.'"[53] When *Parsifal* premiered on Christmas Eve in 1903 at the Met, ticket requests "numbered more than seven thousand, and five hundred people had to stand for the entire five-hour performance." Cosima Wagner, his widow and the director of his musical estate, was concerned that commercialism would corrupt the purity of the sacred nature of the work. According to Kirk, "perhaps she had a point. In New York, for example, a veritable 'Parsifalitis' epidemic broke out, replete with Parsifal hats, Parsifal cigars, and Parsifal cocktails." At least four towns in America have a "Parsifal Place," and statues to the composer stand in Cleveland and Baltimore.[54]

In addition to any temperamental affinities between Wagner and America, immigration certainly played a role. Like Cather's Nebraska—which, as late as 1910 saw foreign-born residents outnumber American-born three to one—New York was an immigrant-heavy society, particularly Germans. Between 1846 and 1855, more than a million Germans immigrated to the United States (the US population in 1850 was a little over 21 million),[55] many of whom settled in New York. In 1880, the census showed 360,000 people of German origin in Manhattan alone, about 30 percent of the population. Had the so-called Kleindeutschland of Manhattan's Lower East Side been its own city, it would have been the fourth largest municipality in the United States; New York was "the third German-speaking metropolis in the world, outstripped only by Berlin and Vienna."[56] This prevalence of Germans in America had an outsized impact on music, particularly in New York. In 1855, 79 percent of the New York Philharmonic was German; by 1892, that figure rose to 97 percent. The American composer and pianist Louis Gottschalk, upon "hearing a military band in 1863 [. . .] sourly asked: 'Is it necessary to say that it is composed of Germans (all musicians in the United States are German)?'"[57]

So it isn't surprising, from a variety of standpoints, that America took to Wagner, but it will certainly be important to remember Wagner's impact during

Cather's most formative literary period, particularly when she was living in New York, the epicenter of Wagnermania at the time. This will bear clues as to her artistic theory and development and help explain, perhaps, why she began to back away from opera as a subject after *The Song of the Lark,* when she'd thoroughly worked through her most Wagnerian tendencies via the story of a great Wagnerian soprano. But it's also important to remember that Wagner wasn't the whole story of Cather and opera. She wrote often of Italian, French, and American opera, as well. Edith Lewis, remembering their early days in New York "remember[ed] that we discussed once whether it would be worthwhile to buy a new coffee-pot, since the future seemed so uncertain. Our practice of economy was, however, accompanied by extravagance. [. . .] Even in those days we went often to the opera, sitting high up, in the cheap seats. The Metropolitan, at any rate, was not economizing then. I recall a performance of *Don Giovanni* in 1908, with Eames, Sembrich, Scotti and Chaliapin in the cast, and Gustav Mahler conducting."[58] Cather was one of the very few Americans of her period to experience opera in its many forms, its highs and lows. She knew the Andrews Opera Company performing *The Chimes of Normandy* two blocks from her home in a tiny upstairs theater "opera house." She knew Eames and Sembrich under the baton of Mahler at the Met. Cather's opera experience, like her work and the history of American opera, is an exceptionally wide spectrum.

RUSTIC CHIVALRY
Opera in Cather's Early Fiction

The end of art is named only by indirection—cryptic suggestions of the 'something
else' which is perceived, or the veiled confusions of words like 'beauty,' or the
trials of metaphor. Imperfect and indefinite—yet all the pieces wheel
like a constellation around some core of light.
—Bernice Slote, introduction to *The Kingdom of Art*

*O*n June 13, 1890, sixteen-year-old Willa Cather was one of three graduates
of the high school in Red Cloud. Each student was required to give a
speech, to be delivered in the performance hall of the Red Cloud Opera
House. Cather was, by all accounts, a talented public speaker, though later in her
career she decried public lectures, the "lecture bug" as she called it, which she
saw as distracting for the serious writer. But that later hesitation to throw pearls
before pigs on the speaking circuit was a learned antipathy. As a youth—and one
who had yet to take writing seriously—, she had no such reservations.[1]

Alex Bentley (a relative of M. R. Bentley, the model for the vicious Wick
Cutter in *My Ántonia*) discoursed on the topic "New Times Demand New
Measures and New Men"—an appropriate topic for a recent graduate. Local
boy John Tulleys delivered a somewhat Trumpian address on "Self-Advertising"
in which he asserted that "a man should blow his own trumpet and the louder
and longer he can blow the deeper impression he will make and the trumpet
he uses should be made of brass and the more brass it contains and the more
vigorously it is blown the louder it will sound."[2] Cather's speech was more cul-
tivated, if no less assertive. According to the *Red Cloud Chief,* she demonstrated
"at once her knowledge of and familiarity with both history and classics of ancient and modern times" in an oration on "Superstition versus Investigation," in

which she spoke of humanity's "exodus from barbarism to civilization" through scientific inquiry. It was in part a defense of controversial scientific practices such as vivisection and in part an attempt to expurgate unfounded belief from religious practice, a bold task no doubt meant to address the provinciality of her hometown.

"Superstition," she declared, "has ever been the curse of the church, and until she can acknowledge that since her principles are true, no scientific truth can contradict them, she will never realize her full strength."[3] Cather advocated a science-backed religion, though not like "the Ancient orientals [who] were highly civilized people but were dreamers and theorists who delved into the mystical and metaphysical, leaving the more practical questions [to] remain unanswered." She proceeded to praise the "practical worth" of the Greeks and condemn the "iron scepter of fear" of the European Middle Ages before declaring that "scientific investigation is the hope of our age." It's a problematic speech, but impressive for an author of sixteen who had limited formal education and was attempting a universal theory of epistemology in approximately 1,200 words. If nothing else, it shows Cather's confidence and ambition. And it shows her early tendency toward philosophical syncretism; as a teenager, science and *true* religion were one knowable truth. To make her case, she leaned on one of the favorite authors of her youth: "Worship as defined by [Thomas] Carlyle is unmeasured wonder, but there are two kinds of wonder, that born of fear and that of admiration; slavish fear is never reverence."[4] Worship for Cather in the spring of 1890 was a matter of admiring the reality of the universe understood concretely, less a matter of fear and trembling. With this speech, Willa Cather solidified her independence from convention while not quite committing herself to what form that independence would take.

Less than one year later, on March 1, 1891, her thoughts on Carlyle would reappear, published simultaneously in *The Hesperian* and the *Nebraska State Journal.* She described Carlyle as "always dreaming," with "one half of his heart [. . .] always in Valhalla." He had "one of the most intensely reverent natures" and "his every act was a form of worship," but his religious universalism, along with his dislike of social convention, would have made him ill-suited for the ministry. He was a truth-teller naturally alienated from popular assumptions. He was "the last of the mammoths, tortured and harassed beyond all endurance by the smaller, though perhaps more perfectly organized offspring of the world's mature years." He was an independent, as was she, regardless of the judgments of the lesser beings in orbit. He who had written about history as a succession of heroic figures and deeds—"The History of the world is but the Biography of great men"—Cather was now writing of as one of those heroes. She wasn't shy about piggybacking on Carlyle's grandiosity with some of her own nascent artistic theories, including the memorable "Art of every kind is an exacting master, more so than even Jehovah. He says only, 'Thou shalt have no other gods before me.' Art, science, and letters cry, 'Thou shalt have no other gods at all.' They accept only human sacrifices." She was using Carlyle as a safety net to express her burgeoning ideas about art.

Though Cather later remembered the essay as "a splendid example of the kind of writing I most dislike; very florid and full of high-flown figures of speech,"[5] its publication was the only push she needed to move from science to letters. In her high school oration, she'd written about the necessity of objective scientific inquiry unsullied by conventional morality or superstition; it was a speech that trod the borderlands between philosophy and hard science. It was commonsensical, but with ever a hint of artistic outburst. The Carlyle essay, less than a year later, not only did literary history the favor of showing Cather her own name published—"what youthful vanity can be unaffected by the sight of itself in print!"—thus prompting her to pursue arts and letters as a career, but it also allowed her to engage her theories of art without the distraction of practical science. In this essay, art and religion become one *unknowable* truth. In "Concerning Thos. Carlyle," we see both the transition from scientist to writer, as well as Cather's first attempt to formulate the "Kingdom of Art" ideas that would continue, in some form, her entire career.

Few major authors have an apprentice corpus as diverse as Cather's. In part, the breadth of her style and subject probably reflects that she was late in coming to her literary aspirations. F. Scott Fitzgerald could get his Old West melodrama—*The Girl from Lazy J*—out of the way in his youth, as could Ernest Hemingway his experiments in poetry—"Blank Verse," a poem composed entirely of punctuation, written in high school—, but Cather didn't know she wanted to be a writer until Professor Hunt had published her Carlyle essay during her prep year at the University of Nebraska. Though she'd read extensively and intensely as a youth, she had ground to cover as a young adult transitioning between a prospective woman of science to one of letters. Accordingly, her fiction of the 1890s gives readers the rare opportunity to see the artist learning her craft from the ground up. Whereas her critical voice was a product of natural inclinations hammered out rather quickly through copious work on the theater circuit, it took her longer to settle on a typically Catherian mode for her fiction.

In college, she published such works as "A Tale of the White Pyramid" (1892), a Poe-esque tale of ancient Egypt; "The Son of the Celestial" (1893), a character sketch of a Chinese immigrant in San Francisco; "The Elopement of Allen Poole" (1893), a local-color story full of thick Southern dialect; "The Clemency of the Court" (1893), a political allegory; and "The Fear That Walks by Noonday" (1895), a football story built around a play-by-play rendering of a game. As prolific as she'd been in Nebraska, her fiction apprenticeship intensified noticeably once she moved to Pittsburgh in 1896 to edit *Home Monthly*. In that year alone, Cather published at least nine short stories, including "A Night at Greenway Court," historical fiction set in colonial Virginia; "The Princess Baladina—Her Adventure," a children's story; "The Count of Crow's Nest," a mystery; "Wee Winkie's Wanderings" and "The Burglar's Christmas," Victorian sentimentalia; and "The Strategy of the Were-Dog," a Christmas fantasy in which a werewolf attempts to sabotage Santa's flying reindeer. Through the end of the century, she began to narrow her focus and style to something more recognizably Cather, though still with experiments like the Wildean "West Bound Train" (1898), a comedic short play, and "The Affair at Grover Station" (1900), a ghost story. And among these many outliers are more recognizable efforts in plains narratives like "On the Divide" (1896) and "El Dorado: A Kansas Recessional" (1896). In all, the thirty-two stories Cather published between 1892 and 1902, when she began to publish those that would appear in *The Troll Garden,* represent a staggering diversity of material, if that material also frequently reveals its author's relatively amateur standing.

Her early fiction tells a story of an author finding her topic and method, allowing readers to see the diversity-in-self that she spent a decade of apprentice work sorting out. Clearly, much of that early fiction was not written with high artistic ideals in mind; often, Cather's uncollected fiction is imitative, careless, or formulaic. But it also bears evidence of her hammering out her artistic guideposts. In 1894, she noted that an artist's work is "all God gave him" instead of happiness, popularity, and friendship.[6] The artist's life was one of renunciation. A year later, that ethic was applied to football, with a character in "The Fear That Walks by Noonday" lamenting that "nobody but hermits and anchorites can play foot ball. A Methodist parson don't have to practice half such rigid abstinence as a man on the eleven," remembering all "the supper parties he had renounced, the invitations he had declined, and the pretty faces he had avoided in the last three months."[7] The hermetic purity required of athleticism as Cather described it no doubt extended from the purity of artistic devotion. Art required not just a renunciation of earthly comforts, but also the giving over of oneself to emotional truth. In 1899, Cather published an open letter to soprano Lilian Nordica in which she chastised Nordica for her "Puritanic aversion for emotional display," noting that her "indifference" to the character of Santuzza in *Cavalleria Rusticana* was "obvious."[8] "Ah!," she wrote, "if you would sometimes let your heart go out with that all-conquering voice! if you would but sometimes be a woman!"[9] Around the same time, she was applying this theory of performance to her soprano characters in "Nanette: An Aside" (1897) and "A Singer's Romance" (1900), writing of Tradutorri in "Nanette" that she "holds back her suffering within herself; she suffers as the flesh and blood women of her century suffer. [. . .] It is this stifled pain that wrings your heart when you hear her, that gives you the impression of horrible reality." Cather was engaged in identifying what, beyond the voice, makes a great soprano great. Measuring *Il Barbiere di Siviglia* against *Cavalleria Rusticana,* she noted in a May 1900 review that "had operatic composition never advanced beyond the frank artifice and blithe triviality of Rossini, operagoing would scarcely have become a serious avocation."[10] This was during the same year she published "Eric Hermannson's Soul," her first story in a national magazine, which references the Intermezzo from *Cavalleria* as a way of introducing the title character to a world of passion and art rather than the artifice and triviality of the moral conventions to which he'd previously submitted himself. In the 1890s, then, Cather was learning to sound like *Cather;* that process of exploration frequently echoed or referenced her emerging understanding of opera.

The first story Cather published that would eventually appear in *The Troll Garden* (1905), her first short story collection and a fair boundary for the termination of her apprentice career, was "A Death in the Desert," published in *Scribner's Magazine* in 1903. Prior to that was a decade of bold exploration and risk-taking, mixed with much conventional fiction of the period. While there are some bright spots and much promise, they clearly represent a period of teeth-cutting for Cather. Even so, they help establish Cather's artistic tendencies that would permeate her career, particularly her attitudes toward music in society. Writing in the *Nebraska State Journal* in 1894, ostensibly in a column on Sarah Bernhardt, she declared that "whole nations have died from spiritual famine as well as from a famine of corn. The world must have ideals and emotions and it cannot always make them for itself. It will pay any price for them, risk any peril for them. They come to us, these actors and poets and painters and singers of sweet music, from somewhere out of the region of the vast unknown, and we give them food and raiment, the best the land affords, and in return they give us our dreams."[11] Where she'd begun the decade with an eye toward scientific inquiry, through the course of a decade she worked out an idea that art was every bit as essential to human survival as an objective understanding of our universe. From her earliest fiction, *art,* more often than not, meant *music;* and by the end of that decade, music was almost always opera.

Her first published short story was "Peter," originally appearing, improbably,[12] in a Boston literary weekly called *The Mahogany Tree* on May 21, 1892. It would become also her second story published in the *Hesperian* on November 24, 1892, after "Lou, the Prophet," which had been published the previous month. "Peter" is a reworking of the story of Bohemian immigrant Francis Sadilek, father of Annie Sadilek who became the model for Ántonia Shimerda, who had one morning taken his shotgun out, ostensibly to hunt, only to turn it on himself. The story as Cather writes it begins not with the family patriarch casually bidding everyone at home farewell, but rather with his being engaged in a disagreement with his son, Antone, who is trying to convince his father to give up his violin. "I need money," says Antone. "What good is that old fiddle to thee? The very crows laugh at thee when thou art trying to play. Thy hand trembles so thou canst scarce hold the bow."[13] Peter stalls, saying that the day is too cold but that he will relent tomorrow. Cather then provides his backstory. Five years earlier, he and his family, including his wife and Antone, the eldest son, had moved to southwest Nebraska to homestead. A mere three years before that, he'd been "second violinist in the great theatre at Prague," where he ate and drank plenty and where he "wore a dress coat every evening, and there were always parties after the play." He remembers hearing Liszt perform, and remembers being captivated by a great French actress: "The last night she played a play in which a man touched her arm, and she stabbed him. As Peter sat among the smoking gas jets down below the footlights with his fiddle on his knee, and looked up at her, he thought he would like to die too, if he could touch her arm once." However, he is injured by a "stroke of paralysis" that inhibits his performance, and he is dismissed from the theater orchestra. Cather leaves the rest of the details to the reader, but, presumably, Peter heard, like so many others, of the easy life and free land in America and immigrated, finding instead "nothing but sun, and grass, and sky." Peter, delicate and foolish, does not succeed as a farmer, but his son Antone, who reached manhood on the frontier, has the iron practicality necessary to survive. He has no tolerance for frivolities like music—the clash of the frontier mores and art will become a trend in Cather's early fiction—and, consequently, Peter learned to fear above all else "the Evil One, and his son Antone."

Realizing that his only happiness is behind him, and dreading the imminent loss of his instrument, he takes the violin and Antone's shotgun out into the moonlight. He thinks about Antone's severe nature—his penuriousness and his demands on the women in the household. He caresses the violin, telling it, "we have seen it all together, and we will forget it together, the French woman and all." Then he breaks the violin over his knee, puts the muzzle of the gun to his forehead, and pushes the trigger with his toe. In the morning, his family finds him frozen through, too bent and stiff for a coffin, so he has to be buried in a pine box. Antone finds his father's violin bow, which Peter had forgotten to break and takes it into town hoping to sell it. "Antone was very thrifty," Cather concludes, "and a better man than his father had been." While Cather clearly and professedly modeled Peter Sadelack on Francis Sadilek, it's worth positing that she might also have had in mind her own father, notably gentle and mannerly, a product of the east, who'd had to move his family into town after struggling through only one season as a farmer. Cather's message is that breaking the land is a task for those who are *of* that land—Antone or Alexandra Bergson—not the first generation who came and strove and, in their inability to leave behind the delicacies of civilization, failed. In particular, Cather's attention to music in "Peter" indicates an inner conflict with regard to art on the frontier. "Peter" sends the message that the beauty of music is incompatible with the brutality of life on the Divide. But the idea that music or art and the frontier are somehow irreconcilable is a notion Cather would abandon later, instead noting in her fiction how often art flourished in the wilds in a truer way than it would in the cities. "Peter" shows us Cather hammering out her ideas about the humanness of art and the humanness of the settler experience. In this story, the inexperienced Cather took the more obvious route and wrote a story in which the harsher experience simply obliterates the more beautiful one. But she would eventually learn to reconcile the two, and the idea that human artistic expression is perhaps better suited for the fields than the forums is, in fact, one of Cather's innovations, one aspect of what made her work different and noticeable in the early twentieth century.

But she didn't only write of art in its rustic iterations. Cather's geographic biography shows a noticeable list toward the urban. She grew up "in town" in Red Cloud, then moved to Lincoln, then to Pittsburgh, then to New York, her primary permanent residence for most of her professional life. Her early fiction begins to follow this trajectory beginning in 1896, as soon as she began working for the *Home Monthly*. And as she increasingly included music in her fiction, her writings on music became increasingly framed by an urban or suburban context, such as "The Prodigies" (1897), a story based on a prairie remembrance that Cather migrated near to the city.

Mildred Bennett writes of Willa and her brother Roscoe visiting the "New Virginia" settlement near Catherton, outside Red Cloud, during the summer when she was twenty years old. It was customary for some of the farm families to hold "literaries" occasionally—sessions in which neighboring families would gather to discuss art and ideas.[14] The topic of the gathering that Willa and Roscoe attended was Emerson and the Transcendentalists, whom Willa claimed the farmers understood far better than her classmates in Lincoln. This notion of great art and philosophy being a sort of record of lived experience is one that remained with Cather throughout her life, as with her 1921 statements that "the old-fashioned farmer's wife is nearer to the type of the true artist [. . .] than is the culture enthusiast" and that the child "who plays by ear on his fiddle airs from *Traviata* without knowing what he is playing, or why he likes it, has more real understanding of Italian art."[15] Such a gathering also illustrates for modern readers the thirst frontier folk had for education and culture. Imagine today a dozen farmers and families gathering to discuss Slavoj Žižek or Judith Butler, particularly before the Information Age, even before Carnegie had dotted the countryside with modern, accessible libraries. If the Westerners were generally less educated, their eagerness to match coastal erudition was certainly a formidable impulse. It should be no surprise, then, that the gathering also featured a musical performance by one of the farmers' daughters. "This unhappy soul," as Bennett describes her, sang twelves pieces with encores. "Willa was ready to explode," both because of the quality of the performance and the banality of the repertoire (Bennett posits that this was the inspiration for Lily Fisher in *The Song of the Lark*), but also, presumably, the stage-motherishness of forcing a child to expose herself performing for gawking—or simply bored—parental acquaintances. While this anecdote occurred in far-flung Catherton, a few years later Cather would transplant it to a suburban neighborhood reflective of her life in Pittsburgh.

"The Prodigies" begins with Harriet and Nelson Mackenzie preparing to leave home to hear the children of a friend perform a recital. The children, Hermann and Adrienne Massey, are noted singers who have already received intensive vocal training under some of the world's great teachers and have been introduced to some of the major players in the opera world. Adrienne has a photograph inscribed to her by Jean de Reszke reading "To the Juliette of the future from an old Romeo." Cosima Wagner gave the children a picture of Richard, as well as a book of Nibelung mythology, possibly Jessie Weston's *The Legends of the Wagner Drama,* probably the best-known English-language analysis of the Wagner sources during the setting of the story. The children also read Grail legends, further aligning them with the Wagners.

Harriet Mackenzie envies the Massey family. She was herself a musician of some skill as a youth, with a career nearly launched by the great Polish pianist Theodor Leschetizky before she improbably settled down with Nelson, a sensible, caring doctor whose only apparent artistic inclination is to play the cornet; in an apparent reference to the tooting of popular brass bands of the time, the fact of his cornetting "alone was certainly enough to disqualify him for becoming the husband of a pianist." Harriet, who notes that the "cruelly exacting life of art" is "offered to [women] at a terrible price," had been willing to forgo her concert career and settle down, but only because she assumed that her offspring would inherit her talent and inclinations and would fulfill her artistic legacy. However, it was not to be. Nelson and Harriet's children are happy and healthy, but musically wholly inept, even to the point that they have difficulty recognizing the "simplest nursery air." They have much to recommend them, being "unusually truthful and well conducted," but they are "thoroughly commonplace," and decidedly unartistic.

The Massey children perform and are applauded enthusiastically. Even Nelson Mackenzie, who had previously uttered a reservation about "exhibiting [. . .] children [. . .] like freaks," congratulates Kate Massey by telling her that she must "feel blessed among women." The aftershow quickly becomes about Kate and her shameless bragging on the children's progress, their European tutoring and performances, and their love of repertoire. She recounts Hermann asking that she instruct their hired girl to stop singing "Sunday school songs and street airs": "Mamma," he said (at least according to his mother), "I don't like to ask you to send Annie away, but please ask her to not to sing to us, she sings such dreadful things." She offers their early love of Beethoven's *Lied* "In Questa Tomba Oscura"—a spiteful song about a dead lover—as evidence of their precociousness. For that evening's performance, she'd had her children singing from Gounod's *Romeo et Juliette* (hence the detail about de Reszke's unseemly claim to be Romeo to little Adrienne's Juliette). In a few nights, she's taking them to see Berlioz's *Damnation of Faust*.

Richard Giannone noted that the music Cather selects for the children is all "painfully inappropriate" and "serve[s] to emphasize the incongruity of young talents weighed down by mature art."[16] A young brother and sister singing a love duet from *Romeo et Juliette* is clearly meant to make the reader uneasy, to worry about the children and side with Nelson Mackenzie as his unease with the children's treatment grows. What's important, though, is not just noting that Cather is using music to illustrate the problematic experience of the Massey children—but that this is the first time in her fiction she uses music in this fashion. "The Prodigies" represents Cather's first foray into operatic intertextuality. In a few of the seventeen short stories she'd published before "The Prodigies," she'd made passing reference to opera as a genre, notably in "The Count of Crow's Nest," where she briefly engaged with the relative merits of the operatic subgenres oratorio and light opera. But never before had she made reference to a specific opera for the purpose of fleshing out a character, establishing a setting, or moving a plot forward. She didn't have the kids perform selections from *Hansel und Gretel*—she had them perform *Romeo et Juliette*. The impact of one title versus the other is very different. Cather would make reference to forty-seven specific operas in her fiction, almost all of them meaningful intertextual references. The first two appear in this story.

At intermission, while their mother is busy accepting praise on behalf of her children, Nelson notices the two children are standing together at a window in an adjacent room. He listens to their conversation, in which they discuss wanting to play outside with the neighbor kids. "They do have awfully good times," says Hermann. "Perhaps that's why they are so common. Most people seem to be who have a good time." However, they cannot—they've already fallen too far behind in their Italian studies. Nelson approaches them and offers to set up a play date with the Massey kids and his own children, but it seems like they won't have much in common. The Mackenzie children aren't musical, and the

Masseys read the *Nibelungenlied* rather than *Swiss Family Robinson*. Nelson returns from intermission somewhat confounded. The children begin to perform the second part of their program, but Adrienne, pale and quaking, collapses to the floor. An ailment, unidentified but clearly connected to the intensity of her vocal training, has felled the girl. Mackenzie attends to her, and she recovers over time, but she will never sing again. Knowing this, Kate turns to her son, telling him "you carry not one destiny in your throat, but two. You must be great enough for both!" Nelson, unable to make Kate Massey see sense, leaves the boy to his mother and fate.

"The Prodigies" is Cather's first significant use of opera in fiction. But, if Cather was beginning to understand how to use opera to her advantage in telling a story, she still had not quite ironed out her attitude toward opera as an art form or how the artist attains greatness. The idea of frailty hand-in-hand with artistic rigor certainly doesn't sound like Cather. We see here an inconsistency, an instance of the author coming into being. Though Cather frequently wrote child characters, she rarely if ever in her mature fiction romanticizes childhood as she does in "The Prodigies." In her later fiction she writes of children essentially as smaller, less-experienced adults, but does not separate them out into some separate sphere of innocence. And when she writes of the connection between music and youth in later fiction, there is seldom, if ever, a sense that artistic endeavor is infringing on an idealized childhood. Philip Kennicott notes that "The Prodigies" "has an uncanny edge to it, a Hawthornesque edge; but it also shows the author's awareness of the simple but easily overlooked fact that music, more than most other arts, demands repetition and study, detachment and isolation. And these things can be debilitating."[17] Certainly this is the point of the story. But by the 1910s, Cather would write of a young Thea Kronborg practicing piano for hours a day, taking after it "like a terrier after rats." She'd write of Olive Fremstad's father abusively forcing his daughter to practice for hours a day so that, even in adulthood, her hands showed the wear of long practice hours; but Cather wrote that such rigor instilled the work ethic that made Fremstad the operatic superstar she became. In "The Prodigies," Cather recognizes the trollishness of Kate Massey, but it's hard to imagine Cather writing the same story twenty years later, when she had for so long espoused, and lived, ideals of artistic purity and sacrifice.

Cather would revisit the idea of practice in the life of an artist many times. In fact, she frequently covered the same or similar material from different angles, even, like many authors, occasionally recycling material. When a story was particularly piquant but underserved, or when her first outing with an idea didn't quite match her expectation as her art matured, she would rework an idea into a new story or as part of a longer narrative. She did this with "Peter," which was fashioned into Mr. Shimerda's suicide in *My Ántonia.* Many parts of "The Son of the Celestial" reappear in "The Conversion of Sum Loo" (1900). And "Nanette: An Aside" (1897), published in *Home Monthly,* became "A Singer's Romance" three years later when published in *The Library.*

Of these latter two, both stories focus on prima donna sopranos at the peak of their career, offering perspective on Cather's emerging interest in the opera star system that would fully manifest itself in her friendships with opera singers such as Fremstad years later, and in her depiction of the rise of fictional soprano Thea Kronborg in *The Song of the Lark.* The stories' similarities are apparent. Both feature sopranos in their prime, both also are situated on those sopranos coping with the loss of young assistants who leave them for men.

In "Nanette," a singer named Tradutorri had, years earlier, taken the daughter of a deceased friend into her employ to tend to her daily needs as she travels. Nanette, having fallen in love, gingerly floats the idea of remaining in New York, where Tradutorri had been engaged in singing the role of Santuzza in *Cavalleria Rusticana.* The older woman balks: "Of course you cannot leave me. Why who could ever learn all the needs of my life as you know them? What I may eat and what I may not, when I may see people and when they will tire me, what costumes I can wear and at what temperature I can have my baths." She is, as she owns, "as helpless as a child," not to mention lonely, given that her husband, suffering a vague illness, has abandoned her for the gambling tables of Monte Carlo. Nanette agrees not to remain with her lover in New York. Then Cather spends several paragraphs justifying Tradutorri's apparent selfishness by explaining her relationship to her art. Tradutorri "is the only woman of [her] generation who sings with the soul rather than the senses." Unlike other "simple and transparent" singers who "vent their suffering," Tradutorri keeps her suffering locked in, making one wonder how "one woman's heart can hold a grief so great." Hers is the "theory of 'repression.' This is classical art, art exalted, art deified." Cather compares Tradutorri to Maria Malibran, who, according to opera lore, sang herself to death (she'd collapsed in exhaustion after a series of encores, yet continued to sing). Someone so wrapped up in the deliberate purity of art could certainly not be expected to fill her own baths. Nevertheless, after a night of thought Tradutorri demands that Nanette leave her for the lover. She has decided that Nanette's purity of emotion is as equally valuable as her own art, and that there are "women who wear crowns who would give them for an hour" of the love that Nanette is experiencing.

"A Singer's Romance" includes several of the same basic elements. A soprano, her devoted assistant, an absent husband malingering in Monte Carlo. And while the soprano in question is now Selma Schumann rather than Tradutorri, her assistant is Antoinette, matching the diminutive of "Nanette" in Cather's earlier story. However, "A Singer's Romance" plays out a bit differently. In it, Schumann is a journeywoman soprano rather than a marquee star. At age forty-two, she reflects that her artistic maturity came too late, that, as with Cather's 1894 interview of Helena von Doenhoff, "art does not come at sixteen"—she's satisfied with her artistic achievement, but saddened by the realization that she's allowed her youth to pass in the process. Schumann has noticed a vaguely latinate man frequently hanging about her theater and dressing room and wherever else she might happen to be. She addresses him, but he never replies, other than to bow slightly. She fantasizes that he is a devotee of her neglected art, and imagines an *affaire de coeur*. To that end, she's given up sweets and champagne, her erstwhile only pleasures, in an attempt to regain her figure. One morning, she overhears Antoinette speaking in an adjoining room. She listens in and hears Antoinette speaking with the Signore, saying, "she is so lonely. I cannot find the heart to tell her that I must leave her." He replies that "she has been like a mother to you, the Madame, she will be glad of your happiness." Realizing that her assistant is soon to leave her for the man she'd assumed was soon to be hers, she weeps, recovers, then orders breakfast and a quart of champagne.

Clearly, as a nascent writer of fiction, Cather spoke, understood, and thought as a child. "Nanette" is a sentimental Victorian story about a mother figure's self-sacrifice for a daughter figure. But, three years later and through a glass darkly, Cather put childish simplicity aside and wrote about a character achieving a measure of independence in facing a difficult truth of life. These stories demonstrate the gulf between, as John Flannigan notes, Cather's youthful artistic creed that "in the kingdom of art there is no God, but one God" and her much later statement that "art is too terribly human to be very 'great.'" Only, the gap between these stories was one of merely three years. In that brief time, Cather had become much more realistic about the life of the artist. In

"Nanette," the title character is willing to forgo her own happiness to facilitate Tradutorri's greatness, and it's only when Tradutorri recognizes that letting Nanette free is itself an act of artistic greatness that the story concludes. In "A Singer's Romance," however, Schumann faces the hard fact that the Signore was in fact not enamored of her artistic skill but rather of the simple, youthful beauty of Antoinette. Schumann represents the artist alone. As Cather would quote Fremstad a decade and a half later, "you need never be afraid any one will take [your art] away from you, for the chances are nobody will ever know you've got it." This idea of the untranslatable greatness and the inherent loneliness of the artist's quest will appear frequently in Cather's later fiction, both in her artistically inclined characters like Thea Kronborg, Nelly Deane, and Lucy Gayheart and in characters who make unappreciated discoveries, like Tom Outland in *The Professor's House*.

Though she wrote frequently of citified music folk, Cather never overlooked the place of art in the rustic for long. Published in *The Cosmopolitan* in April 1900, "Eric Hermannson's Soul" was Cather's first story published in a major national literary magazine. It begins with the title character attending, at the badgering of his mother, a Free Gospeller revival. Eric has been a known dancer, fiddler, and general carouser. The Free Gospellers, led by a man named Asa Skinner, know that Eric's a big fish—converting him could have substantial implications for the legitimacy of Skinner's group: "Never had Asa Skinner spoken more earnestly than now. He felt that the Lord had this night a special work for him to do. To-night Eric Hermannson, the wildest lad on all the Divide, sat in his audience with a fiddle on his knee, just as he had dropped in on his way to play for some dance." The violin, "an object of particular abhorrence to the Free Gospellers [. . .], singing forever of worldly pleasures and inseparably associated with all forbidden things,"[18] is Skinner's focus. Getting Eric to forsake that instrument would be a tangible assertion of salvation. During the service, Eric's mind wanders through earthly delights: "a girl named Lena singing to him while playing guitar, a girl who had never worked in the fields and had kept her hands white and soft, her throat fair and tender, who had heard great singers in Denver and Salt Lake."[19] But the preacher, imploring "what right have you to lose one of God's precious souls?" is too much. Eric, overcome with religious fervor, takes the violin by the neck and smashes it over his knee: "To Asa Skinner the sound was like the shackles of sin broken audibly asunder."[20]

The story then shifts to Wyllis and Margaret Elliot, siblings of a well-to-do family from the east, who had been sent west to the family's ranch in an apparent attempt to tame Wyllis, as it was "customary for moneyed gentlemen to send their scapegrace sons to rough it on ranches in the wilds of Nebraska or Dakota" to force them into maturity. The two of them had experienced the West in its fullest, sleeping in sod houses, making the "acquaintance of the personnel of a third-rate opera company on the train to Deadwood, din[ing] in a camp of railroad constructors at the world's end," riding, fishing, dancing "where the lost souls who hide in the hills gathered for their besotted revelry." Margaret, an adventurous sort who has a "strain of gypsy blood," is primed for a prototypical Western experience when she happens to meet Eric, who has been helping thresh wheat. She reveals an incipient attraction to Eric, calling him an "interesting" Norwegian, to which her brother replies, "who, Siegfried?" "Siegfried," she responds, in Cather's first meaningful treatment of Wagner in her fiction, "He looks like a dragon-slayer." Wyllis has jokingly compared Eric to the hero of the *Ring*, and Margaret is more than willing to buy into the fantasy.

She recounts playing a parlor organ only to have Eric "stumble in" (Cather uses this phrase twice in short succession to indicate Eric's apparent stupefaction) at hearing the music, and, "in some inarticulate manner made [her] understand that he wanted [her] to sing for him." She sings, then plays the Intermezzo from *Cavalleria Rusticana*. "I *heard* his tears," she says, describing his reaction. Eric, transported by the music—music of which he'd been robbed by his religious conversion—, recounts tragic events, "as if to himself." The music "gave him speech, he became alive." The Intermezzo reawakened Eric Hermannson's true soul, allowing him to reclaim his heroic birthright as a superhuman Siegfried figure as the story plays out. *Cavalleria* and the *Ring*, despite their relative contemporaneity, are very different operas, one an ironic take on the "rustic chivalry" of Sicilian peasants, an opera that takes only about seventy-five minutes to perform. The other is a sprawling four-part, fourteen-hour sequence of operas, an allegorical comment on humanity at the crux of history built roughly on the rise and fall of its hero Siegfried. But both have a raw emotionality that Cather would tend to exploit in her writing. They have none of the "frank artifice and blithe triviality of Rossini."

Opera plays two roles in "Eric Hermannson's Soul." The *Cavalleria* Intermezzo reawakens Eric's emotional understanding; it frees him from the self-abnegation that his conversion had precipitated. The repeated references to

Siegfried serve to explain Margaret's feelings about Eric, and, more broadly, the West, as a place of outsized mythology. *Cavalleria,* peak *verismo* opera, is the peasant world of the Divide writ in stark emotional terms. "What is *Cavalleria Rusticana* but a mélange of the folk music of southern Italy?" wrote Cather in 1897. In this instance, that folk sensibility is universal. Mascagni's opera, Cather wrote in 1900, the year of "Eric Hermannson"'s publication, "is music that means something more than pleasing sound, here is music that becomes a notable emotional language, the speech of the soul."[21] John Flannigan has noted that Cather intentionally used the Intermezzo because of its "dramatic placement" in the opera, appearing when the "overlapping sexual and religious tensions at work in the opera"[22] are at their highest point. Cather certainly intended this, given the sexual and religious tension that would cloud Eric's relationship with Margaret for the remainder of the story. But Cather was also sending a message that this "mélange of the folk music," an "emotional language," has the capacity to engender Wagner-level mythology. The Intermezzo, as the story progresses, will have the impact of making Eric into Siegfried, a Nietzschean Übermensch completely freed from moral obligation.

After Margaret performs for Eric, the two begin spending time together in a brief, unconsummated love affair (Margaret is engaged to a man back east who sends her flowery, decidedly non-Hermannsonian love letters). They ride horses, at one point Eric rescuing her in the midst of a stampede of wild equines. They discuss music, he asking her if he might hear music like the *Cavalleria* Intermezzo if he were to move and find work in New York—she discourages him from doing so, unable to imagine him out of his Western context. For a week they fulfill for each other what the lives of each have lacked: for her, raw adventure, for him, music and culture. When Margaret hosts a dance on the evening before she is set to leave, Eric wrestles with whether to attend. He hasn't danced or played a fiddle since his conversion. But he relents, and in doing, regains himself: "He was no longer the big, silent Norwegian who had sat at Margaret's feet and looked hopelessly into her eyes. To-night he was a man, with a man's rights and a man's power. To-night he was Siegfried indeed." He thinks, "with an almost savage exultation," of trading his soul for that moment, wondering whether "any man had ever so cheated Satan, had ever bartered his soul for so great a price." Encountering Asa Skinner the next morning, he cheerfully confesses his crime, then "drew himself up to his full height and looked off to where the new day was gilding the corn-tassels and flooding the uplands with light."[23] Music has restored him. And in this instance, we see for the first time, Cather using music in general, and opera specifically, not as something out-of-place on the prairie, but as something that specifically aligns with the raw emotion of the West.

Interestingly, Cather's apprentice career begins and ends with smashed violins. In "Peter," the instrument represented a token of civilization incompatible with the wilds of the frontier. Within a decade, the violin would come to represent the ability of a frontiersman to connect with his truest self. In the course of her apprentice fiction, Cather increasingly relied on music to fully communicate her meaning, and, by the end of the 1890s, that music was opera more often than not. She also began during this period to iron out her thoughts on art and the life of an artist using vocalists as her subjects. By the publication of "Eric Hermannson's Soul," Cather was still breaking violins, but doing so not to illustrate the oppressiveness of the prairie, but to show that that oppressiveness could be overcome.

CHAPTER 4

✽

CATHER AND HER ARTISTS
Evolving Short Fiction

[. . .] a man out in the open on a dark night, and before him, on a hilltop, a light shining.
Between this man and that light there were woods and brambles and sloughs and
marshes and deep rivers. But the man was so unconscious of all this that it seemed to
him he could already put out his hand and touch the light. This kind of man,
I felt, would in some fashion get what he started out for.
—*The Autobiography of S. S. McClure,* ghostwritten by Willa Cather

The February 26, 1904, edition of the *Nebraska State Journal* included a
column from Cather's former professor and editor Will Owen Jones, in
which he took her recently published story "The [sic] Wagner Matinee"
to task. "Miss Cather," he wrote, "like most of the writers who go out from the
west, seems to take pleasure in using the forbidding material furnished by the
struggles of the pioneers." According to Jones, in the story Cather presents an
unnecessarily bleak version of the frontier "with brutal liberality, and her picture
reminds one of darkest Russia."[1] Cather wrote him a letter in response to the
"ringing slap" he'd given her. After speculating that he'd been disingenuously writing for the benefit of the Red Cloud crowd, she noted that "A Wagner Matinée,"
featuring an old pioneer woman reconnecting with her musical roots over the
course of a Wagner concert, had occurred quite organically and honestly. She'd
corresponded with a woman who became the model for Aunt Georgiana, then
went to a concert, and had worked out the plot before she'd left the performance
hall. She simply added some details from her earliest memories of the farmhouse
that the Cathers had occupied when they had first moved to Nebraska, and
voilà—the story was born.

She certainly hadn't meant to exploit or exaggerate the pioneer experience.

"I though[t] everyone admitted that those pioneer days were desolate," she claimed, "and I was misguided enough to think the story a sort of respectful tribute to the courage of those uncomplaining women who weathered them." The frontier was bad enough, she noted, when she was a girl—it must have been far worse a decade or so earlier when Georgiana would have settled there.[2] Nevertheless, the story met chastisement, not only from Jones but from Cather's family as well, who assumed she'd modeled Georgiana on her own Aunt Frances given that, like Georgiana, Frances had New England roots, having graduated from Mt. Holyoke, and had studied music before marrying George Cather and moving west. But Cather adored "Aunt Frank," and, so far as depicting Nebraska, she was giving a frank and fair picture of the plains. It *was* a hard life, and, no, there hadn't been easily accessible Wagner concerts, as there were on the coasts. She was a bit puzzled as to why people were angry. As James Woodress describes her predicament, "she seemed to have done something horrid without realizing it."[3] Even so, she accepted that the depiction might have rubbed some the wrong way and made modest adjustments to the text. For example, hearing the first strains of Wagner on stage breaks "a silence of thirty years; the inconceivable silence of the plains" for Georgiana in the first publication of the story, whereas later editions drop everything after that semicolon—there would no longer be anything particularly *inconceivably* bad about the plains.[4] Cather was eager to reconcile her shot-from-the-hip version of Nebraska that perhaps played too much to urban prejudices with her deep-seated and earned reservations about culture on the Divide. She was working out the relationship between her Nebraska roots—which she cherished—and the coastal, urban, sophisticated context of her professional years. Increasingly, she was using opera as a way of sussing out her identity by using it as a way for characters to figure out their own. Cather, like many of her characters, was torn between her own exceptionalism—her separateness from and her felt superiority to her homeland—and her desire to speak to the majesty of the West and the determination of its people. Specifically in her short fiction of the first two decades of the twentieth century, Cather's opera-related characters, performers and enthusiasts, constitute an outlier species of humanity whose natural habitat is the extremes of human emotional experience. Cather's Alexandra and Ántonia, for example, are comfortable watching the cycle of growth year-to-year in ruralia. But in a subset of characters, best represented in her short fiction from *The Troll Garden* to the *Youth and the Bright Medusa* years, Cather made clear that some people are made differently and require the sort of outsized stimulation that only an art form like opera can provide. She simply struggled to express the trials of the artistic soul without incidentally insulting her family heritage.

"A Wagner Matinée," first published in *Everybody's Magazine* in March 1904, was the earliest of Cather's mature stories to meaningfully engage opera as a central aspect of the text, and one of the first stories from the time when she seemed to have begun taking her craft of short fiction more seriously. She would eventually publish two collections of short fiction during the first half of her career, *The Troll Garden* (1905) and *Youth and the Bright Medusa* (1920); most of the stories that appear in these two collections were originally published in magazines between 1903 and 1920 (four were original to those collections). Four of the seven stories in *Troll Garden* center substantially on opera, and seven of the eight stories in *Youth* do so as well. The latter collection contains four of the stories from the former, slightly reworked (the original plan for *Youth* was to be a reissue of *Troll Garden).*[5] Of those four, three—"A Death in the Desert," "Paul's Case," and "A Wagner Matinée"—were stories in which opera played a major role, and a further four stories—"Coming, Aphrodite!," "The Diamond Mine," "A Gold Slipper," and "Scandal"—focused specifically on opera singers.

Despite the fact that they share four titles, the relative critical reception of the two collections differed significantly. *The Troll Garden* was received as "more the work of promise than fulfillment" and full of "mere dummies, with fancy names, on which to hang epigrams." However, there's little doubt today that several of the stories, now frequently anthologized, are standouts of American short fiction. When the same stories were republished alongside "Coming, Aphrodite!" and "The Diamond Mine" fifteen years later, they were roundly appreciated, one reviewer backhandedly referring to the collection as "the triumph of mind over Nebraska."[6] In both collections, Cather featured opera prominently, intentionally ensuring that her widest possible audience associated her with musical drama. Opera permeates her uncollected fiction of the period as well, in stories such as "The Joy of Nelly Deane" and "The Bohemian Girl." This is the period during which Cather rose to prominence through her novels as a writer whose subject was the Great Plains experience. But her short stories tell differently. If some bias against rural fiction had prevailed, leaving Cather's plains fiction in the ashbin of literary history in the good company of so many other great authors who happened not to push the right buttons at the right time, and her short fiction of the period, which certainly has every bit the raw literary quality of the novels, were all she were known for, then no one would think of Willa Cather as a Nebraska writer. Based exclusively on her short fiction of the time, Cather would be known as a writer of opera stories.

The narrator of "A Wagner Matinée" is a man named Clark, presently a resident of Boston. He'd grown up, however, on or near his Aunt Georgiana's homestead in Red Willow County, Nebraska, fifty miles from the railroad (incidentally, Red Willow County is about fifty miles west of Red Cloud, so Cather might have intended that figure to represent a place particularly removed from civilization as she'd known it). Georgiana was a New England native and had taught music at the Boston Conservatory before taking up with an "idle, shiftless boy of twenty-one," Howard Carpenter, with whom she'd eventually eloped to the frontier in the late 1860s. Given that Nebraska was opened for homesteading in the 1860s and became a state in 1867, we are to understand that Georgiana's new environment was particularly harsh and isolated from anything like the rich cultural offerings of Boston. Nevertheless, she doggedly maintained the artistry and erudition of her erstwhile life. As Clark remembers, "it was to her, at her ironing or mending, that I read my first Shakspere, and her old text-book on mythology was the first that ever came into my empty hands."[7] She also taught him to play music on the parlor organ she'd convinced Carpenter to buy her after fifteen years on the prairie, during which time she had not "so much as seen a musical instrument." Georgiana is, even if by necessity, a person of focus, faith, and patience, essential characteristics for pioneer survival. Removed from art, she maintains a belief in the necessity of art and a determination to bring it to this new country. However, despite the emotional calluses formed by deprivation, music remains a tender subject. Though she teaches Clark the technical aspects of how to play the keyboard, she rarely speaks to him about music. He remembers once "doggedly beating out some easy passages" from a score of Carl Maria von Weber's *Euryanthe* when Georgiana approached him, "saying tremulously, 'Don't love it so well, Clark, or it may be taken from you.'"[8] Georgiana is vaguely aware that Clark might be like her—particularly susceptible to music. While no doubt she senses that a love of music like *Euryanthe* might propel Clark to reach his potential by reaching out past the borders of the farm, she's also acutely aware of how devastating it can be to the psyche to have had it and lost it.

Georgiana has traveled to Boston to settle the terms of a will, her first trip out of Nebraska in three decades, and the story, as the title suggests, centers on Clark taking her to a performance of orchestral arrangements from various Wagner operas. He chooses this performance based on a memory from his childhood wherein Georgiana had recalled attending a performance of Meyerbeer's *Les Huguenots* in Paris. Despite his apparent sensitivity, however, this choice only serves to establish that Clark is in fact not a proper inheritor of Georgiana's love of opera. Though Meyerbeer was somewhat German in his orchestrations, his vocal approach was distinctly Italian, and he was also the great solidifier of French grand opera. Combined with the fact that the Boston performance was to be a series of selections from various Wagner operas, Clark linking a full Parisian performance of *Huguenots* to a Wagner medley in the colonies would be akin to inviting a visiting relative to go mountain biking because you knew he had a Harley-Davidson in his garage. Such things are similar only to the uninitiated. But the proverbial broken clock is right from time to time, and Georgiana was luckily a long-deprived fan of Wagner.

Clark asks her whether she's heard any Wagner operas and she admits she hasn't (the subtext is that she hasn't been near enough to any performances since they'd become common in the United States), but that "she was perfectly familiar with their respective situations, and had once possessed the piano score of *The Flying Dutchman*." As Richard Giannone notes, this is a clue to readers about Georgiana's artistic temperament. The first Wagner performances in the United States happened in the 1850s, but they were few; Wagner wasn't a frequently performed composer in the country until the 1880s. So for Georgiana, a music teacher of the 1860s, to have possessed a Wagner score is remarkable.[9] Clark's claim that her training "had been broader than that of most music teachers of a quarter of a century ago" is clearly an understatement. This in turn lets us know that her separation from music upon leaving New England was more tragic than the simple loss of a hobby or job; it was the devastation of a core part of her identity. Clark notes the social space of the performance hall. He worries that she might suffer some "trepidation" due to her "queer, country clothes." But she does not. Rather, she is like "old miners who drift into the Brown hotel at Denver, their pockets full of bullion"—the old miners are rough but have confidence, because they know they are richer than anyone else there. Despite their look, they have the privilege to regard everyone else as a poseur. Georgiana's pocketed bullion is her deep connection to music. Unlike the culture enthusiasts throughout the audience, she *knows* the art on a fundamental level that they don't.

The performance cycles through the *Tannhäuser* overture, the *Tristan* prelude, an unspecified piece from *Dutchman*, and the "Prize Song" from *Die Meistersinger von Nürnberg*. When the *Tannhäuser* overture breaks the "silence of thirty years," Georgiana clutches Clark's coat sleeve. He senses "the waste and wear we are so powerless to combat," the "tall, naked house on the prairie, black and grim as a wooden fortress." But though that imagery is as bleak as Will Owen Jones had claimed, Cather tempered it with the pond where Clark had learned to swim, dwarf ash seedlings, a cornfield that "stretched to daybreak" and a corral that "reached to sunset" and in between the "conquests of peace."[10] Clark's understanding of Nebraska is abruptly as unified and complex as the shared space of the sacred and profane that *Tannhäuser*—an opera strung between a garden of earthly delights and the saintliness of the Elisabeth character—represents. During the love stories—*Tristan* and *Dutchman*—Georgiana is enigmatically quiet, but Clark notices, on the same hands that once played the *Dutchman* score, a "thin, worn band that had once been a wedding ring"—music and romantic possibility have been replaced with wearing domesticity. She weeps during the "Prize Song" from *Meistersinger*. At intermission, Clark asks her about it, and she recounts knowing a "tramp cow-puncher" who sang the "Prize Song" and had sung in the chorus in Bayreuth when he was a boy. If we assume he was in Nebraska in the 1870s or 1880s and had sung in Bayreuth as a child, then he had performed likely in the eighteenth-century Margravial Opera House, not in Wagner's Festspielhaus, which opened in 1876. He knew Wagner, but was more original to Wagner's capital than the composer himself. He was more Wagner than Wagner. Georgiana's relationship with him (there is the thinnest suggestion of infatuation) further situates her emotional investment with Wagner as more profound than that of those who adopted the composer during his later American heyday. That musical cow-puncher would have been a real and romantic connection to the music during Georgiana's most desperate years, not a trendy enthusiasm for the *Ring*, but rather a bond with a then-obscure European composer that yielded postadolescent rebirth of hope and love.

After intermission, the orchestra performs four selections from the *Ring*. Cather provides little commentary on Georgiana's reaction in the second half of the performance, however, other than that she wept quietly but continuously, looking occasionally up at the stage lights, apparently absorbing herself in pure sound. The *Ring* is an epic opera cycle metaphorically centered on the willing extermination of the self; Georgiana seems to understand this process on a personal level now, late in life. Clark contemplates that he has no idea "how far [the music] bore her, or past what happy islands [. . .] into some world of death vaster yet, where, from the beginning of the world, hope has lain down with hope and dream with dream, and, renouncing, slept."[11] In the "deluge of sound" Georgiana allows her annihilation into something more profound ("Paul's Case" will end with a variation of this theme). When the performance concludes, the other concertgoers file out, but she makes no gesture of exiting. She sits until the auditorium is empty, until the stage itself is "empty as a winter cornfield." Then, as soon as Clark speaks, she bursts into tears and pleads, "I don't want to go, Clark, I don't want to go!" Clark understands: "For her, just outside the concert hall, lay the black pond with the cattle-tracked bluffs; the tall, unpainted house, with weather-curled boards, naked as a tower; the crook-backed ash seedlings where the dish-cloths hung to dry; the gaunt, moulting turkeys picking up refuse about the kitchen door."[12] This isn't Georgiana not wanting to return to Nebraska, but rather her not wanting to go back into the world to face the fact that she has lived her life without the music she needed to really live. Cather would go on to write many opera-bound characters, characters invested in an emotional reality far beyond what most people experience and far beyond what most people expect. Her opera characters, much unlike her farmers, are those happy to live, in Geraldine Farrar's terms, "ten years thick [rather] than twenty thin."[13] Georgiana, Cather's first such character, simply happens to be one who has lived thirty years very thin.

"A Wagner Matinée" is a story about the consequence of relinquishing ideals, about setting off into an adventure only to find mundanity and not having the will to escape. Just over a year later, Cather published a sort of companion piece in which a young person, unlike Georgiana, refuses to compromise ideals, but finds that the only escape from mundanity is annihilation. "Paul's Case" appeared in *McClure's Magazine* in May 1905. About a year later, Cather joined that publication's editorial staff, resulting in five years of continuous employment, immense professional development as an editor, and a fruitful stretch of in-house publication leading to her first novel, *Alexander's Bridge* (1912). The story follows a boy named Paul, the motherless son of a working-class father whose abusiveness is never quite spelled out but is heavily implied in Paul's consistent fear of the man, even to the point that he briefly fantasizes about dying at his father's hands as being the only way his father would appreciate him. It begins with Paul's teachers, who, as with his father, don't understand or appreciate him. They find him insolent (Cather keeps his specific offenses vague) but haunted. As one instructor simply remarks, "there is something wrong about the fellow." Paul is like most of Cather's opera-infatuated protagonists, who simply don't *click* with normal people and who intractably move in the direction of some ineffable higher ideal that most people don't sense. Paul seems unaffected by the lack of understanding that his father and instructors show, however; after a tribunal in which the teachers discuss how to discipline him, he skips away gleefully whistling the Soldier's Chorus from Gounod's *Faust*.

Paul works as an usher at Carnegie Hall, where he has been exposed to opera—though mostly, if not entirely, as excerpts (in addition to *Faust*, the story also references *Martha* and *Rigoletto*). One evening, the "soloist chanced to be a German woman, by no means in her first youth, and the mother of many children." Despite her age, Paul adores her, partly due to her costume, a satin gown and tiara, but, more than that, her "indefinable air of achievement, that world-shine upon her." In the earliest version, eventually published in *The Troll Garden*, that "air" makes her "a veritable queen of Romance." Years later, for *Youth and the Bright Medusa*, Cather switched out that phrasing for an air "which always blinded Paul to any possible defects."[14] The difference is important. In the later version, Paul loses agency—he is simply incognizant of salient facts and behaves according to his ignorance. But in the original version, Paul was affirmatively able to create a Romantic queenliness out of sheer idealism. The text's evolution displays a bit of Cather's evolution with regard to opera over the period; the earlier version presents Paul's wide-eyed adoration, the latter his inability to read and manage his feelings on the performance. An older Cather would describe her own youthful infatuation with opera in similar terms, for example, in Lucy Gayheart's wide-eyed response to her first full orchestra concert. Regardless, in either version of "Paul's Case," Cather lets us know that Paul is beholden to the imaginative possibilities of the theater. As with many characters, Cather uses the tension between the life-imagined-in-art versus life-as-lived to raise questions of personal identity, to posit whether the emotional reality felt in art is somehow more real than lived experience. Paul is one of Cather's elect who senses something greater in music than what most are capable of sensing.

Paul and his father live on Cordelia Street, somewhere east of downtown Pittsburgh, roughly in or around the East Liberty neighborhood where Cather lived for some of her Pittsburgh years. It is a staid, solidly middle-class neighborhood, where on Sundays the women sit gossiping on porch rocking chairs, children play in the street, and men sit on the stoops with "their legs well apart, their stomachs comfortably protruding, and talk[ing] of the prices of things, or [telling] anecdotes of the sagacity of their various chiefs and overlords."[15] Paul's father holds some of the men with whom he works up to his son as models—not the chiefs and overlords, but rather their underlings. He wants Paul to aspire to middle management. However, it is the stories of the barons that piques Paul's interest, their palaces in Venice and yachts on the Mediterranean. But Paul's vast distance between the complacency around him and the finer things represented by these practically abstract creatures of wealth has yielded an internal crisis. He feels he belongs there, but he is stuck on Cordelia Street. His imagination will have to fill in the gap.

Paul's teachers had speculated that the boy's bad behavior indeed came from an imagination "perverted by garish fiction." But the sort of books he has around his house, where "art" is represented by portraits of Washington and Calvin, is unlikely to spark flights of fancy, and Paul isn't all that interested in literature, anyway. He is a creature drawn to music, "from an orchestra to a barrel organ. He needed only the spark, the indescribable thrill that made his imagination master of his senses, and he could make plots and pictures enough of his own."[16] Aside from his job at Carnegie, he was friendly with Charley Edwards, the lead boy actor of a stock company in town, who let Paul hang around backstage. At his ushering job, he was exposed to opera: "The moment the cracked orchestra beat out the overture from *Martha,* or jerked at the serenade from *Rigoletto,* all stupid and ugly things slid from him, and his senses were deliciously, yet delicately fired." Through his friendship with Charley Edwards, those delicately fired impulses are made substantial. In the larger concert hall, Paul gets some sense of the possibilities of opera at scale; on the smaller stage, however, he's presented with the rush of actual live theatrics. These two forces, combined, motivate him to fateful acts, willing into being an unearned existence beyond the life he was born to.

Paul had, for some time, exaggerated his relationship with actors of the local stock company, and suggested to his school friends, in "fervid and florid inventions," that he was a part of the company. These lies filtered up to the teachers and then to Paul's father, who, alarmed by Paul's runaway imagination, pulls him from school, forces him to quit his work at the Carnegie and his association with Charley Edwards and to take an office assistant job at the Pittsburgh firm of Denny & Carson. Paul refuses to accept his fate and, one day, absconds with nearly a thousand dollars—well over $20,000 in today's dollars—which he'd been entrusted to deposit. Paul then, over the course of a few short days, lives his best life. He takes the train to New York and a room at the Waldorf. He buys a wardrobe and luggage to go with it. He takes a loge at the opera. He orders flowers for his sitting room, bathes and naps leisurely, and goes to supper wondering "that there were honest men in the world at all": "This was what all the world was fighting for, he reflected; this was what all the struggle was about."[17] At this point, it's probably natural for a reader to dislike Paul. His short-sightedness, solipsism, materialism, thievery—all are despicable. But Cather doesn't endorse the boy's behavior or attitude. He's no more a palatable character than is Melville's Bartleby. That earlier character, preferring not to do anything, was an enigmatic figure of perfect individualism. Most people would prefer not to do drudge work for petty pay, and Bartleby's coworkers, who do their work dutifully, suffer alcoholism and dyspepsia as a result of going along with what is expected. Bartleby is simply the one person who politely clarifies and stands by his actual preferences. Likewise, Paul, with a most routine attitude, takes money as it's made available to him and acts according to his personal nature without compromise.

Be that as it may, Paul understands that his sojourn in paradise is never to be permanent. Eight days into his time in New York, he reads of his crime in a Pittsburgh newspaper. His father had repaid the money, and Denny & Carson had no intention of prosecuting, but Paul's capture and return seem inevitable—his father is following a lead that says that the boy had been seen in a New York hotel. Paul dresses once more in his finery, gets drunk, sleeps and wakes, then takes the train to Newark. He disembarks and takes a cab out into the countryside. He walks alongside a train track until he hears a locomotive. When the moment is right, he jumps in front of it. His body is thrown and "the picture making mechanism" of his mind—that picture making mechanism fired to life by music—is crushed, and "Paul dropped back into the immense design of things." Cather never indulges in an exploration of Paul's cogitations, whether self-pity or fear. In quasi-naturalistic form, she simply presents Paul as an exceptional person exposed to the wanting stimuli of an unexceptional world and allows him to behave accordingly. Paul's "case" is a study in what happens when the Romantic confronts a world without Romantic gratification.

"A Wagner Matinée" and "Paul's Case" travel opposing arcs in some ways. Georgiana was musically sophisticated before her remove to Nebraska; her return to the urban east reconnects her with music. Paul, on the other hand, is naïve and untutored but with an apparent natural compulsion to music; unlike Georgiana, however, his sojourn in the larger city is unmusical other than the unexplored loge he takes at the opera, as though something about the opulence of his experience has satiated his Romantic appetite. Paul is a dandy with overdeveloped tastes; Georgiana is a long-suffering woman of depth. Despite these differences, however, each story makes reference to opera to underline the characters' outsider status. In both "A Wagner Matinée" and "Paul's Case," Cather does not write of a universal human condition, but rather a special class of individuals bound by a profound connection to music. Paul's father and teachers, like Georgiana's husband, are routine. Paul and Georgiana thrive on a mode of human expression that transcends the routine experience that others seem to accept as a matter of course. Cather was herself a person frequently out of step with the common mode, from dressing in masculine fashion and signing her letters "Wm." as a young person; as a young woman who wanted to be a doctor in a world where only males were doctors; as a teenager who wrote that "amputating limbs" was her "idea of perfect happiness" and "slicing toads" was her "occupation during a summer's vacation";[18] later as the only female (and hardest worker) on the *Hesperian* staff in college; and later still as a girl in her late teens and early twenties who didn't shy away from writing hard-hitting, "meat-ax" criticism about seasoned professionals of the stage. Cather, herself a perpetually odd duck, no doubt related to this strange compulsion to the greater end of human expression as a sign of differentness from the world around her. Music broadly, but opera in particular, is an unnaturally extreme expression of normal human emotion. Georgiana and Paul become martyrs on the cross of exceptionalism, Georgiana in her accidental sojourn into brute survival and the brief recovery of her fundamental self, Paul in his absolute refusal to accept normalcy as a way of life. In these early characters, as in later characters, Cather used the innate extremity and oddness of opera to allow characters to express an innate queerness of personal identity.

While most of the stories in *The Troll Garden* and *Youth and the Bright Medusa* take place in or around urban cultural hubs—"A Death in the Desert" and "The Sculptor's Funeral" being notable exceptions—the period intervening the two collections saw Cather engage, if somewhat obliquely, with opera in a plains context in stories such as "The Joy of Nelly Deane" (1911) and "The Bohemian Girl" (1912). "Nelly Deane" reads a bit like a shorter, inverse version of *The Song of the Lark,* how Thea Kronborg's life might have ended up had she stayed in Moonstone. It begins with a performance of Handel's oratorio *Queen Esther* in a small town Baptist church on Christmas Eve. The country folk have come from miles around through the snow to see the performance, in particular Nelly's singing of Esther. Nelly is a much-beloved local girl, pretty with a sunny disposition and great optimism for the future. But the future, as Cather reminds us repeatedly in the story, is not in our hands. Nelly's "joy" will endure only as long as fate allows it. The story begins with Nelly and the narrator, Margaret, ready to go on for the last act of the performance, evading the three dressers, Mrs. Dow, Mrs. Freeze, and Mrs. Spinny, backstage. These three women align with the three *morai,* the mythological fates that draw out thread to determine destiny: Spinny as Clotho, the spinner, who creates the thread; Dow as Lachesis, the measurer of the thread; and Freeze as Atropos, the unturnable, who cuts the thread at death. Like Queen Esther, who famously left her fate to the will of God, Cather loads the first paragraph with insinuations of inevitability. Throughout the story, Spinny will facilitate the extenuation of Nelly's life, Dow will observe, and Freeze will appear once again when Nelly's life is ending.

As Esther, Nelly performs up to expectations, outdoing the tenor, her schoolmaster, who had tried his best to "eclipse her in his dolorous solos about the river of Babylon." After the performance and much congratulation, Nelly invites Margaret to stay with her overnight. The two mean to go to sleep, but in their excitement stay up talking into the early morning. "One is not a prima donna the first time for nothing," Margaret recalls, "and it seemed as if we could not go to bed." Among other things, they discuss Nelly's various love interests, including Scott Spinny, son of Mrs. Spinny and her husband, a penurious man who runs a local store, and Guy Franklin, a traveling representative for a dry goods company. Nelly reveals that she is engaged to Franklin, a fact she is keeping secret from her parents. When Margaret hesitates over this relationship, Nelly reassures her. "He's so *different* from our boys," Nelly pleads, "and he's just terribly in love with me. [. . .] I'm awfully fond of him, too. Awfully." She also reveals that part of her infatuation is the prospect of moving away with Franklin: "I'm going to live in Chicago, and take singing lessons, and go to operas, and do all those nice things."[19] Proper singing lessons and performances are part of life beyond the small frontier town. Nelly is looking for something, in her word, *different* than what she's been given. Again we see Cather's tortured ambivalence about towns like Red Cloud. Whereas she treats Nelly's home as a place of great community solidarity and warmth, full of caring people, for a rare few, like Nelly or Paul or Georgiana, the only way to artistic fulfillment is to leave.

The remainder of the story plays out in a series of Margaret's episodic reconnections with her hometown via visits and letters. When they graduate the following spring, Margaret goes off to college and Nelly stays home. But the engagement with Guy Franklin wilts. He is assigned a different sales territory and loses contact with Nelly, marrying instead the daughter of a rich cattleman from the northern Nebraska town of Long Pine. Nelly's father's business fails, and she takes a teaching job to help the family. In a letter, Mrs. Dow reports that Nelly doesn't like teaching. "The children try her," she writes, "and she is so pretty it seems a pity for her to be tied down to uncongenial employment." In the absence of Guy Franklin, Scott Spinny has begun courting Nelly. Scott isn't a particularly bad individual, but he lacks any sense of romance, and most assume that he will become a hard, miserly man like his father when he takes over the family store. Nevertheless, Nelly, emotionally destitute, consents to marry him, partly in exchange for Scott employing her father. Ten years on, Margaret, whom fate has given a happier lot (she's "been in Rome for a long time"), receives a letter from Mrs. Dow that reports, among other town news, that Nelly has passed away. She'd had a curable sickness, but Scott had alienated the two most capable doctors in town, leaving Nelly in the care of "young Doctor Fox, a boy just out of college and a stranger." The small-town life, with its ruthlessly demanded compromises, has led to Nelly's death, the fated Mrs. Freeze in attendance. Like Paul and Georgiana, Nelly is a person who needs art to be fulfilled. Jilted by Guy Franklin and left to her hometown, she lacks the faith and persistence of Georgiana, and she withers accordingly. She has forgone the singing lessons and operas she'd hoped for in the city and instead subsists on a teaching job that leaves her unfulfilled. When she falls ill, it is her husband's smallness, having engaged in a variety of petty economic scraps with the more seasoned doctors, that leads indirectly to her unhappy death. Nelly was happy when she was performing musical drama—life seemed promising, specifically with more singing and opera to come. Without that, her fate is disappointment and death.

Why did Cather situate these characters' fates on opera? Opera was one of the dominant cultural mediums of the time, certainly, and more familiar to people from all walks of life than what we might assume now, more familiar even than painting or sculpture would have been then—an opera company might travel to Red Cloud, but a Rossetti exhibition certainly would not—so referencing it might have made sense in terms of audience accessibility. It represented a culmination of a variety of forms, a *Gesamtkunstwerk*, so Cather could use it as a catchall to represent art broadly, appealing to those interested in music, drama, and everything else that gets wrapped into an opera performance. By the early 1900s, Cather had no doubt seen hundreds of operas. Long before was her 1895 trip to see the Met's company perform in Chicago; since that time, she'd had substantial exposure to opera in Pittsburgh, and, from 1906 onward, in New York. It would have been a natural point of reference for her. But beyond all these reasons, opera served as a sort of artistic ideal, the highest point of a gothic flying buttress, reaching forever into heaven. In the platonic sense of it, what opera *was* could be sensed by those in far-flung regions of western Nebraska through church performances and Main Street opera houses—but that sense only gave the impression of some more perfect realization of art beyond earthly experience, something one had to sacrifice to attain. Cather didn't mean to demean the small-town experience. She often wrote of it warmly, and her rural-born characters tend to be more richly imagined than her city folk. But opera gave her special characters something greater to hope and strive for.

This trend continues, though somewhat masked, in "The Bohemian Girl," published in *McClure's* in August 1912. The title is an apparent reference to a light opera of the same name by Michael William Balfe, first performed in 1843 and popular throughout the late nineteenth century. Other than the title and a few snippets from the aria "I dreamt that I dwelt in Marble Halls," however, the story has few facial similarities to the plot of the opera, and, accordingly, commentary has tended to breeze past any connections between the two. In his definitive Cather biography, James Woodress merely notes that "the story borrows its title, though not its plot, from the romantic nineteenth-century opera of the same name."[20] Similarly, Richard Giannone notes that "'The Bohemian Girl' is a tale of a daring lover retrieving his trapped beloved. Beyond this basic likeness, however, what is important is their dissimilarity. [. . .] Though the story roughly parallels the last two acts of the opera and borrows several of its songs as motif, the works are opposite in tone."[21] For Giannone, the matching titles are simply Cather's ironic way of telling us that her Nebraska story is to be a realistic contrast to the silly fantasy of the opera.

And it is a silly opera, as many light operas are. In his introductory remarks to a 1902 Schirmer reissue of the opera's score, *New York Times* music critic, and Wagnerian (is it possible to think of a critic less positively predisposed to light opera than a Wagnerian?) Richard Aldrich noted the "hopeless disagreement between the critics and the public" as to the opera. "Few operas have been so generally faulted, both by reviewers for the press at the time of its production and by more deliberate critical writers since," yet, "for the [theater] manager who wishes to give English opera," it is an "indispensable resource," guaranteed to bring in an audience.[22] The opera's story originates with a Cervantes tale, which was transformed into a French ballet called "La Gipsy," which in turn formed the basis of an unproduced opera libretto by the Marquis de Saint-Georges titled "La Bohémienne," which, translated, means "The Gypsy Girl." But Balfe's librettist, Alfred Bunn, apparently knew little French, and translated that title as "The Bohemian Girl," despite the fact that the heroine is, in fact, Hungarian, and that no part of the story takes place in Bohemia or has anything to do with, in Aldrich's phrasing, "that strange section of society that has appropriated its name" (he seems to want to remind us that "The Bohemian Girl" and Puccini's then-ascendant *La Bohème* are in no way related). Given that it was one of the most popular operas of the time, Cather certainly knew it well, and given her close relationships with actual Bohemians in Nebraska, she was no doubt aware of the pointlessness of the title reference. She still, however, felt it appropriate to reference the opera in her story.

Her story, as it happens, *is* about an actual Bohemian girl, Clara Vavrika, and her relationship with the son of a Norwegian family, Nils Ericson. The story begins with Nils returning home after a long time away—we'll learn later that he has returned to Scandinavia and has made a success of himself in the shipping industry. He comes home and catches up on family business. His brothers have done well in farming and politics, and his mother is a semi-wealthy firebrand, motoring about in one of the few electric motorcars in town, known, especially, for frequently running off the road. Clara, Nils's childhood crush, has in the meantime married Nils's brother, Olaf, a bluff and bearish farmer-turned-politician with whom Clara has little in common; Olaf's interest in Clara seems primarily in the fact that she can help deliver the Bohemian vote. As the story progresses, Nils reconnects with Clara and her father, Joe, who runs the local saloon. Nils has always had a closer connection to both of them than to his own family. Whereas his mother finds the saloon disreputable, Joe loves having

Nils around to play flute with whichever other musicians might be hanging about. Whereas Nils's family is focused on propriety and acquiring the county acre-by-acre, Clara sports an adventurous personality that needs release into the wider world. Eventually, Nils convinces Clara to leave his brother and run away. He confides in her that he has become financially well-established in the old country, and has no interest in or need of family money, as his brothers have assumed. He tells her she reminds him of a wild bird, caught in the hand, its heart beating so hard "you were afraid it would shatter its little body to pieces." "You used to be just like that, a slender, eager thing with a wild delight inside you. That is how I remembered you. And I come back and find you—a bitter woman."[23] Recognizing the truth of what he says, she consents, and they leave. In a brief coda to the story, Nils has also facilitated the escape of his youngest brother, Eric, whom he knows to have a spirit as adventurous as his and Clara's. He leaves him a note outlining how to leave town and find him, as well as money to do so, promising, as well, a position with his shipping company once they all reach Europe. Eric rides the train out of town, but panics and returns. Meeting his mother on the porch, she accepts him without emotion. "I've come back, Mother," he greets her. "Very well," she replies.

The story has musical elements, though it's certainly not Cather's most opera-focused story. The bond between Nils and Joe is largely precipitated by Nils's musicianship, and this is partly why Joe tacitly consents to his daughter's flight. Nils sings snippets from *The Bohemian Girl* at key moments to rekindle Clara's affection for him. Other than that, music is sublimated to a more overt statement of the theme that a select few suffer spiritual death in the absence of adventure. Here, then, Cather doesn't use music generally, or opera specifically, in the way she does with the other stories to illustrate the emotional demise of characters. Even so, the title and passages from the opera deserve investigation. The operatic reference is more than a casual remark or an ironic and unnecessary push-back against the goofiness of the source text. While "The Bohemian Girl" is actually about a young woman of Czech origin, and hence generic enough to be a coincidence, the references to specific arias from the opera combined with the ubiquity of the opera performed by traveling troupes during Cather's youth means that Cather likely meant readers to engage with the opera and consider the relevance of that text to hers. The idea that Cather titled "The Bohemian Girl" as a throwaway reference or as simple irony would be akin to an author today titling a novel *The Empire Strikes Back* and not expecting audiences to consider, on a page-to-page level, the reference to the film.

The opera, in brief, is about an exiled Polish noble named Thaddeus who saves the daughter of the Count of Arnheim, Arline, from a deer (yes, a deer). In a celebratory banquet, Thaddeus refuses to toast the Austrian emperor, earning the Count's ire and forcing him to flee, which he does with the help of his gypsy friend, Devilshoof (yes, Devilshoof). The gypsies also kidnap Arline (because gypsies do such things in opera). Twelve years later, Arline, having lived with the gypsies ever since, has forgotten her noble upbringing. Her gypsy companions rob the Count's drunken nephew. Somewhere along the way, Arline reveals a vague memory of her youth ("I dreamt that I dwelt in marble halls") to Thaddeus, and the two profess their love. The Queen of the Gypsies, jealous, frames Arline for the nephew's robbery, and Arline is sentenced to death, but the Count recognizes her as his daughter due to a scar from the deer attack and commutes her sentence. In the following celebration, the Queen of the Gypsies seeks revenge and is killed in a scuffle when she attempts to kill Arline.

If Cather's story was drawn in no direct sense from the opera, there is a thematic thread tying them together nonetheless. Both distinctly involve a clash of worlds. The characters Nils, Clara, Thaddeus, and Arline each are inheritors of dual and mutually exclusive environments between which they must choose. Just as Arline must choose the purported gypsy Thaddeus (his noble blood is only revealed later), so do both Nils and Clara have "roving" and "Tartar or gypsy" blood themselves, and must elect lives of freedom and adventure or the settling down that is expected of them. E. K. Brown described the Eric Ericson coda as "unexpected and unsatisfactory," because it describes the painful contrary choice, remaining in place when one feels out of place.[24] But that misses the point. In this story, Cather was merging the threads of her earlier opera stories into one. Nils, like Paul, risked everything to pursue his true self. Clara faced a crisis whereby she would follow either Nils's or Nelly's example and chose the former. Eric is a Georgiana-to-be. A reader familiar with Cather's opera stories should recognize this spectrum of possibility and experience. Certainly, Cather was reflecting not only on the Nellys she'd known, but also on her own course had she not ventured out under her own charts.

Cather references the "marble halls" aria to represent a sense of displacement, the idea that one simply isn't where one is meant to be. "I dreamt that I dwelt in marble halls," the aria begins, and it follows with dreams of vast riches and innumerable suitors. "But I also dreamt, which charmed me most," it concludes, addressing Thaddeus, "that you loved me still the same." Cather doesn't write these lines, but, given the popularity of the aria at the time, many of her readers would have been able to fill in the idea that wealth and stability—the things represented by Nils and Clara's home environment—are less satisfying than love. The text is a rejection of the middle-class expectations and mores that would keep the two apart. Shortly after Clara sings "marble halls," she sings "for memory is the only friend / That grief can call its own." These lines are from the aria "The heart bow'd down," sung by Arnheim, reflecting on the loss of his daughter. Clara juxtaposes the hopeful aria against one that reflects on the nature of unfulfilled hope, the idea that memory and grief are companions. She's unhappy with her situation, remembering the possibilities she'd passed over in her own past. Cather uses those two well-known passages from the opera to signal to her audience that sadness is less a matter of one's current situation than it is the knowledge that one's present sadness could have been changed had one followed a different course. It is a subject that Cather would revisit more than a decade later; the idea behind the "Marble Halls" aria will recur in *The Professor's House,* in which the titular professor's favorite opera is Ambroise Thomas's *Mignon,* an opera that also features a heroine of noble birth who has lived with gypsies since a young age and is attempting to reconnect with her homeland and family. Its most notable aria is *"Connais-tu le pays,"* a song in which Mignon remembers, much like Arline through "I dreamt that I dwelt in marble halls," the home of her youth. In that novel, it underscores the protagonist's fixation on the idea of what constitutes a "home" and his desire to return to that earlier, happier moment. Cather was evolving an idea regarding the relationship between home and identity, and the notion that separation from one's home was somehow separation from one's happiness, a theory misaligned with her other stories in which leaving home represented a movement toward personal fulfillment. Whereas her stories tend to point to leaving home as a necessary obligation of happiness, she can't quite get away from the idea that a mythologized concept of returning to an ideal homeplace is always the ultimate goal.

Through the early 1910s, Cather used opera to explore the idea between home and destiny, between happiness and failure to reach one's potential. But she also used opera to explore the practical aspects of the artist's life. No other author was ever as preoccupied with the figure of the prima donna as a literary type as was Cather. No doubt, this was to do with Cather's fixation on the rela-

tionship between art, the artist, and society, and, whereas most artistic endeav-
ors remained male-dominated, operatic performance was distinctly the realm
of the female superstar. This fact, coupled with Cather's lifelong appreciation
for opera, made the opera singer a natural fit for her writing, despite Cather's
limited musical experience as a practitioner. Her singers begin with Tradutorri
and Selma Schumann in her early stories and reach their fullest manifestation
in Thea Kronborg in *The Song of the Lark*, but there are other memorable singers
along the way. They are all successful sopranos, redoubtable women with confident, forceful personalities and improbably pretty names like Cressida Garnet,
Kitty Ayrshire, and Eden Bower. Each of them is distinct in her life situation
and how she faces a variety of personal and professional hurdles, and through
them we get an understanding of how Cather viewed the relationship between
art and artist, the artist's craft, and the surprising practicality with which Cather
understood the business of opera.

That Cather was not a fawning fan of the opera superstar is important. She
was never a prima donna cultist or particularly swayed by the celebrity wave
that overtook many operagoers. Wayne Koestenbaum has noted that "choosing
a diva to love is like inaugurating any erotic arrangement" and that "fans have
no minds of their own. They only figure as emanations of the diva's will, as
mind readers," which is to say that those who fixate on particular performers
divest their own will to a pretend, reconstructed will of the objects of their admiration. He records a girl who stalked Mary Garden and committed suicide
over her inability to connect; crazed fans who tore pieces of Jenny Lind's shawl
as relics; a Russian man who tore Nellie Melba's autographing pencil to bits
and distributed the splinters to friends.[25] It's impossible to imagine Cather engaging in such sentimental nonsense. She was a legitimate friend of Fremstad,
to whom she referred as a "battered Swede" with "suspicious, defiant, far-seeing
pioneer eyes"; she equated Fremstad with real women she knew. She referred to
a singer in "Paul's Case" as "a German woman, by no means in her first youth,
and the mother of many children." In *Lucy Gayheart*, Lucy hears a singer performing below the station her talent might have allowed her; she was "slender
and graceful, but far from young. She sang so well that Lucy wondered how she
had ever drifted into a little road company like this one. Her voice was worn,
to be sure, like her face, and there was not much physical sweetness left in it.
But there was another kind of sweetness; a sympathy, a tolerant understanding."
Even in the odd moment that Cather indulged to comment on diva cultism,

as in "Scandal," it was always from backstage and from the perspective of the celebrity herself. All of her singers, fictional and factual, were real women who also were artists. Their art was inherently performative, public, and ephemeral where Cather's was permanent and private; but Cather recognized that they rolled out of bed in the morning, too, same as she, and connected to their artistry and all that went with it.

In "The Diamond Mine," published in *McClure's* in October 1916, we are introduced to Cressida Garnet, the "diamond mine" leaned upon for financial stability for a long series of siblings and husbands. Though the story is based loosely on the life of soprano Lillian Nordica,[26] Cressida was, like Olive Fremstad, a "worker, not a dreamer." She was "not musically intelligent; she never became so," but by her "driving power" and the vocal coaching of Miletus Poppas (the object of painfully anti-Semitic description and characterization) she is able to rise to global prominence. Cather introduces Garnet as recently engaged to her fourth husband-to-be, Jerome Brown. Cressida was a talented girl from a large family from Columbus, Ohio. Her first husband, Charley Wilton, was a handsome but frail local man who played organ in the church and had died a few years into their marriage. Her second, short-lived, marriage was to a tractor magnate named Ransome McChord. That relationship died when he forced her to choose between their marriage and her vocal coaching under Poppas, effectively asking her to choose between him or musical success. Her third husband, the subject of about half of the story, was a Bohemian avant-garde composer named Blasius Bouchalka she'd met in New York after she'd ascended to prominence as a diva. He was an ambitious man until he inherited her life of luxury and became complacent. He is painfully uxorious, or so it seems until Cressida returns home unexpectedly from a tour and surprises him in flagrante with the Bohemian cook, Ruzenka. The long-suffering Cressida dismisses him quietly, giving him enough from their marriage settlement to support his modest lifestyle. Jerome Brown would prove the worst of her husbands, burning through vast sums of her money in ill-fated investment schemes; other than her oldest brother, Buchanan Garnet, "he was the most rapacious of the men with whom she had had to do."[27] When Cressida dies—a victim of the *Titanic,* no less—her estate is picked over and disputed by her various siblings and Brown, who are outraged that she'd left $50,000 to Poppas. As Cather notes, "it seemed never to occur to them that this golden stream, whether it rushed or whether it trickled, came out of the industry, out of the mortal body of a woman."[28]

What's particularly notable in this story is how little opera the story actually references. It is about twelve thousand words long and focuses entirely on the life of an opera singer. And yet only a few sentences are devoted to her craft and stage career. Early it is noted that she struggled to gain notoriety, that she is a worker whose craft comes by sheer will. To that end, Cather references only an early performance as Brangena in *Tristan und Isolde*. The story concludes with a brief correspondence from Poppas in which he quotes the final lines of *Das Rheingold:* "*Traulich und Treu / ist's nur in der Tiefe: / falsch und feig / ist was dort oben sich freut!*" ("Faithful and true / is only in the deep: / false and fearful / is what makes joy above"). In between is only a brief reference to Cressida's hearing a bit from Massenet's *Manon* and an upcoming performance of *Don Giovanni*. Brangena is Isolde's handmaiden, Manon is a naïve, ill-used woman, and the passage from *Rheingold,* sung by the Rheinmaidens, reminds us that only in the depths, as in the cold North Atlantic where Cressida meets her fate, can truth and fidelity be found. Cressida Garnet is a singer who uses just enough talent, coupled with an immense work ethic, to produce immense fortune and fame. But Cather reminds us, through her willing resistance to reference opera in the story, that worldly concerns still have found the artist and have robbed her of delight in her craft. The only concrete nods to opera in the story are those that remind the reader that Garnet's life is one in which the artist, especially one noble and forgiving, is liable to be cut down by a world that doesn't fully understand or appreciate her craft. When Cather writes of other operatic heroines in the 1910s like Kitty Ayrshire, Thea Kronborg, and Eden Bower, their occasional hard-heartedness must be weighed against the fate of the very willing and compassionate Cressida Garnet.

Cather wrote only one recurring character in her fiction, Kitty Ayrshire, the protagonist of "A Gold Slipper" (1917) and "Scandal" (1919). Kitty, modeled on soprano Mary Garden, is a classic diva: pretty, confident, daring, and perfectly willing to outrage an audience—"to shock the great crowd was the surest way to get its money," she believes.[29] She is a fascinating, witty personality—Kate Hepburn might well have cited her as a character influence. But her two stories are not particularly great. "A Gold Slipper" involves Kitty dressing down a staid businessman who thinks opera is for the birds. He's a strawman who sets up a variety of common arguments against the arts that Kitty suavely puts down. In "Scandal," Kitty has succumbed to some ailment of the throat and in her convalescence has an acquaintance tell her a story about another businessman who'd hired a Kitty look-alike to follow him around town so as to wow potential accounts. Cather had little confidence in either story, trying to call "Slipper" back before publication because it was a "trifling little story," but she let it run because it paid $450.[30] "Scandal," the weaker of the two, is disconcertingly racist, with the businessman in question, an Austrian immigrant named Siegmund Stein, being a caricature of a Jewish department store owner; despite the story, by any objective evaluation, describing his rise as the result of hard work and astute observation, he's nevertheless characterized as having "one of those rigid, horse-like faces that never tell anything; a long nose, flattened as if it had been tied down; a scornful chin; long, white teeth, flat cheeks, yellow as a Mongolian's; tiny, black eyes, with puffy lids and no lashes; dingy, dead-looking hair" and elsewhere as "a deep, mysterious Jew who had the secret of gold." This follows on the tail of her descriptions of Miletus Poppas, a "vulture of the vulture race [who] had the beak of one." We're never told what sort of nose Ántonia Pavelka or Claude Wheeler had, or invited to attach a moral significance to such description had one been provided. Regardless, the story is a weird sort of schadenfreude in which the reader is invited to gawk at the embarrassment of the Jewish businessman in the company of his "Old Testament" friends. If no great author is necessarily worthy of disqualification for such sins, no great author is immune from having them pointed out as errors, either. Beyond that, "Scandal" deals little with opera specifically other than to call to account the silliness of celebrity culture that had grown up around the most prominent divas.

"A Gold Slipper" begins with Marshall McKann, a coal company executive, who, against his better judgment, has been dragged by his wife to a Kitty Ayrshire recital in Pittsburgh. The show had sold out, but McKann's wife has learned that additional seating, in the form of wooden chairs, is to be added to the stage itself. McKann believes firmly that high art of Kitty's sort is an emperor's new clothes situation; people go and pretend to like it due to social pressure. McKann considers himself impervious to such influence.

As the recital begins, Kitty appears in an outrageous gown, a "reviling, shrieking green which would have made a fright of any woman who had not inextinguishable beauty," the "repartee of a conscienceless Parisian designer." It was bare-shouldered and "split back from a gold-lace petticoat, gold stockings, gold slippers." The train is attached to both ankles, causing it to keep "curling about her feet like a serpent's tail." McKann, however, is not aghast. Such shenanigans are to be expected from such a woman. It's not until intermission, after her singing of pieces from Handel, Mozart, and Beethoven, that he begins to be affected by her. As she's walking offstage, she brushes against him, looks down, and murmurs "pardon!" At that moment, he "seemed to see himself as if she were holding a mirror up before him. He beheld himself a heavy, solid figure, unsuitably clad for the time and place, with a florid, square face. [. . .] Not a rock face, exactly, but a kind of pressed-brick-and-cement face, a 'business' face upon which years and feelings had made no mark." He thinks of Kitty. She's not like other singers, whom he'd imagined all to be "fat Dutchwomen." Rather, she has the figure of a "young girl, supple and sinuous and quick-silverish; thin, eager shoulders, polished white arms that were nowhere too fat and nowhere too thin." McKann, leering and self-satisfied, is early made to be a parody of post-Gilded Age capitalist masculinity. We know not to like him. In the second half of the performance, when Kitty sings a series of romantic German songs more to her particular skills than the earlier classical pieces, she looks at McKann and catches him yawning, and he notices that she frowns a little at the sight. Rather than feeling embarrassed, it makes him feel important.

She wraps up her recital with a selection of modern French songs. Then, though she will have to rush to catch her train to New York so that she can sing *Faust* the following night, she avails the audience with an encore: the most popular aria from a French opera that had "become synonymous with her name—an opera written for her and to her and round about her, by the veteran French composer who adored her." This clue is the most telling connection between Kitty and her basis in real life: Mary Garden. Garden, a Scottish soprano admired for both her singing and acting, had worked closely with the French composer Jules Massenet during the composer's later years. He wrote one of his later operas, *Chérubin,* with Garden in mind, and she originated the title role in Monte Carlo in 1905.[31] If Cather's readers might not have been quite aware of that particular fact, they would certainly have been aware of the scope of such qualification and would have associated it with a popular, well-known figure such as Garden. Kitty was an artiste par excellence. After the encore, both McKann and Kitty rush away, McKann annoyed by how "his fellow-townsmen [had looked] owlish and uplifted" by her performance.

Both of them are bound for New York out of the East Liberty station. By chance, McKann's car happens upon Kitty's, broken down on the way. He is persuaded to deliver her to the station. Once on the train, she insists they enter into a dialogue. She had noticed his obvious displeasure at the performance and asks why he disapproved. What follows is a Socratic dialogue in which Kitty seeks not to win McKann over to a love of art songs and opera, but rather to prove her superiority. What was it that he found so problematic about the performance? The gown? The lights? The uncomfortable chairs? McKann proudly declares he knows less about fashion than about music. And of course the seating was uncomfortable and the lights blinding. But Kitty persists, noting that she felt from him something "quite hostile and personal." Finally McKann comes out with it. "I'm a hard-headed business man," he says, "and I don't much believe in any of you fluffy-ruffles people."[32] She asks him his line of work. He replies "coal." She says that she doesn't have any natural distrust of business people and could become interested in coal; is she, then, more open-minded than he? He laughs at this and says that she has been so inured in a world of fakery that none of her kind know when they are or aren't interested in something. "They imagine they do, because it's supposed to be the proper thing," he claims. In essence, no one really likes opera, but rather many pretend to in order to signal a note of cultural superiority. Kitty then asks whether people attend church for the same reason: "Don't people go to church in exactly the same way? If there were a spiritual-pressure test-machine at the door, I suspect not many of you would get to your pews." McKann evades this question by calling her question an evasion, which, to be fair, it is. If Cather, in this instance, treats the relationship between art and religion somewhat flippantly, she didn't always. Cather famously equated the two and treated both seriously in *The Professor's House*, noting, as elsewhere, that "art and religion (they are the same thing, in the end, of course) have given man the only happiness he has ever had." Kitty then describes Tolstoy's theory of art, that art and truth are a matter of starving baser hungers so as to reveal a more profound hunger at the base of existence. She claims that this idea is "even the subject of the greatest of all operas, which, because I can never hope to sing it, I love more than all the others." This is clearly a reference to *Tannhäuser*, Wagner's opera about the rejection of the joys of Venusberg, a representation of worldly delights, so as to attain spiritual perfection; when the story was published in 1917, Wagner's operas had been widely banned from performance in the United States after the nation's entry into World War I, so she, despite her German music bona fides, would have had no hope of performing it. McKann simply replies that he thinks Tolstoy was "a crank." Kitty knows that she hasn't defeated McKann in the sense that she's changed his mind. But his blanket stonewalling of the artist's argument leaves her satisfied enough that she has proved him a failure.

The Kitty Ayrshire stories are frustrating in that they create an interesting character (it should be worth noting that the anti-Semitism of "Scandal" comes less from her than from her friend telling the anecdote), but they don't give her notable narratives. During the First World War, Cather was writing stories for a commercial market to offset the one-third increase in her expenses during that period,[33] using her well-honed editor's eye from her *Home Monthly* and *McClure's* years to produce viable commercial fiction. If Kitty couldn't have been Cather's Nick Adams, Hemingway's famous recurring character, she might have been her Basil Lee or Pat Hobby, Fitzgerald's serial story characters of the following decades. But even if Kitty's stories underwhelm, Cather, as with Cressida Garnet, uses the character to explore another side of the opera singer's life, apart from the struggles of artistic perfection. In these stories, she analyzes the singer's quotidian struggles with popular perception—both the rumors in "Scandal" and the unreceptive tastes of the bourgeois public in "A Gold Slipper."

Cather was freer with subject in her short fiction in many ways: not only during the wide-latitude experimentation of her apprentice years, but in her later stories as well. Notably, her stories were much more amorously preoccupied than her novels. This was to be expected in her early stories, when, by and large, she was copying the market expectations for short fiction; she wrote stories of love and loss then because people bought stories of love and loss. But her mature short fiction is also far more engaged with matters of romance than were her novels of the same period. While *O Pioneers!* includes the tragic love story of Marie and Emil, Alexandra's relationship—and eventual marriage—with Carl is notably platonic. Ántonia's relationship with Jim is, as well, and her eventual marriage is presented much as an afterthought. Thea gets married to Fred, apparently, in *The Song of the Lark*, but that event warrants only a sentence in the epilogue, recounted in passing by Aunt Tillie. In *One of Ours*, Claude's marriage to Enid is positively stillborn. And so on. Joan Acocella, in her introduction to *Willa Cather and the Politics of Criticism*, makes the point that Cather was something of a pioneer in this regard. Thea Kronborg's statement that "who marries who is a small matter, after all," Acocella identifies as "a turning point in the history of Western literature," noting that "who marries whom, or at least who goes to bed with whom, is not only a small matter, it is the subject" for virtually all women previously portrayed in literature. "*The Song of the Lark*," she concludes, "is the first completely serious female *Künstlerroman,* the first portrait-of-the-artist-as-a-young-woman in which the heroine's artistic development is the whole story, with sex an incidental matter."[34] But while Cather's short stories have a Kitty Ayrshire here and there, someone whose narratives have little to do with sex, they are far more likely than her novels to engage with romantic love directly, often with frank eroticism.

"The Garden Lodge," published only in *The Troll Garden,* features Caroline Noble. She's a musician, brought up in a painfully bohemian (not *Bohemian*) household run by her father, a "music teacher who usually neglected his duties to write orchestral compositions for which the world seemed to have no especial need [. . .], writing interminable scores which demanded everything under heaven except melody."[35] Her mother, believing him to be the "music lord of the future"—a reference to Wagner's essay "The Music of the Future"—is wholly deferential and meekly tends to the house, in addition to mollifying the students he ignores. Caroline's brother is a fez-wearing painter without any particular talent or drive who hangs about the house with other artsy young men who likewise prefer mocking other artists and popular tastes to actually producing art. He shoots himself at age twenty-six. Caroline, however, manifests a practical streak missed by her family. She sets up a music-teaching studio, proves to be a talented instructor, keeps regular hours, and becomes a sensible, modest success. In time, she marries Howard Noble, a wealthy man of Wall Street and a widower sixteen years her senior. Caroline, by all outward appearances, maintains the unsentimental practicality that had allowed her to lift herself up from poverty.

On the grounds of Caroline and Howard's property is the titular garden lodge, a quaint structure in quiet environs. By a mechanism not fully revealed in the story, the lodge had recently served as a retreat for the famous tenor Raymond d'Esquerré. He'd stayed there during the month of May before sailing for the London opera season, Caroline accompanying him in the lodge while he rehearsed. Her friends are horrified—d'Esquerré isn't only a famous tenor but a global sex symbol as well, and the eminently sensible Caroline, of all women, was the only one they knew incapable of appreciating his nonmusical talents. It was, they thought, "another striking instance of the perversity of things." His arrival had been the "signal for a feminine hegira toward New York." Women from all walks of life came to hear him at the Met. Shop girls and businesswomen and women with doctoral degrees came to see him: "There were the maimed, even; those who came on crutches, who were pitted by smallpox or grotesquely painted by cruel birth stains. [. . .] Stout matrons became slender girls again; worn spinsters felt their cheeks flush with the tenderness of their lost youth. Young and old, however hideous, however fair, they yielded up their heat—whether quick or latent—sat hungering for the mystic bread wherewith he fed them at this eucharist of sentiment."[36] But if anyone could not appreciate him, it would have been Caroline. The phrase "eucharist of sentiment" is meaningful, because it demonstrates that d'Esquerré's draw isn't reduced to handsomeness. Rather, his musical talent combines with animal magnetism to elevate his audience to a quasi-spiritual higher plain of emotional awareness. The maimed, matrons, and spinsters are reawakened sentimentally, returned to a place of feeling they had long lost as though they'd touched the holy train. The grotesque and pitted are given the fantasy of loving fulfillment by his work. The passionless are impassioned.

One evening two weeks after d'Esquerré had departed, Howard asks Caroline how she would feel about tearing down the lodge and installing a new guest house—"a big rustic affair where you could have tea served in mid-summer," he asks. When she brings up that it perhaps should stand because the famous performer had used it, Howard replies, "are you going to be sentimental about it?" and they laugh, acknowledging that her perfect level-headedness would never allow her to be sentimental. Even so, Caroline can't sleep that night, thinking about the lodge and the man who'd stayed there. Quietly, she slips out of the house and visits the lodge. A storm is about to break, and "everything seemed pervaded by a poignant distress; the hush of feverish, intolerable expectation. The still earth, the heavy flowers, even the growing darkness, breathed the exhaustion of protracted waiting." She sits at the piano and begins to play through the first act of *Die Walküre*, the last piece they'd practiced together. She comes to the duet at the end of act one, when Siegmund and Sieglinde, soon to join and produce the hero Siegfried, sing "thou art the spring for which I sighed in winter's cold embraces." Notably, she recalls these words being sung by d'Esquerré, though they belong to Sieglinde in the opera—a subtle evocation of the oneness of the two.[37]

She remembers rehearsing once with d'Esquerré when he put his arm around her as he would have held Sieglinde on stage, "one hand under her heart, while with the other he took her right hand from the keyboard [and] drew her toward the window." Caroline had not relented to the advance; "she had been wonderfully the mistress of herself at the time; neither repellant nor acquiescent" and had "rather exulted, then, in her self-control."[38] She had been tacitly invited to sex but had declined. Remembering that moment, she falls on the couch and begins to sob. "It was not enough," she mourns, "this happy, useful, well-ordered life was not enough. It did not satisfy, it was not even real. No, the other things, the shadows—they were the realities." She considers that even her parents and brother were nearer an authentic, fulfilled reality than she had been, wealthy and secure, with Howard. Like so many others, her emotional reality was awakened by d'Esquerré—only two weeks too late. She cries herself to sleep, then, in "a moment between world and world," neither quite conscious or unconscious, "she felt her dream grow thin, melting away from her, felt the warmth under her heart growing cold." Something slips away from her, which she tries to grab with "fluttering hands," but it is gone.

The next morning at breakfast, Howard notes that Caroline looks tired and suggests she retreat to the mountains until the warm weather passes. He then asks if she were serious about letting the lodge stand. "No," she replies, "I find I was not very serious. I haven't sentiment enough to forego a summer-house." Howard responds that he is "rather disappointed": "I had almost hoped that, just for once, you know, you would be a little bit foolish." They laugh.

Where Cather's other stories of opera singers tend to focus on the practical realities of the singer's life—finances, social imbroglios, audience reactions—in this story the singer himself is a ghost. D'Esquerré is never a physical presence in the story, only a memory. But his fixed place in Caroline's mind shows the lingering impact of operatic art. Published in *The Troll Garden*, "The Garden Lodge," like its companion pieces, demonstrates a personal devastation in the absence of access to art. Caroline is Georgiana, only on a shorter timeframe. While d'Esquerré's appeal is clearly tied to sexuality, his net effect is not dissimilar to what Georgiana experienced at her Wagner matinée—especially given that Georgiana remembered Wagner in part through psychic glimpses of her handsome cow-puncher. In addition, while Cather seemed to have blamed provincialism for the death of art, be it the provincialism of small rural towns as in "Nelly Deane" or working-class urban neighborhoods as in "Paul's Case," a story like "The Garden Lodge" reminds us that wealth and sophistication alone do not suffice to provide artistic satisfaction. Caroline is from New York. She marries a well-do-do New York man. She goes to the opera and even has a great opera singer reside on her property. But her failure to metaphorically engage the operatic possibilities of that moment—here represented by an affair with the famous tenor—is no less a rejection of artistic ecstasy than Georgiana or Nelly remaining out west. In tying sex to opera, "The Garden Lodge" sets up a complex nexus between physical and emotional reality that she would more fully explore fifteen years later.

"Coming, Aphrodite!" originally appeared in *The Smart Set* in August 1920, though it was originally published as "Coming, Eden Bower!" The Eden character had been loosely based on Mary Garden, who had recently performed in Camille Erlanger's opera *Aphrodite;* the story is by far Cather's most sexually explicit, and George Jean Nathan, who accepted the story for publication, feared a libel suit (he also required Cather to tone down some of the more overt sexual descriptions in hopes of dodging Anthony Comstock's Society for the Suppression of Vice).[39] The story is certainly one of Cather's finest, and was universally praised when published without bowdlerization in *Youth and the Bright Medusa.* One reviewer described it as such:

> without a superfluous word or an ounce of sentimentality [Cather] tells here the story which has tempted a hundred others, the story of two young artists, in a Washington Square garret, Don Hedger, the painter, and Eden Bower, the singer, who drift together for a passionate interlude, and then drift apart. The thing is told with the utmost skill, and the deftest strokes of descriptive incident. The two contrasted personalities are projected as firmly in a few strokes as if a whole novel had been filled with the details of their careers.[40]

In her famous 1922 essay "The Novel Démeublé," Cather advocated for an unfurnished prose style. For a story situated in and preoccupied with the sparse furnishing of a New York city apartment, this review couldn't have been more appropriate. Were it not such a long story (nearly sixteen thousand words), it would probably be one of Cather's widely anthologized stories alongside "A Wagner Matinée" or "The Sculptor's Funeral."

The story begins with Don Hedger, a painter, who rents an upstairs room off Washington Square. The upstairs has been parceled out into two apartments, the second of which has recently been evacuated by a playwright who, as playwrights might, failed to pay rent. The new inhabitant is a woman of twenty, Eden Bower. For the first few days of their shared existence, the two interact sparingly. She chastises him for using their shared bathtub to wash his dog; in retaliation, he barks at her to clear a trunk she'd left in the hallway. Otherwise, he only knows her from hearing her sing. From the rooftop one May night he hears a woman's voice singing the "tempestuous, over-lapping phrases of Signor Puccini, then comparatively new in the world, but already so popular that even Hedger recognized his unmistakable gusts of breath."[41] The main action of the story takes place in the summer of 1902 (the story's coda takes place eighteen years later, which we can assume is contemporaneous with the story's 1920 publication). Puccini's *La Bohème*—which, given the bohemian lifestyle of Don and Eden, is probably what Cather intends to evoke—was first performed in New York's Wallach's Theatre in 1898 and didn't make it to the Met until November 1900.[42] By referencing this opera, Cather is signaling a story of willfully impoverished young artists falling in love. Hearing her, Don tells his dog, "It may not be so bad."

One day, Don is sifting through his clothes closet, which shares a wall with Eden's living room. He notices a ray of light shining through a knot hole in the wall, and, without thinking, crouches to look through. There, "in a pool of sunlight, stood his new neighbor, wholly unclad, doing exercises of some sort before a long gilt mirror." Hedger watches, not realizing how "unpardonable" his behavior is, in part because, as an artist, he'd worked with nude models often, and in part because Don is generally asocial and incognizant of codes of human conduct. He observes her "as she swung her arms and changed from one pivot of motion to another, muscular energy seem[ing] to flow through her from her toes to her finger-tips. The soft flush of exercise and the gold of afternoon sun played over her flesh together, enveloped her in a luminous mist which, as she turned and twisted, made now an arm, now a shoulder, now a thigh, dissolve in pure light."[43] Hedger's hand begins to behave as though he were holding a crayon, darting about as though he were drawing her, and "the charcoal seemed to explode in his hand at the point where the energy of each gesture was discharged into the whirling disc of light, from a foot or shoulder, from the up-thrust chin or the lifted breasts." Certainly no author has described autoeroticism so tastefully.

While Don's voyeurism is described as "unpardonable" and later "detestable," Cather mitigates his violation by making it partly an act of artistic enthusiasm and partly a derivative of Don's background. He had been a foundling, rescued and educated by a priest, then turned loose into the world at a relatively young age. He took his education as an artist, and lives in simple poverty, wanting nothing more than independence to paint what he wants to paint. He is, as he says later in the story, "painting for painters," rather than a general public, "painting for painters,—who haven't been born."⁴⁴ Eden, on the other hand, is a singer who knows that she needs an admiring public. From childhood, she's trained herself to sing and act and now, at twenty, she's fled her hometown of Huntington, Illinois, where her father sells tractors, to seek her fame. She had gone first to Chicago—where all of Cather's aspirant singers get their starts— where she'd attracted the attention of a wealthy newspaper publisher named Jones (perhaps an homage to Will Owen Jones), who had agreed to finance her further study in Paris. She's now in New York to await her trip over in the fall.

Eden, as it turns out, is aware of Don's peeping. One night as he watches her sitting by her window, smoking a cigarette, she stands, "look[s] about her with a disdainful, crafty smile, and turn[s] out the light." While it's unclear how long she's been aware of Don's transgression, it is clear that she's tacitly endorsed the invasion. For her, like every aspect of her life, it is a performative experience. It's not a surprise, then, when the two begin to chat. Meeting at first in Washington Square Park, they discuss his art; she reveals her zest for life. They begin to meet for dinner and drinks. Eventually, he invites her to Coney Island to see a model friend of his, Molly, perform a stunt whereby she rides up in a hot air balloon, then descends, scantily clad, on a trapeze. After seeing this once, Eden evades Don and convinces Molly to let her do the next show. She performs to the admiration of the crowd, but to the perturbation of Don. Not winning him over with her stunt disappoints her greatly. Afterward, they go to eat, and she asks him about a new painting she's seen him work on. He says it's based on an ancient Mexican legend, but balks at recounting the story to her because he doesn't "know if it's the proper kind of story to tell a girl." "Oh, forget about that!" she responds, "I've been balloon riding today." She's up for anything.

The legend, "The Forty Lovers of the Queen," is about a Mexican princess who has the power to bring rain. Part of her gift, however, requires she remain a virgin until marriage, a stipulation that the King can only maintain by keeping a close guard on his amorously inclined daughter. When he returns from a war party with captives, the Princess notices a particularly strapping young chief who's been taken prisoner. His body is covered with tattoos, and she pleads for his life so that he can adorn her in the same fashion. But the Princess is "without shame before the Captive," and, overcome by lust, he forces himself on her briefly before being stopped; his punishment is the removal of his tongue and testicles (Cather's version reads "gelded"—the *Smart Set* publication limited the term to "maimed"). Afterward, he is given to her as a slave. In time, a nearby Aztec king hears of the Princess's gift and marries her so that she can make rain for his kingdom. He gives her a fortress on the edge of the city where she can live in privacy. Nightly, the new Queen instructs her captive to bring her men, with whom she sleeps for a day or two, then orders killed. Having once found a man who satisfies her, she elects to spare his life, and, through this, she is found out. The King, furious, has her and the slave burned to death. The story concludes, simply but disconcertingly, "and afterward there was scarcity of rain."

Eden is horrified not by the story itself so much as by the savagery with which Don tells it: "to antagonize and frighten her," she thinks. "Now she was looking at the man he really was. Nobody's eyes had ever defied her like this. [. . .] He was testing her, trying her out, and she was more ill at ease than she wished to show." They walk home "like people who have quarrelled or who wish to get rid of each other." Even so, both unable to sleep, they chance to meet on the rooftop later that night. He puts his arms around her and "they began to talk, both at once, as people do in an opera." What follows is a "flood of trivial admissions" in which he apologizes for his behavior, and she forgives him. He helps her climb down into the dark hallway: "When his feet were on the carpet and he reached up to lift her down, she twined her arms about his neck as after a long separation, and turned her face to him, and her lips, with their perfume of youth and passion."[45] At once, they consummate both rivalry and love.

Having begun a sexual relationship, they open the door that separates their apartments and for a period of weeks cohabitate. But it is not to last. Eden, ever the girl about town, has made the introduction of Burton Ives, a famous artist to whom she offers to introduce Don in the hopes of getting an endorsement and a wider audience for his work. Don, however, thinks Ives is a popular hack and refuses. What ensues is an argument in which they reveal their mutually exclusive artistic ambitions: She sees art as a path to wealth and celebrity; he is insistent about maintaining strict artistic independence, poverty be damned. He leaves to visit a friend on Long Island for a few days, during which time he realizes his error and returns to reconcile with Eden. She, however, has gone on to Paris. In a brief coda, Eden has returned to New York eighteen years later, now a prima donna assoluta, to perform in an opera titled "Coming, Aphrodite!" and takes some time to check on Don. Though she doesn't find him, she does chat briefly with an art dealer who confirms that Don has had a successful career, but only in the sense that he is highly influential among younger painters: He is "one of the first men among the moderns. [. . .] Madame," the dealer assures her: "there are many kinds of success." Eden, for her part, has reached the pinnacle of her field, but it seems not to have made her happy. Rather, she is able only to *perform* happiness: "Leaning back in the cushions, Eden Bower closed her eyes, and her face, as the street lamps flashed their ugly orange light upon it, became hard and settled, like a plaster cast," but, tomorrow night, "this mask would be the golden face of Aphrodite. But a 'big' career takes its toll, even with the best of luck."

Like Cressida Garnet, and to an extent like Thea Kronborg, Eden has left the small town to achieve world renown and near artistic perfection as an opera singer. But satisfaction eludes her, and now, in middle age, she is realizing, as perhaps Cather was realizing around 1920, that "art is too terribly human to be very great." Regardless, Cather's short fiction of these middle years of her career consistently involves characters with an artistic temperament feeling compelled to leave their humble roots to pursue their personal truths through art. But Cather seemed to struggle with how to represent this concept without unduly deprecating her hometown and state, and, eventually, she struggled with what sort of satisfaction fleeing one's upbringing might actually bring. Opera, performed humbly on the plains and in grand fashion only in the cities, represented a spectrum of artistic achievement. If that Rossetti exhibition had happened in Red Cloud, it would still have been Rossetti. But the *Trovatore* performance would have been very different there than what she would have found in Chicago. Opera, in its forms and complexity, was a suitable vehicle for helping her understand and express the spectrum of art and artistic temperament. Cather will always be known as an author of the plains. But she's not. At least not exclusively. In her short fiction of her best short fiction years, she's an author who wrote about opera as a way to explore human exceptionalism. Her stories of the period between 1903 and 1920 focus consistently on opera as a way for characters to demonstrate qualities that separate them from home by connecting them to who they really are.

⚘

CHAPTER 5

ENTR'ACTE
Alexander's Bridge

There have been notable and beautiful exceptions, but I think usually the young writer
must have his affair with the external material he covers; must imitate and strive to
follow the masters he most admires, until he finds he is starving for reality and cannot
make this go any longer. Then he learns that it is not the adventure he sought, but the
adventure that sought him, which has made the enduring mark upon him.
—Cather's preface to the 1922 reissue of *Alexander's Bridge*

*J*n May 1912, *Collier's* published Cather's short story "Behind the Singer
Tower." The story documents a conversation between a handful of
professional men—two reporters, an engineer, a draftsman, a lawyer,
and a doctor—as they consider the disaster of the fictional Mont Blanc hotel,
which had burned to a shell the day before, taking, as of the latest count, hundreds
of lives.[1] Despite being a gem of deft style and measured revelation of plot—and
something of an outlier in Cather's writings as a story with an abrupt, ambiguous
ending (Cather loved an epilogue, even when she didn't announce them)—the
story rarely merits a mention in Cather scholarship. Woodress dismisses the
vignette quality of the story as making it "muddled," and he writes that, though
the story is best categorized as "social-protest fiction," its narrator undercuts the
protest theme by claiming that the waves of immigrants who sacrifice themselves
building the city must be doing so to build "something wonderful" (though a fair
reading of the story might consider that remark ironic).[2] Sharon O'Brien writes
that the story is "more than social criticism" and that it also represents, metaphorically, Cather's career at that moment. The skyscrapers in the story represent
Cather's literary aspirationalism, but the all-male cast of characters coupled with
the destruction of the Mont Blanc suggests an anxiety about Cather's beginning

her move into the male-dominated world of novel writing.[3] (In reality, Cather had operated in the male-dominated world of magazine publishing for years.) When commentary reacts to "Singer," such dispositive, sociopolitical assessments are typical; generally, however, commentary ignores "Singer" altogether.

The story begins with the six men in a launch heading up the North (Hudson) River. Though they are described as being in "a kind of stupor" because of "that terrible day," the event itself is left undisclosed. They pass an Italian steamer, the *Re di Napoli*, heading to its pier; the reporter notes that the Italians are proud of their new docks and that they "feel they've come up in the world." The harbor has a "brooding mournfulness [. . .] as if the ghost of helplessness and terror were abroad in the darkness." Behind them, the city "seemed enveloped in a tragic self-consciousness," the towers "grouped confusedly together, as if they were confronting each other with a question [. . .], like the great trees left after a forest has been cut away." The city itself is "an irregular parallelogram pressed between two hemispheres, and, like any other solid squeezed in a vice, it shot upward." Throughout this long, three-paragraph introduction, Cather insinuates much, but tells little; the Mont Blanc hasn't been mentioned at all, but the city is described as reeling, tense, guilt-ridden from a shock. Then, in a short paragraph, the narrator notes that his companions don't speak because there's nothing more to say. Abruptly and without transition, he notes that "before we left town the death list for the Mont Blanc had gone above three hundred."

Then the narrator, Fred Hallet, the engineer of the group, describes the scope of the disaster, not only the sheer volume of lives lost, but the specific human capital: the presidents of half a dozen trusts, two state governors, and a major European ambassador, along with so many businessmen that Wall Street had been forced to shut down for the day in a vacuum of leadership. Also among the dead are a few "pampered opera singers." Body identification was difficult, both because of the charred corpses and because a fair number had jumped from one of the thirty-five stories of the hotel into the "cobwebby life nets" stretched hundreds of feet below; the ineffective nets left the bodies a mess. Among the jumpers had been the famous tenor Graziani, identified not by his body, but by his hand, sheared off and left to hang on the rail of a fire escape as he'd tried to grasp it while falling past. It was identified "by a little-finger ring, which had been given to him by the German Emperor. [. . .] I had seen it often enough when he placed it so confidently over his chest as he began his 'Celeste Aida.'"

After enumerating the essential facts of the devastation, Hallet shifts to a narrative describing his early days as an engineer, which happened to have been helping to lay the foundation of the Mont Blanc. He was under the direction of Stanley Merryweather, a cost-cutting construction manager whose cheapness (as in other stories of the decade, Cather makes this anti-Semitic by having Hallet identify Merryweather as Jewish) ultimately results in a snapped cable that crushes a team of Italian workers. The particular worker with whom Hallet shared a connection was Caesarino, from the small island of Ischia near Naples. By speaking a few words of Italian, Hallet had been able to earn a sort of desperate affection from the man, who knew little English and had no family stateside, but was sending money back to his mother and siblings. On the night of the construction incident, "with drills puffing everywhere and little crumpled men crawling about like tumble bugs under the stream from the searchlight," Hallet's team can't hear the clamshell digger full of sand above them or hear when it snaps, burying them all before they know they're in danger. When the ambulance orderlies dig Caesarino out, he's alive, but they dismiss him to focus their attention on others more likely to survive. "He saw the look," Hallet recalls, "and a boy who doesn't know the language learns to read looks." He knows from their look that he's going to die. "*Ma perche?*" he asks Hallet—"but why?"

When the story concludes, Hallet wonders aloud about the whole experiment of Manhattan, a steel hub of an island, cramped with humanity from all over the world: "Why do we do it?," he asks. "And why, in heaven's name, do *they* do it? *Ma, perche?* as Caesarino said that night in the hole. Why did he, from that lazy volcanic island, so tiny, so forgotten, where life is simple and pellucid and tranquil, shaping itself to tradition and ancestral manners as water shapes itself to the jar, why did he come so far to cast his little spark into the bonfire?" The engineer wonders why the thousands like Caesarino, from "islands even smaller and more remote" come "like iron dust to the magnet, like moths to the flame?" After a moment of silence, one of the reporters says, "we are the people who are doing it, and whatever it is, it will be ours," to which Hallet says something about "don't call anything ours" while their companion, the Jewish doctor Zablowski, is around. The reporter then turns to Zablowski and says, "why don't you *ever* hit back?" And the story ends.

The strange nugget of anti-Jewishness in the last lines might seem tacked on, but, unlike Merryweather's Jewishness, it actually helps to underscore Cather's point in the story, that Manhattan, where she'd lived for six years at the time, was a mix of peoples, ethnicities, social and economic classes, religions, politics, etcetera, but that that mix might not be hospitable to itself. The casual racism in the story, both anti-Semitic and the frequent use of *dago* to describe the poor Italian workers, serves to underline the ingrained prejudices of a society that appears, on the surface, to be building something extraordinary, but that harbors a litany of demographic prejudices that must be overcome before the skyscrapers are anything more than hollow monuments to human potential; for them to be meaningful, the people they represent must overcome their own moral shortcomings. Indeed, the subtle reference in the beginning of the story to the *Re di Napoli*, suggesting an independent city-state on the Italian peninsula, now in the context of a unified Italy, could represent the difficulty of discrete cultural identities forming a cohesive society. That moment of anti-Semitism at the end of the story is meant to bear evidence of how hard that transition would be, that, when the six had spent an hour contemplating disaster and meditating on the melting pot, one might still so casually violate the epiphany they were all expected to reach.

The story was likely inspired in part by the Triangle Shirtwaist Factory in Greenwich Village in March 1911. That disaster, the largest of its kind in New York and one of the largest ever in the nation, took 146 lives—123 women and 23 men—mostly recent Jewish and Italian immigrants working for about ten dollars per week. But whereas Triangle was a disaster for the working people of New York, the Mont Blanc burns with diplomats and industrialists in its rooms. The deaths of the Italian workers predate the disaster at issue in the story by many years. Perhaps Cather had in mind the destruction of the Windsor Hotel (1899, nearly ninety dead) or some other famous fire that had taken the lives of prominent citizens. Regardless, the death of Caesarino and his comrades is foundational to the demise of the titans of art and industry that perish in the Mont Blanc years later. Particularly important is the Italian resonance of the story, the *Re di Napoli* indicating the upward destinies of Italian immigrants, Caesarino's death leading eventually to the death of Graziani. In the story, Cather's references to opera singers suggest the transition from the rustic to the royal, insinuating the peasant's aspiration to become the "Celeste" Caesar celebrated among emperors, but who has the power, if abused, to bring down the mighty, including the "pampered opera singers" like Graziani.

"Singer" is an unusual story for Cather in both style and substance, but it's not alone. *Alexander's Bridge* (1912), her first novel, ends with a bridge collapse, this one likely based on the 1907 failure of the Quebec Bridge, which fell while under construction, killing eighty-six workers. Paired with "Singer," the novel represents Cather's growing mistrust of urbanism and accompanying feats of applied science. We build extraordinary structures, but out of hubris and at the expense of human life. In 1912, she'd lived in New York for six years and had lived in Pittsburgh for most of the decade preceding. Whereas the girl from Red Cloud knew the dreamy joy of Nelly Deane, where Chicago or some other city could represent, abstractly, the highest human potential, Cather of 1912 knew the city in its grittier reality and knew that the physical, steely monuments to human ingenuity had a darker side. It's no surprise, then, that she would turn to the plains for most of the subsequent decade, an elemental balm for the hubristic humanism of the city.

These stories, so unlike most of Cather's other writings, also portray a moment of crisis for her growing artistry. In 1912, Cather was an editor and a vaguely known short story writer and poet. Cather-as-novelist was without form and void. Consequently, her first novel shows a Cather who might have been, one who tries to follow the established path rather than create her own, and her subsequent plains fiction can only really be understood as a divergent outgrowth of the process of artistic realization that *Alexander's Bridge* represents. Given how preoccupied with the process of identity finding Cather would be for the next decade, and given, especially, how important opera would be for her within that process, a novel centered on an engineer trying to find his true self by having an affair with a musical theater performer should not be overlooked.

Cather dismissed *Alexander's Bridge* almost immediately after its publication and took potshots at it for years after. Most famously, in her 1931 essay "My First Novels (There Were Two)," she refers to it as a "studio picture"—that is, not drawn from a living, candid subject.[4] She'd set the story in London, she writes, because "London is supposed to be more engaging than, let us say, Gopher Prairie; even if the writer knows Gopher Prairie very well and London very casually." She was trying to write "interesting material" of the sort that she'd grown accustomed to dealing with in the commercial magazine market, much like the "interesting material" that characterized much of her uncollected short fiction. It wasn't until after the novel was published, when she spent several months in the Southwest, that she came to regard *Alexander's Bridge* as "unnecessary and superficial." In Arizona and New Mexico, "a country [she] really did care about, and among people who were a part of the country,"—so she claimed—she rediscovered authenticity. Then, at least according to the retconned personal history Cather used to explain her transition, she began to "write a book entirely for myself; a story about some Scandinavians and Bohemians who had been neighbors" in her youth: *O Pioneers!* This is a nice personal mythology, and one she'll use in *The Song of the Lark,* when Thea Kronborg's sojourn in Panther Canyon awakens her true artistic self. But it should be noted that Cather isn't claiming a return to authenticity in the wake of visiting Nebraska, but rather the greater Southwest; Taos and Red Cloud really aren't that similar, and Cather's youth was as alien from New Mexico as it was from New York. There should have been nothing in the Southwest to particularly reconnect her with her truer, youthful self. Rather, the gulf between *Alexander's Bridge* and *O Pioneers!* more likely represents the typical process of an author kicking the tires on a new form of art, experimenting rather than being somehow untrue to herself in the first attempt. In that sense, *Alexander's Bridge* actually has a greater claim to be the first novel, just like wobbly first efforts from other writers.

Certainly Cather's reluctance to endorse the novel is partly to blame for the fact that it remains critically underassessed. It's not a perfect book, and it sounds little like Cather's canonical fiction, so if she gives commentators permission to overlook it, then it's easy for commentators to do so. But though her freshman effort is not her best, her own thoughts on it shouldn't be grounds for dismissing it entirely. An artist can never see her own work with perfect clarity. For instance, Cather would similarly dismiss *The Professor's House* as a "nasty, grim little tale" and "certainly not my 'favorite' of my own books"—yet it's one of her finest novels. Cather's embarrassment with regard to *Alexander's Bridge* certainly has to do with the fact that she was attempting a well-wrought story in a transatlantic urban setting with a heavy flavoring of Henry James's narrative approach. The novel was unsuccessful, but her follow-up, a loosely-plotted novel set in the plains without a whiff of James was a surprise hit. It was natural, then, that she would claim *Pioneers* as her real first novel. Even so, that doesn't mean that the novel she wrote first ought necessarily to be consigned to the remainder pile.

At the beginning of his essential reference guide to opera, *100 Great Operas and Their Stories,* Henry Simon includes a preface entitled "An Apology for Smiling." It begins by acknowledging the prevalent conviction among those who pay attention to opera that the opera libretto is "practically the lowest form of literature" and that there is "nothing quite as ludicrous as an opera story."[5] This damnation of the opera plot is one of those not easily dislodged critical defaults. Because libretti are typically judged alongside other forms of narrative art, particularly spoken drama, they tend to fall short of the standards used to judge those other forms. But taken on their own terms, libretti are seldom actually *bad*. As Simon explains, "every one of the stories in this book is—or, at least, once was—good. I say this with confidence because no composer who ever lived would take the time and trouble to write a score for a story he knew to be bad." He goes on to enumerate the opera stories that were good in their original iterations (e.g., the many Orpheus, Elektra, Trojan, and biblical stories, and the great plays suitably converted to opera), as well as to explain how some stories that were originally good were recontextualized by history and made absurd. *La Traviata,* for example, was a shocking assault on sexual mores for a few decades; then sexual mores changed and the drama became indulgently sentimental. *Un Ballo in Maschera* was an edgy treatment of regicide—until regicide fell out of interest as monarchies fell out of power. These aren't bad stories, just stories that force us to recreate in our own minds the worlds of which they were part. *Alexander's Bridge* isn't a bad novel at all. Like Verdi sitting down with source material from Dumas, *fils,* to hammer out the *Traviata* score, Cather wouldn't have put the months into writing the book if it weren't a worthwhile story to tell. And it should be assessed not by the habits and standards of *My Ántonia* or *Death Comes for the Archbishop.* These are very different novels, and, while greater than *Alexander's Bridge,* their less successful older sibling is only lesser in their company. Given that the novel, regardless of quality, is Cather's first attempt at novel writing and reflects many of her own personal anxieties about that transition, it deserves more attention than what it's typically been given.

The novel begins with Lucius Wilson, a former professor of Bartley Alexander's, coming to visit the Alexander household in Boston. Bartley has yet to arrive home, and Wilson is invited in by Bartley's wife, Winifred, who is just getting in from a concert. Winifred is an amateur musician herself, a pianist, and, when Bartley arrives, she performs Schumann's "Carnaval" for Wilson and Bartley's entertainment. "Though I don't practice a great many hours," Winifred admits, "I am very methodical."[6] While the novel is not particularly preoccupied with music, Winifred's musicianship and concert attendance will prove a subtle characterization; Bartley's later love interest, Hilda, is an actor in London's musical theater scene. Cather is setting up Winifred—concert goer and parlor player—against Hilda—center-stage vocalist—using musical personalities to illustrate what will become Bartley's mutually exclusive personal desires. Before Bartley arrives, Winifred and Wilson engage in a vaguely flirty colloquy. Cather never establishes an affair between the two of them, though Wilson's willingness for such is hinted at a few times in the novel; Winifred's polite repudiation of Wilson's advances establishes her moral reliability. Feeling somewhat awkward with the wavering daylight, Winifred asks Wilson to relate some anecdotes of Bartley's college years. "What you want is a picture of him, standing back there at the other end of twenty years," says Wilson, "you want to look down through my memory."[7] Compare this with Jim Burden's admission after two decades of not keeping in touch with Ántonia: "In the course of twenty crowded years one parts with many illusions."[8] Cather is throughout the 1910s preoccupied with the span of a twenty-year memory—from her vantage point of 1912 and 1918, respectively, looking back to the years of her leaving Nebraska, reflecting on that moment of crisis where she would choose to leave home to pursue some yet-nebulous fantasy life in the city. Wilson has little to say about Bartley in concrete terms. When Bartley finally arrives home, Wilson makes vague comments that Bartley had been a young man of great promise, but whom he'd assumed would short-circuit his own potential: "The more dazzling the front you presented, the higher your façade rose, the more I expected to see a big crack zigzagging from top to bottom [. . .] then a crash and clouds of dust."[9] He claims that Bartley has become sensible, which makes Bartley uncomfortable. The crash metaphor, along with the fact that Bartley resists the idea that he has calmed, mostly gives the novel away in chapter 1.

Bartley travels to London on business. Though he is an engineer by trade, his earlier education in Europe had connected him to many of the London literati; Cather had herself recently visited London and had met much of the artistic in-circle there.[10] He and an acquaintance attend a performance of a new musical comedy called *Bog Lights,* featuring a performer that revives a memory of Bartley's youth: Hilda Burgoyne. As it happens, they'd had an affair years earlier, when both were in Paris, he learning his trade and she an aspiring actress, but the affair had ended when he took a job in Canada, where he met Winifred. (Incidentally, he'd offered to confess his doings with Hilda to Winifred, but she declined, saying that they would make her too jealous. The novel is awash in such repressions.) Bartley had all but forgotten Hilda until he chanced upon her performance in London, but being reminded of her reminds him likewise of his earlier, more adventuresome self. Wilson's comment that Bartley had changed and is now content to "leave some birds in the bushes" has primed him for a midlife affair. Of course, the fact that Cather is writing about a midlife crisis while trying to reinvent herself as a writer of urbane psychological novels in her late thirties should not go overlooked.

The timeline of the novel is a bit troubled. In the present action of the story, Bartley is forty-three years old. Upon seeing Hilda again, he thinks that she looks about thirty, making her more than a decade his junior. He elsewhere notes that his career had taken off six years earlier, when he was apparently around thirty-seven. In another conversation, Hilda notes that "we are neither of us twenty now"; while this is likely a general statement of their advancing years, it also indicates that they at least perceived themselves as youthful during their years together. Bartley's past is somewhat murky, but he's said to have come from the West someplace, presumably where Wilson had been teaching at a western college, where he'd been for a little over twenty years at the start of the novel. With these in mind, we can surmise that Bartley got a late start to college (hence his close relationship with Wilson, with whom he would have been a contemporary in age), then traveled to Europe to study sometime around his thirties, where he began what was an apparently multiyear affair with Hilda. Having then lucked into a contract to design the Allway Bridge in Canada, which made him a professional success, he began a relationship with Winifred, forgot Hilda, and moved on with life. This isn't a particularly convincing timeline, given the improbability of an engineer getting such a late start to a career yet finding himself at the pinnacle of the field by his early forties. Whatever the precise timeline, however, Bartley is now firmly in middle age and suffering a reckoning of identity. Hilda might not be twenty now, but she's still quite a bit younger than Bartley and causes him to fixate on his younger self: The word "youth" appears sixteen times throughout the novel, almost always in reference to Bartley's desire to experience again his unbridled past self, especially as he remembers it during his time with her.

Bartley thinks of himself now as "only a powerful machine," trained to do a job effectively, but not free. This is in contrast to "the boy he had been in the rough days of the old West, [. . .] the youth who had worked his way across the ocean on a cattle-ship and gone to study in Paris without a dollar in his pocket."[11] It was during that youth, which, as noted above, is best treated as a relative concept, that he'd first known Hilda, and "he thought of how glorious it had been, and how quickly it had passed; and, when it had passed, how little worth while anything was." Overcome with this desire to reconnect with his past self and seeing a reconnection with Hilda as a way of doing so, he facilitates a reunion with her, which begins innocently but quickly turns amorous. The remainder of the novel is situated on Bartley's indecision as to whether to leave his wife for Hilda or forsake Hilda and return to his stolid marriage. There are scenes in which the Alexanders clearly seem to be drifting apart from one another, but also scenes in which Bartley's deep affection for Winifred makes the thought of Hilda torturous. The only certainty in the novel is that Bartley, despite every apparent worldly success, is destined to be miserable. If he remains with Winifred, he is effectively abandoning the adventurous, youthful side that he believes to be his truest self; if he leaves Winifred, then he is abandoning everything that youthful side had worked hard to achieve. By any reasonable standard, Bartley has opportunities for happiness and satisfaction, but he's perpetually second guessing himself. The novel's genius is that, while Bartley eventually makes a decision, the reader is never privy to it. Cather has him drowned before he can take action.

He had been called to attend to an engineering problem at the Moorlock Bridge, his current major project and the feat that was to immortalize him. The longest cantilever bridge in existence once complete, the project had been hampered by cost-cutting (much like the Mont Blanc hotel), and Bartley laments ever having taken the job. Before catching the train to the building site, he'd written a letter to Winifred, apparently divulging his relationship with Hilda and expecting a permanent break from his wife. But he doesn't send the letter. "There would be nothing for him afterward," he thinks, "forever going on journeys that led nowhere; hurrying to catch trains that he might just as well miss; getting up in the morning with a great bustle and splashing of water, to begin a day that had no purpose and no meaning; dining late to shorten the night, sleeping late to shorten the day."[12] Though he clearly anticipates leaving his wife, it seems he can't envision a happy future with Hilda to replace what he'll lose. He begins to think of his relationship with Hilda as "a mere folly, a masquerade." But then he considers that he'd already promised to meet her in London in midsummer. From the construction site, he telegraphs Winifred to come to him, believing that confessing in person might be easier, but also buying himself time to rethink his situation. He inspects the bridge to find that his calculations hadn't scaled up properly and that the bridge's lower chord was about to buckle. He and the construction superintendent quietly begin to usher the workers off the bridge.

When the bridge collapses, Cather's first great moment as a novel writer happens. Whereas the rest of the novel had been very inward-looking, lacking in tactility or immediacy, emotions often puffed up with impassioned dialogue or desperate contemplations, the failure of the bridge happens with brutal efficiency, much like the construction pit disaster in "Singer." Bartley has walked to the end of the river span, then turns to see the cantilever arm "give a little, like an elbow bending." There is no "shock of any kind" but rather a freefall of thousands of tons of iron work sinking "almost in a vertical line, snapping and breaking and tearing as it went, because no integral part could bear for an instant the enormous strain loosed upon it." Bartley falls into the water clear of the bridge. In a split second he thinks "what it would mean to die a hypocrite," but then realizes he will live "to tell her and to recover all he had lost." Then the bridge crashes into the water behind him and the water is suddenly full of drowning men: "A gang of French Canadians fell almost on top of him. He thought he had cleared them, when they began coming up all around him, clutching at him and at each other. Some of them could swim, but they were either hurt or crazed with fright. Alexander tried to beat them off, but there were too many of them. One caught him about the neck, another gripped him about the middle, and they went down together. When he sank, his wife seemed to be there in the water beside him, telling him to keep his head, that if he could hold out the men would drown and release him. There was something he wanted to tell his wife, but he could not think clearly for the roaring in his ears. Suddenly he remembered what it was. He caught his breath, and then she let him go."[13] It's a day before they find his body. In his pocket is the letter he'd written. It is "water-soaked and illegible, but because of its length, [Winifred] knew it had been for her."

The novel is relatively light in terms of operatic references. The plays in which Hilda appears and sings are not opera, and hardly even, it seems, musical dramas. They are plays with some music. While Hilda might well represent youthful artistic abandon in a somewhat operatic fashion, given the number of prima donnas Cather was collecting in her fiction during this period, she might very well have made Hilda one and assigned her any number of real operatic parts. Indeed, Cather almost seems to have made it a point not to make Hilda an opera singer. Otherwise, when Hilda and Bartley have taken a day trip out of the city and are returning to the "distant gold-washed city" of London (Cather's idealized rendering of the city), Bartley notes that street performers have come out in droves thanks to favorable weather. "We've had five miles of 'Il Trovatore' now,'" he notes.[14] Cather is rarely very flattering of Verdi, especially of *Trovatore*. For example, in "A Wagner Matinée," Clark says to Georgiana "we have come to better things than the old *Trovatore* at any rate,"[15] putting Verdi's troubadour distinctly below Wagner's Meistersinger. Similarly, in *The Song of the Lark,* Spanish Johnny, getting a sing-along together, says, "sure we can sing 'Trovatore.' We have no alto, but all the girls can sing alto and make some noise." *Trovatore* is music for noise making, for friends and buskers. The only other explicit reference to opera in *Alexander's Bridge* is Hilda commenting on Bartley's well-publicized venture to Japan, where he helped spread Western bridge-building techniques, thereby building bridges between East and West. Hilda says she'd read about Bartley being decorated by the Japanese emperor with the title of "Commander of the Order of the Rising Sun," which she says sounds like something from *The Mikado.* Clearly this reference to a Gilbert and Sullivan spoof falls something short of awestruck. Both the *Trovatore* and *Mikado* references serve to lighten their respective moments, though neither seems to invite more thorough intertextual investigation.

However, given that Bartley is based in Boston and that Cather published the novel initially in serial installments in *McClure's* as *Alexander's Masquerade,*[16] it is tempting to draw a line between the novel and Verdi's *Un Ballo in Maschera* (*A Masked Ball*), an opera improbably set in colonial Boston. *Ballo* had been meant to depict the murder of Sweden's King Gustave III, but shortly before its première an attempt was made on the life of Napoleon III; authorities in Naples, where the opera was to open, skittish about depicting regicide and either inspiring other such attempts or inspiring the displeasure of monarchs who were none too fond of the topic of political assassination, insisted that the setting be moved to Boston and depict the killing of the governor of Boston instead (this of course being one of the famous absurdities of opera given that there never was a "governor" of Boston, and certainly not one named Riccardo who was also the Count of Warwick). The narratives also share plot points; aside from the Boston setting and the coincident use of *masque* in the title, both involve love triangles and the death of the protagonist happening after the performance of a noble deed. In the Verdi opera, Riccardo is murdered by Renato, his close friend and the husband of Amelia, Riccardo's love interest; despite knowing that Renato plans to kill him due to his love for Amelia, Riccardo has nonetheless written Renato an absolution that allows for him and Amelia to return, free of legal culpability, to England, even after Renato publicly stabs Riccardo to death at the titular ball. Alexander is far less decisive than Riccardo, obviously, but his letter to Winifred was an attempt to set things right, confessing his affair and either leaving her to her grief or begging for reconciliation. The fact that both Riccardo and Alexander die with letters on them that somehow rectify the damage done from a love affair certainly invites the possibility that Cather had *Ballo* somehow in mind. The opera had premiered at the Met in 1889 and had been performed as recently as 1905, the year before Cather moved to New York, and was performed again at the Met in 1913, the year after *Alexander*'s publication; it was in the air. Though not one of Verdi's most prominent operas, it's certainly more familiar than Verdi operas like *Alzira* or *Stiffelio,* and quite likely known enough to Cather to have been an influence.

The novel might not be her finest and certainly contains a few follies (has anyone ever risen to household-name fame as a bridge engineer, much less after beginning a career in his thirties?). But it *is* a decent novel with moments of subdued brilliance. And it's helpful for sorting out the puzzle that Cather can be. Part of her *wanted* to be a writer of psychological city fiction, and she tried the genre out capably. Though she gravitated toward writing from her youthful experience—twenty years and more before she wrote *Alexander's Bridge*—the Damascene conversion she claims in her subsequent trip to the desert is probably a bit overplayed. More likely, *O Pioneers!* was simply another experimental attempt at a novel, only one that worked out surprisingly well. Regardless, though, of her first novel's position in Cather's work, it's useful in understanding how she approached fundamental questions of life. Does one pursue passion at the expense of civility or civility at the expense of passion? The sensible hobbyist piano player or the actor-singer who has bet her life on the pursuit of artistic success? Cather, ever enigmatic, kills Bartley before he can act decisively. Though Cather would find her most recognizable mode a year later, her first novel shows her to be the artist capable of—or compulsively torn between—inhabiting multiple modes of human experience and expression. *Alexander's Bridge* shows Cather at a moment of crisis, a point at which she reckoned with and defined herself. Bartley Alexander was faced with a choice: the polite parlor piano of Winifred or the Broadway belting of Hilda. Likewise, Cather was facing a decision as to what sort of novelist she would be: the Jamesian writer skirting characters' various repressions over tea or the expressive primitivist celebrating life under the Big Sky. Cather chose the latter; or perhaps the latter chose her.

CHAPTER 6

PROSE OPERAS

O Pioneers! and *My Ántonia*

[Ivar] best expressed his preference for his wild homestead by saying that his Bible
seemed truer to him there. If one stood in the doorway of his cave, and looked off
at the rough land, the smiling sky, the curly grass white in the hot sunlight; if one
listened to the rapturous song of the lark, the drumming of the quail, the burr
of the locust against that vast silence, one understood what Ivar meant.

—*O Pioneers!*

sk twenty people today what opera is, and expect as many answers.
Among them will be inclusive, technical definitions—"opera is
a form of drama in which singing aids in expressing situational
emotion," historical, demographic definitions—"opera is a form of musical
drama that grew to prominence in Europe in the 1700s and spread to European
colonies to become a global form," faux profundities—"opera is *life*" or "opera
is *humanity*," and some hesitant stammering about big city concert halls, fancy
dress, and roundish women in horned hats and pointy brassieres who sing loudly.
There will be biases in which devotees feel honor bound to defend the form or
in which skeptics lay into its absurdities and unnaturalness.

What all these responses will share is the idea that opera is, in some sense,
"the combination of musical repletion with certain highly stylized features of
presentation."[1] Those words weren't used, however, to describe opera specifically,
but rather were how Mary Jane Humphrey, in her essay "'The White Mulberry
Tree' as Opera," compared Cather's second novel, *O Pioneers!*, to opera. The
novel, like opera, is replete with music and one might consider it "highly stylized," as well, at least in the context of much of Cather's other work. Humphrey
begins by noting that Cather, in her introduction to the 1925 edition of Gertrude Hall's *The Wagnerian Romances*, admitted to once having attempted, with

difficulty, "to transfer the feeling of an operatic scene upon a piece of narrative," essentially to try to write opera in prose form. Cather, frustratingly, neglected to name the novel in which she'd attempted to do so. Most commentators assume in passing that that statement refers somehow to *The Song of the Lark*, but, as Humphrey notes, that novel is *about* opera without being particularly *operatic*. Opera is "the kingdom of star-crossed love, tormented passion,"[2] not the "prosaic" and almost entirely unexplored romance between Thea and Fred. Rather, in certain key, stagey regards, the "White Mulberry Tree" section of *O Pioneers!* is a more likely candidate, with its frustrated passion, its lushly described settings and costumes, and its high, tragic drama.

Cather seldom leans on theater technique, and operatic overdoing specifically, in her plains novels to express her emotional situation. While not as austere as *Death Comes for the Archbishop* or *Shadows on the Rock*, her plains stories are characteristically matter-of-fact, increasingly so as the 1910s progressed. A libretto must compress a novel's worth of information into about thirty pages of script—so that only the truly emotional bits of story remain, which is then drawn out over about three hours of musical expression. The effect is typically one of extended, exaggerated feeling. Emotion isn't only intense but is defined by *sustained intensity*. Cather's plains novels, however, are typically subtle; they operate on resonant echoes of implied emotion. The longest section of *My Ántonia* is "The Shimerdas," which encompasses the vast majority of Jim and Ántonia's relationship. It is a narrative of operatic scope on its own. Each of the following sections, "The Hired Girls," "Lena Lingard," "The Pioneer Woman's Story" (which is actually several pioneer women's stories), and "Cuzak's Boys," contains enough developed narrative to cover the needs of a libretto, yet none of them has the emotional density of opera. This is characteristic of most of Cather's mid-to-late career work, and perhaps why composers and librettists have been so reluctant to use Cather as source material for opera. To date, only "Eric Hermannson's Soul" has been the subject of a musical drama—and it's somehow been used twice.[3] While much of her early short fiction, as well as *Alexander's Bridge*, is conventionally sentimental and designed to provoke emotional reaction, Cather became more restrained and deliberate as she matured. But emotional expressiveness, including that of romantic love, remained present in her work, albeit used more judiciously.

At some point, it became commonplace to refer to *O Pioneers!*, *The Song of the Lark*, and *My Ántonia* as Cather's "Plains Trilogy." This is a vaguely useful critical notion. It sidesteps the touchy problem of fitting *Alexander's Bridge* into the Cather oeuvre, while distinguishing those three from *One of Ours*, a war novel, and the impressive diversity of topics Cather tackled thereafter. But it's also an arbitrary and somewhat misleading construct. Cather wrote about the plains throughout her late career as well; *Lucy Gayheart* is a reconsideration of *The Song of the Lark*'s major themes—an aspiring singer leaving a small prairie town for the city—published nearly twenty years later. *The Song of the Lark* is as much about Thea's career in the city as it is about her life in the country, and that novel's proportion of rural-to-urban setting is roughly the same as that within *One of Ours*, Cather's fifth novel. More accurately, the four novels after *Alexander's Bridge* could be thought of as Cather's "Plains Tetralogy"; if Thea's story qualifies, Claude's should as well, given that both are dissatisfied with their small-town roots and flee to seek fulfillment in higher ideals and new geographies. But even that structuring of Cather's earlier novels is less than perfect. Instead, a grouping of *O Pioneers!* with *My Ántonia*, both pure plains narratives, and *Song of the Lark* with *One of Ours*, novels that begin in the West before moving to the wider world, makes sense. The first pairing represents Cather's paean to the plains, embracing the primitive, earthy world of the settler experience, while the latter two show her compulsion to send rural characters into the civilized world (a term that has to be used somewhat ironically here) to find their personal truths, a sort of reversed Leatherstocking narrative progression.

But if *O Pioneers!* and *My Ántonia* share some similarities of setting and attitude, they are still very different books. *O Pioneers!* is a slim and story-driven 55,000 words. *My Ántonia*, conversely, is a much weightier 81,000 words, less driven by story than by character, told in a long series of brief episodes. The early novel is a family epic, ending with the triumph of Alexandra Bergson; the later novel is a memoir built around one man trying to reconstruct a girl he knew in his youth, from whom he is largely estranged, with whom he shares little in common, yet who represents a fundamental prairie character he feels he's lost by growing up and moving away. Alexandra wins by conquering the frontier; Jim loses by leaving it. *Pioneers* is about the triumph of agriculture, *Ántonia* the triumph of life. The fact is, there's really no easy way to iron out Cather's corpus. She's no more *just* a plains writer than she is *just* a city writer, but even her plains stories and novels tend to say very different things using very different methods. If we were listing common elements of all her novels, however, on that list has to be that Cather persistently uses music to suffuse her various landscapes with a sense of higher emotional truth.

If Alexander hadn't done very well for Cather, maybe Alexandra would. There's no escaping the relationship between the names of Cather's first two novelistic protagonists. The name *Alexander,* as Cather, a classicist of sorts, would have understood, is not just the name of the first major conqueror of the West. It comes from two Greek words, αλέξειν, a verb meaning "to ward off or protect," and the genitive of ἀνδρός, "man," or, at least in the biblical Greek that would have cross-pollinated Cather's Greek, "husband." The fact that she chose the masculine and feminine versions of the same root name is no coincidence. Alexander is the quasi-ironic name of a man engaged in conquering the world, building bridges (actually incursions) into virgin territory, doomed to fail at the cusp of success; he's no protector of men—he can't even protect himself. Alexandra, however, is ironclad. The men in her life—her father, her brothers, her eventual husband—all rely on her for their survival (if not always *literal* survival, then the survival of their family line). She is both an Alexandrine conqueror and one who shields others in her orbit. No doubt Cather meant her follow-up novel to be a strong contrast with her debut in more ways than one, signaled by the complementary names of their protagonists; and where *Alexander's Bridge* took place in cityscapes that might have been replete with music but weren't, *O Pioneers!* is in a rural world that is surprisingly full of music.

The novel begins with an invocation, a poem titled "Prairie Spring."[4] Nineteen lines long, the first half of the poem is crowded with ponderous imagery of the prairie: "the flat land, / Rich and somber and always silent," "toiling horses" and "tired men," "sullen fires of sunset," and "the eternal, unresponsive sky." Then, "against all this, Youth," described as "flaming," "singing like the larks," "sharp desire," and "singing and singing, / Out of the lips of silence, / Out of the earthy dusk." Eternal and silent versus flaming youth, singing and singing like birds out of a silent earth. Cather begins the novel with this series of juxtapositions, contradictions that are nevertheless presented as a unity, earthiness into ether, song from the "lips of silence." She is sending a message that this will be a novel of complexities, both the violent immediacy of human jealousy and the ponderous growth of an alfalfa field (Alexandra's chosen crop), music bringing it to life.

Cather wrote the novel in 1912. After the failure of *Alexander's Bridge,* she traveled to the West, where, watching a wheat harvest, she conceived the idea for "The White Mulberry Tree," then as an independent story, a prairie rework-ing of the Pyramus and Thisbe myth. Returning home, she realized that the story could overlap with another recent effort, "Alexandra," and be combined and expanded into her next novel. Since she had just written "The Bohemian Girl," Cather's return to prairie writing after years of Jamesian civility, a Ne-braska novel was probably inevitable. In fact, Woodress notes that Alexandra is a version of Nils's mother from that story: She simply "drops thirty years, her widowhood, and becomes Alexandra Bergson."[5] But it wasn't as simple as splicing "Mulberry" and "Alexandra" together. Those are the last two sections of the novel and comprise only about a third of the total text. Cather wrote three sections to set up the emotionally charged finale—a murder and a marriage—a classic five-act structure and reminiscent of grand opera.

Part I, "The Wild Land," begins memorably: "One January day, thirty years ago, the little town of Hanover, anchored on a windy Nebraska tableland, was trying not to be blown away."[6] The town is introduced and described in fine de-tail, before the introduction of several of the principal characters: Emil, whose kitten is stuck up a telegraph pole in the freezing weather; Alexandra, Emil's sister, wearing a man's ulster coat "not as if it were an affliction, but as if it were very comfortable and belonged to her; [carrying] it like a young soldier"; Carl, who comes to the rescue of the kitten; and Marie, a little Bohemian girl fawned over by the men in the general store. In this presentation, Cather is being de-liberately theatrical: a scene set, the two romantic pairs of the novel introduced. Alexandra and her brother have come into town to fetch a doctor for their dying father. By the end of the first part, the father has died, giving Alexandra, rather than her brothers, control of the family property, a few years have passed, and Alexandra has begun aggressively acquiring other lands in the county so as to plant alfalfa, a new crop to the area.

Part II, "Neighboring Fields," begins sixteen years later. Alfalfa had been a prescient move, and the farms are doing well. This section begins with Emil home from college, tending to the Norwegian cemetery. While cutting the grass with a scythe, he whistles what Cather offhandedly identifies as "the 'Jewel' Song," the common referent of "*Ah, je ris de me voir*," an aria from Charles Gounod's *Faust* in which Marguerite sings about the jewels that have been planted in her room by Méphistophélès. It's a bold choice, given that the part is technically challenging and originally meant for a coloratura soprano. *Faust*, enduringly popular and over half a century old at the time of the novel, would quite possibly have been performed in Lincoln during Emil's time there, but the Jewel Song isn't the sort of aria typically sung in saloons and frat houses and other places college boys find themselves, so Emil choosing this piece in particular must be meaningful. Richard Giannone posits that Cather is signaling Emil's demise. In the song, Marguerite marvels at herself in the jewels, and "this romantic power makes the girl susceptible to Faust's flattering advances, and both lovers are destined to be destroyed by the blinding force of their lust[.] [. . .] [It] not only expresses the birth of physical love but also discloses its destructiveness."[7] According to this reading, Emil singing this thematically foreshadows his affair with Marie and the vengeance taken upon the lovers by Marie's husband, Frank. However, Emil's love for Marie is nascent, and, besides, the aria is about a woman feeling attractive, not a man finding a woman attractive. And there's nothing ominous about it, either. In an opera that goes to some very dark places, the Jewel Song is rather playful, both in music and text. More than love and death, it's about hope and positive transformation. Emil whistles the song while tending to the cemetery of the first pioneers, a clear signal about passing from one generation to the next and the transformation that the land—and the Bergson family's fortunes—have taken. This positivity and optimism doesn't forebode Emil's tragedy, but rather enhances it by making it a farther fall.

In the intervening years, Carl also has left Hanover, trying to make it as an engraver in Chicago (Cather's artists *all* go to Chicago), but has returned in some state of defeat. While he is speaking to Alexandra, who is now well on her way to wealth, she claims to admire his freedom. She is bound to her family farm, as well as to her brother Emil—to whom she is close—as well as to her brothers Lou and Oscar, who mistrust her and resent that their father had given her control of the family's assets upon his death. Carl, however, disagrees that personal independence is, on its own, a good thing: "Freedom," he says, "so often means that one isn't needed anywhere. Here you are an individual, you have a background of your own, you would be missed. But off there in the cities there are thousands of rolling stones like me." He says that he and the other artists are "all alike; we have no ties, we know nobody, we own nothing. When one of us dies, they scarcely know where to bury him." They are mourned "only by their landlady and the delicatessen man," and they leave behind nothing "but a frock-coat and a fiddle, or an easel, or a typewriter, or whatever tool we got our living by."[8] "Freedom" as Carl has experienced it, is merely the freedom to pay "the exorbitant rent that one has to pay for a few square feet of space near the heart of things. We have no house, no place, no people of our own. We live in the streets, in the parks, in the theatres. We sit in restaurants and concert halls and look about at the hundreds of our own kind and shudder." To some extent, Cather was writing from experience. At this point, she was a mildly successful writer with a book of short fiction, a book of poems, and a novel to her name, with only the short stories commanding much respect, living in an expensive city and tossing artistic caution to the wind by writing about Gopher Prairie rather than London. Carl, too, is eager to return, physically, to the land of his youth, where he feels purpose and security. If so many of Cather's texts evoke the prairie as a cultural wasteland, here we see her looking back to roots with admiration. Carl, quite philosophically, mentions a line from a song, "wo bist du, mein geliebtest Land?" ("where are you my beloved country?"), from "Der Wanderer" by Franz Schubert, noting that he "liked the old country better." Even so, he observes that "now the old story has begun to write itself over there," listening to the sounds of the garden. "Isn't it queer: there are only two or three human stories, and they go on repeating themselves as fiercely as if they had never happened before; like the larks in this country, that have been singing the same five notes over for thousands of years."[9] On the one hand, he misses the old country; on the other, he admits that the human experience is universal, with only two or three stories, presumably repeated across all countries old and new. Importantly, he says that those few stories are told in song, like the larks singing the same five notes for millennia. When Mary Jane Humphrey wrote that *O Pioneers!* was a work of "musical repletion," this is what she meant. Not only does music recur throughout the novel, but Cather insists that even characters' attitudes and the behavior of the land itself is musical. Nebraska *itself* is an opera.

As Part II plays out, Emil's infatuation with Marie develops, and Carl chooses to leave Hanover for new opportunities in Alaska (the allure of the Gold Rush will recur in *My Ántonia*); the dangerous relationship nears and the sensible relationship grows distant. And then the novel goes into a sort of brief hibernation, with Part III, "Winter Memories," focusing on the silence around Alexandra as Lou and Oscar have turned their backs on her, and Emil and Carl have left Nebraska. Alexandra experiences a recurrent fantasy from her youth in which she is carried by a giant man, "like no man she ever knew [. . .] much larger and stronger and swifter" and who smelled "of ripe cornfields."[10] It is a dream that evokes the power of the land to sustain her when others let her down. This middle section does little to move the plot forward, but is a stylistic rendering of the novel's major themes. It is to the novel what the ballet was to grand opera, appearing in the middle, deprived of plot but pantomiming the attitude of the story that frames it.

Then comes Part IV, "The White Mulberry Tree," which Humphrey identifies as the particularly operatic portion of the novel. In quick succession, we see the marriage of Signa, a house girl, and the death of Amédée Chevalier (a name that means *beloved knight*, but ignobly brought down by a bout of appendicitis); love and death are portended. By this point, Emil, returned from Mexico, and Marie have professed but not consummated their love. Emil attends a mass built around Rossini's *Petite Messe Solenelle* but beginning with Gounod's "Ave Maria." It's either a pleasant coincidence or none at all that Emil is tied twice to Gounod. That composer lived an improbably blessed younger life, growing up at the Palace of Versailles, being a musically inclined youth whose mother happened to be a music teacher, being exposed to opera at a young age, winning the Prix de Rome. Emil, unlike his older brothers Lou and Oscar, was born late enough to enjoy the family's good financial fortune and to have a family matriarch who supported his academic dreams and peripatetic nature. He, like Gounod, had a biography built for success. Gounod's "Jewel Song" tells the reader that Emil is living in a moment of happy, even oblivious, transition, if, as Giannone posits, it also portends his death. Gounod's "Ave Maria," a "meditation" built on a prelude of Bach's, reminds us of that prayer's importunity for sinners now and at the hour of death, offered, no less, to Marie's namesake.

Emil is overwhelmed by the passion of the "Ave Maria." As Raoul Marcel sings it, Emil wonders why Marie hasn't come to the service and begins "to torture himself with questions about Marie. Was she ill? Had she quarreled with her husband? Was she too unhappy to find comfort even here? Had she, perhaps, thought that he would come to her? Was she waiting for him?"[11] Listening to the music, he "emerge[s] from the conflicting emotions which had been whirling him about and sucking him under. He felt as if a clear light had broken upon his mind, and with it a conviction that good was, after all, stronger than evil, and that good was possible to men." He is rapturous, and "the spirit he had met in music was his own." He knew that Frank Shabata, if he lived a thousand years, would never know the passions that this music brings about for Emil, and that Frank is an unworthy partner for Marie: "And it did not occur to Emil that any one had ever reasoned thus before, that music had ever before given a man this equivocal revelation," and on the force of this revelation, he leaves the church to go to her.

In perhaps Cather's most brutal passage, Frank discovers the two, hearing "a murmuring sound, perfectly inarticulate" in the shadow of the mulberry tree between his farm and the Bergsons'. The sound of sex is inarticulate, like music evoking sensation without literalizing it. He "began to act, just as a man who falls into the fire begins to act," purely by reflex. Though Frank is a typically brutish man, Cather assigns him no guilt. Rather, he acts on pure emotion, just as Emil had done. He fires his gun thrice, and the two figures roll apart, the man's hand "plucking spasmodically at the grass." Suddenly the woman begins to cry out and drag herself across the grass. She cries out again and again, and Frank, panicked, hides behind a hedge briefly, listening in guilty wonder, before running away and leaving her to her doom. Ivar finds them the next day, Emil shot through the heart, Marie having had one shot through her right lung and the other through her carotid artery, from which she gushed blood as she'd pulled herself toward the hedge.

Cather doesn't often go in depth in such instances. In "Peter," the title character is last seen pushing the trigger with his toe; then Cather cuts to his family hauling his body off. When Claude Wheeler is shot in *One of Ours*, a bullet "caught him in the shoulder. The blood dripped down his coat but he felt no weakness." If only every shooting death could be so comfortable. Claude's companion is "blown to pieces" around the same moment, but his death is no more graphically described than that, and the only result is that Sergeant Hicks ran alone thereafter. Lucy Gayheart resigns herself to death in icy waters without any particular violence. Cather's characters die, and often painfully, but she seldom made it a gruesome affair at the sentence level. She does, however, with the deaths of Emil and Marie. The whole novel is around 55,000 words, of which Emil and Marie's death scene (including Ivar's postmortem) comprises nearly two thousand. This is operatic. This is the end of *Traviata* or *Bohème*, where characters are dying of tuberculosis and sing themselves to death over the span of twenty minutes. This is a moment of emotion drawn out intentionally—and effectively. It's not gratuitous, but rather a meditation on and investigation of a spike of emotion. As a contrast, Cather spends only a few sentences on the family committing to alfalfa, an act that lasts for, and impacts, generations.

The novel isn't entirely operatic, though. One peculiarity of opera is that it tends to end at the peak emotional moment: Tosca plunging from the rampart. Don Giovanni hauled to Hell. Dido dying upon Énée's sword. Carmen slain by José. Until mid-twentieth-century opera, this was nearly always the case, and certainly was a given for most opera performed during Cather's life. But the catastrophe of Frank, Emil, and Marie, doesn't end *O Pioneers!*. A fifth section, "Alexandra," incidentally the first written portion of the novel, concludes the narrative. In it, Alexandra begins to reconcile herself to Emil's death and consents to marry Carl. Cather's work is in many ways aligned with opera. But Cather craved an epilogue. Opera doesn't. Nevertheless, Mary Jane Humphrey is right that *O Pioneers!* is certainly the most operatically intense of Cather's novels and predicated on raw emotion in a way that evokes operatic intensity.

Pioneers is so conventionally theatrical that its five parts follow fairly neatly a classical five-act dramatic structure, though Cather wouldn't follow such conventions so closely thereafter. But while *My Ántonia* doesn't have the same sense of narrative inevitability or cohesiveness that *O Pioneers!* does, it's equally theatrical. Cather evoked the stage when she wrote Jim Burden's introduction to the prairie. "Cautiously I slipped from under the buffalo hide," he remembers, "got up on my knees and peered over the side of the wagon. There seemed to be nothing to see; no fences, no creeks or trees, no hills or fields. [. . .] There was nothing but land: not a country at all, but the material out of which countries are made."[12] This is the play's introduction to the audience, the buffalo hide rising like a curtain, stage lights low, no country at all—only possibility. Jim's experience on the prairie isn't only theatrical, but heroically so: "All those fall afternoons were the same," Jim recalls of his childhood days with Ántonia,

> but I never got used to them. As far as we could see, the miles of copper-red grass were drenched in sunlight that was stronger and fiercer than at any other time of the day. The blond cornfields were red gold, the haystacks turned rosy and threw long shadows. The whole prairie was like the bush that burned with fire and was not consumed. That hour always had the exultation of victory, of triumphant ending, like a hero's death—heroes who died young and gloriously. It was a sudden transfiguration, a lifting-up of day.[13]

Shortly after, as if to illustrate, is Jim's mock-heroic "dragon slaying" battle with the rattlesnake. But if theatrical in some sense, the novel is far more meditative than *Pioneers,* lacking the "highly stylized features of presentation" as Humphrey described them; as Jane Smiley began her introduction to the one-hundredth-anniversary edition of *Ántonia:* "Cather was not a flashy stylist."[14] But if *Ántonia* is less emotionally intense than *Pioneers,* less operatic, Cather nonetheless evokes theatrical conventions and returns to opera specifically on a few important occasions.

Considering that Cather's previous book had been *The Song of the Lark,* a novel focused on the progress of an opera singer, which happens to mention fourteen operas across a spectrum of styles and periods, it's no surprise that *My Ántonia* mentions only five, almost all in passing. Jim remembers Mrs. Harling playing "the old operas for us" on weekends, calling every Saturday night "like a party."[15] He remembers, specifically, Harling playing from *Martha, Norma,* and *Rigoletto,* no doubt a clue as to the seriousness of the engagement with opera. *Norma* is a serious opera, to be sure (it's source text was a play subtitled "the Infanticide"), but its best-known aria, "Casta diva," is one of the truly popular arias, known even to those who don't know opera. Likewise, with *Rigoletto*'s "Caro nome" and "La donna e mobile," danceable party songs, despite the twisted natures of their libretto's tales. *Martha,* on the other hand, is an opera comique, much more appropriate for a light-hearted Saturday, and it includes the popular Irish song "The Last Rose of Summer" as both a set piece and a motif. Cather references these three operas specifically not to suggest that Mrs. Harling is offering a conservatory-in-brief full of Wagnerian seriousness (Cather had worked out her Wagnerism in the previous novel), but rather she is playing well-traveled pieces accessible to a general public. Two years earlier, Cather had offered up opera in all its weighty ambition in Thea's story. In *Ántonia,* she's giving opera its moment as a rousing, oddly folky pastime. With one exception, this is how opera functions in the novel, something that is prevalent but not prevailing, common but not affecting. The Black Hawk Opera House has no actual opera in the novel, but rather hosts high school commencement exercises and a performance by Blind d'Arnault, the sightless Black performer of popular melodies.

But when Jim goes to college, Cather makes two additional operatic references, both of which, though brief, are important intertextual references. In Lincoln, Jim reconnects with fellow Black Hawkian Lena Lingard, who lives independently and is thriving as a dressmaker. Though Lena rebuffs Jim's romantic advances, showing an indifference to amorous relationships typical of Cather's heroines—Alexandra/Carl, Thea/Fred, Lucy/Harry—they nevertheless engage in a close friendship bound by their mutual insistence to transcend Black Hawk. Among other activities, they frequently attend theater performances. Lena hangs "upon the lips of the contralto who sang, 'O Promise Me!'" from Reginald de Koven's light opera *Robin Hood.* A lesbian reading of Lena's character could find much in the lyrics of this aria, in which the lover begs that she and the beloved will take their "love unspeakable" to "some sky / Where we can be alone and faith renew, / And find the hollows where those flowers grew."[16] Reading "hollows" along with the flower imagery reveals an imbedded yonicism of feminine sexuality, and Lena's apparent fascination with the contralto and the eroticism of "hanging on her lips," suggests at minimum a sexual interest on Lena's behalf, as well as a measure of sexual independence, Jim later remembering that "Lena gave her heart away when she felt like it, but she kept her head for her business."[17] Cather seemed to like Lena as a sexually empowered woman. Commenting in a letter to Ferris Greenslet in 1918 about W. T. Benda's illustrations for the novel, she wrote, "I will send you three Benda drawings tomorrow; the two full figure ones, of Antonia and Lena Lingard—the latter fairly busting out of her clothes—I think extremely good."[18] The picture, featuring Lena in a field with a dress profoundly unbuttoned, certainly shows a measure of physical self-possession.

The other reference, following immediately thereafter, occurs when Lena and Jim go to see Alexandre Dumas's *La Dame aux Camélias,* a play based on his novel of the same name, in English translation as *Camille,* with incidental music taken from Verdi's *La Traviata,* which was itself adapted from the play. The play, like the opera, centers on a tubercular courtesan who falls in love with a young gentleman, whose father objects to the union, forcing them apart, though the gentleman doesn't know his father's role in her rejection. They reconcile only minutes before her death. As Carolyn Abbate and Roger Parker note in *A History of Opera,* Verdi gravitating to Dumas's play, with its emphasis on social issues and setting in the present, represented a deliberate break with Italian opera's tradition of "Romantic plots of heroism and love, set in a remote historical past." It is Verdi tilting toward Verismo. It also has the incidental effect of empowering its female lead. As Abbate and Parker note, "The misogyny of Dumas's novel, which is told throughout from the male point of view, is inevitably softened in the play, where Violetta appears as a character onstage; and it is softened even further in the opera. [. . .] Verdi's version of the story makes 'voice-Violetta' the unambiguous centre of attention. The composer was evidently more interested in her than in the male principals, who are wooden and one-dimensional by comparison."[19] Cather was certainly attuned to this progression, from the male-described story of the fallen woman in the novel, to the woman given agency on the stage to describe her situation in the play, to the woman given primacy of expression through singing in the opera. Though Jim and Lena see the play, Cather's repeated invocation of the Verdi music, as well as how she describes the actor who performs Marguerite (Violetta in the opera) and the total effect of the performance, clearly indicates she intended the force of Verdi, something beyond speech.

"Our excitement began with the rise of the curtain," Jim remembers, at the first lines of dialogue, about which "there was a new tang [. . .]. I had never heard in the theater lines that were alive, that presupposed and took for granted" —essentially text that introduces a story without exposition, bringing the audience in a living story. Jim appreciates that this was a work of realism. It was "the most brilliant, worldly, the most enchantingly gay scene I had ever looked upon." He describes the scene:

I had never seen champagne bottles opened on the stage before—indeed, I had never seen them opened anywhere. The memory of that supper makes me hungry now; the sight of it then, when I had only a students' boarding-house dinner behind me, was delicate torment. I seem to remember gilded chairs and tables (arranged hurriedly by footmen in white gloves and stockings), linen of dazzling whiteness, glittering glass, silver dishes, a great bowl of fruit, and the reddest of roses. The room was invaded by beautiful women and dashing young men, laughing and talking together. The men were dressed more or less after the period in which the play was written; the women were not. I saw no inconsistency. Their talk seemed to open to one the brilliant world in which they lived; every sentence made one older and wiser, every pleasantry enlarged one's horizon. One could experience excess and satiety without the inconvenience of learning what to do with one's hands in a drawing-room! When the characters all spoke at once and I missed some of the phrases they flashed at each other, I was in misery. I strained my ears and eyes to catch every exclamation.

He remembers Marguerite being played by a woman "already old, with a ravaged countenance and a physique curiously hard and stiff," playing against an Armand who was "disproportionately young and slight" and handsome. "But what did it matter?" he wonders. She portrayed a character "young, ardent, reckless, disillusioned, under sentence, feverish, avid of pleasure." Seeing her illness, "the handkerchief she crushed against her lips, the cough she smothered under the laughter," "wrung [his] heart." He wants to run onstage and push Armand aside and take Marguerite, even in all her age and infirmity, for his own, especially when she rejects Armand accompanied by the Traviata duet "Un dì, felice" (which Cather identifies as "misterioso, misterios'altero"). Between acts, the orchestra "kept sawing away at the 'Traviata' music, so joyous and sad, so thin and far-away, so clap-trap and yet so heart-breaking," leaving them "no time to forget" during breaks. When Jim leaves to smoke after the second act, he leaves Lena "in tearful contemplation of the ceiling"—not unlike Georgiana's speechless awe after the Wagner concert—, and congratulates himself for not bringing some callow "Lincoln girl" who would have talked about local dances and gossiped. In her emotional attachment to the performance, "Lena was at least a woman, and I was a man."

The totality of the *Camille* scene is around 1,200 words, full of ecstasy, replete with music and highly stylized features of presentation. When Armand's father insists Marguerite leaves, Jim recalls, "Lena wept unceasingly, and I sat helpless to prevent the closing of that chapter of idyllic love, dreading the return of the young man whose ineffable happiness was only to be the measure of his fall." The play features a "heartless world [. . .] so glittering and reckless." Jim remembers the chandeliers and gaming tables piled with gold, Marguerite with "such a cloak, such a fan, such jewels—and her face!" When Marguerite swoons, Lena "cowered beside me." In the final scene "there wasn't a nerve in me that hadn't been twisted [. . .] nothing could be too much now. I wept unrestrainedly. Even the handkerchief in my breast-pocket, worn for elegance and not at all for use, was wet through by the time that moribund woman sank for the last time into the arms of her lover."

My Ántonia is generally a somber and unflorid novel, but this scene, more than any other in the novel or perhaps in any Cather novel, wallows in emotion. And not for a lost crop or a dead child or a flood or a blight, but for a play performed over the course of a few hours. Both Jim and Lena are in tears over an actor pretending to die in the perfect safety of a capital city theater. It's the combination of the story and the words and the acting and the music, Cather borrowing Verdi not because of the coincident source texts of the play and opera, but because that opera music, as Jim reminds us, ties the total work of art together.

After the play, Jim accompanies Lena home and then walks to the rural part of town in which he resides. He remembers the smell of the lilacs blooming after the rain, "the new leaves and the blossoms together, [blowing] into my face with a sort of bitter sweetness." He "tramp[s] through the puddles and under the showery trees, mourning for Marguerite Gautier as if she had died only yesterday, sighing with the spirit of 1840, which had sighed so much, and which had reached me only that night, across long years and several languages, through the person of an infirm old actress"—just as Carl's larks had sung the same songs for millennia, so this story is an eternal, living story for Jim that no lifetimes or languages can corrupt. It has become an "idea is one that no circumstances can frustrate. Wherever and whenever that piece is put on, it is April."[20]

When Cather wrote in 1925 that she'd once tried to write a scene in a novel that captured the intensity of opera, she could have referred to a few novels. Possibly *The Song of the Lark,* her novel most heavily steeped in opera. Possibly, as Mary Jane Humphrey argues very convincingly, the Emil and Marie section of *O Pioneers!,* drawing from Wagner's great love story, *Tristan und Isolde.* But the allowance should be made that she was thinking of this scene in *My Ántonia,* a novel that otherwise tends not to revel in emotion, a scene in which the full arsenal of theatrical possibility—a true *Gesamtkunstwerk*—creates a deep, sentimental reckoning.

❧

CHAPTER 7

BITTER CONTEMPT

The Song of the Lark and Cather's Wagnerism

> Wotan wanders further; and a mortal woman bears him twins: a son and a
> daughter. He separates them by letting the girl fall into the hands of a forest
> tribe which in due time gives her as wife to a fierce chief, one Hunding.
> With the son he himself leads the life of a wolf, and teaches him the only
> power a god can teach, the power of doing without happiness.
> —G. B. Shaw, *The Perfect Wagnerite*

*T*itles are an underappreciated aspect of literature. The handshake introduction of any text, they set a tone and establish aspirations. Despite
their importance, many authors struggle to write them well. Literary
history is littered with titles that uncreatively identify the protagonist or the
setting by name (*Wuthering Heights, McTeague*). For every *A Midsummer Night's
Dream* or *Love's Labour's Lost,* Shakespeare gave us plenty of *Othello*s and *Henry
X*s. Some simply declare the major theme of the text (*War and Peace, Atonement,
Persuasion*). It's been popular for over a century now to draw a snippet of poetry
or scripture meant to import a range of feeling and meaning for a text, stately
and validating (*Tender Is the Night, For Whom the Bell Tolls, A Passage to India*).
Hemingway quoted a three-thousand-year-old Jewish monarch to remind us that
the sun also rises on each generation as it always has—despite the fact that he
was self-consciously setting his generation apart as something new and different
upon which the sun had not yet risen. Some authors have relied on in-jokes like
"catch-22" that you have to read the book to understand.

Good titles, though, are evocative, original, and multivalenced (*Cane, Arms
and the Man, Leaves of Grass*). They are worth exploring in themselves.

Though she came up with a few good ones, Cather, too, struggled with titles. Self-aware, she wasn't happy with *The Song of the Lark,* which she'd borrowed from a painting, apparently because the moniker tended to be misinterpreted. "The title of the book is unfortunate," she wrote in the preface to the 1937 autograph edition of the novel. "Many readers take it for granted that the 'lark song' refers to the vocal accomplishments of the heroine, which is altogether a mistake." Instead, she admitted, the title was taken from a "rather second-rate French painting" by Jules Breton that features a young woman in the fields in the early morning who pauses abruptly to hear a lark. It was "meant to suggest a young girl's awakening to something beautiful."[1] Not that the lark's song was *not* beautiful, but it wasn't that the girl was going to learn to sing as beautifully. Rather, she was to come to a fundamental appreciation for beauty, setting her on an infinitely impossible but noble quest to create beauty herself. There's much to unpack in Cather's statement. John Flannigan noted that Cather "retained a strong populist streak in her musical tastes that enabled her to enjoy, without embarrassment or irony, art, be it great or modest"[2]—apparently that populism didn't extend to visual art. Breton's painting might not be an acknowledged masterpiece, but it's certainly striking and beautiful, and calling it "second rate" is a bit severe. Such an evaluation suggests a continued self-consciousness on Cather's part, a bit of imposterism by which she, even in her late career, felt somehow outside of artistic legitimacy. She felt the need to apologize for the novel in its intermediate position between *O Pioneers!* and *My Ántonia;* it wasn't as good, she thought, starting with the title itself. But in a metasense, that's part of the novel, which posits that a great artist only ever struggles infinitely upward; she'd set out to describe the artist's progression only to find that her own great was never good enough. The bitter perfectionism that drives Thea Kronborg is a projection of Cather's own sensibility.

Certainly, *The Song of the Lark* lags behind *My Ántonia, Death Comes for the Archbishop,* and *O Pioneers!* in reputation if not in actual effect. In Cather's catalog, it's considered a solid second-tier novel, like *My Mortal Enemy* or *The Professor's House,* and it is seldom read or taught today. Cather's first biographer, E. K. Brown, lamented that "in retrospect it seems curious that the novel in which Willa Cather is most explicitly engaged with artists and the artistic process is the least artistic of her works."[3] According to Brown, it's *about* art, but not so much art *itself.* James Woodress, piggybacking on early reviews, calls the novel "enormously interesting and attractive [but] not without its flaws," referencing some critics who had called the novel, at a ponderous 146,000 words in its original iteration (earlier drafts had topped 200,000 words), "overwritten." "She had not yet," he posits, "formulated the principles she proclaims" in "The Novel Démeublé," where she advocates for a careful pruning of novelistic detail.[4] Hermione Lee claims the novel, though it is situated between the undisputed masterpieces *O Pioneers!* and *My Ántonia*, "feels quite unlike them," being the sort of "thick, heavy, straggling, detailed narrative she would only allow herself once again, in *One of Ours*."[5] In *Music in Willa Cather's Fiction*, Richard Giannone names eight chapters after specific novels, but the chapter that includes *Song of the Lark* is merely titled "The Lyric Artist" and focuses as much on Cather's relationship with Fremstad and her Kitty Ayrshire stories as it does on Thea's story.

Cather was hard on the book, but she tended to be severe with herself; she all but forgot her uncollected short fiction, famously disowned *Alexander's Bridge,* and referred to *The Professor's House* as a "nasty, grim little tale."[6] Cather tended to see her own work through the lens of her critics, not knowing the sound of her own voice. Of course, *Alexander's Bridge* is a well-crafted, professional novel, and *The Professor's House* is certainly one of the overlooked gems of American literature. Even much of her early, uncollected short fiction works as well as stories of the period that tend to be anthologized. In evaluating *The Song of the Lark,* probably Cather was reflecting on both the success of *Ántonia*, as well as early criticism from her editor, Ferris Greenslet, who had balked at the novel's structure in its first manifestation with the initial parts "disproportionately long" and a "lack of coherence" between the early, realistic sections and the later, more romantic story.[7] Cather wrote that "the chief fault of the book is that it describes a descending curve," that Thea's triumph is the novel's undoing. "The full tide of achievement," she wrote in 1937, "is not so interesting as the life of a talented young girl 'fighting her way,' as we say. Success is never so interesting as struggle."[8] Where Alexandra still has a world to conquer at the end of her novel, where Ántonia still has half a life of farmy mothering to tend to, Thea ends as the world's greatest Wagnerian soprano. But Cather forgets her own character; Thea, though triumphant, is never satisfied. For her, the artist's greatest disappointment is reaching the pinnacle only to find herself alone and with no more mountain to climb. Or if there is a peak left to ascend, only she, she knows, will ever see it—no one can share the great artist's greatness.

At least one commentator, however, has acknowledged the mastery of the novel. John Dizikes, a historian, identifies *The Song of the Lark* as "the finest

American novel about art and the artist, one of the most undervalued of Willa Cather's novels."[9] He praises the depiction of Thea's backstory in Moonstone, Colorado, and the realism with which Cather documents it, especially the provincialism and divisions between the various segments of town, the protestant Anglo-Americans on one side of Main Street and the immigrant Catholics on the other. Dizikes focuses on characters like Lily Fisher, "the angel-child of the Baptists," and Thea's own sister Anna, who felt that "nothing was decent until it was clothed by the opinion of some authority," to emphasize what he sees as Cather's indictment of small-town life with regard to opera, forcing Thea to flee to the city. He notes that a theater in Moonstone would have been "kept busy with dances, bazaars, temperance lectures, high-school bands, basketball games, and elocution contests" more so than it would have been likely to feature opera. Thea's teacher, Herr Wunsch, "evoked with unerring accuracy," is one of those who created an American operatic tradition, but he is an aberration in Moonstone. Dizikes has a profound respect for the novel, but its importance goes beyond the depiction of the small-town milieu as troubled environs for art, a depiction that is equivocally presented. Thea does, in fact, flee Moonstone for the well-being of her artistic ambitions, but she also reconnects with her hometown periodically throughout the novel, and especially finds inspiration and authenticity through the opera-singing residents of Mexican Town. *The Song of the Lark* is "the finest American novel about art and the artist" not because it lays bare the barriers to artistic success, but rather because it fairly surveys the artist in every context. Dizikes might have been prescient. Twenty-seven years later, Alex Ross devoted an entire chapter of his book *Wagnerism: Art and Politics in the Shadow of Music* to Cather, noting specifically that it evinces Cather as "an acute observer of city culture" in addition to her small-town, prairie settings. More than that, "among major authors, only Thomas Mann knew his Wagner better, and he lacked Cather's acumen on the subject of singers."[10]

The Song of the Lark is itself permeated not only by opera, but specifically by Wagner, whose phenomenal rise and popularity through the latter half of the nineteenth century was so ubiquitous that "Wagnerism" is "rarely included among the roster of *isms*" emerging during the period—Wagnerism is simply implied. As Jed Rasula describes it, "the epochal upheavals of the twentieth century have blunted our ability to recognize what a force Wagner was: in the century of Hitler, it became harder to imagine that Wagner, in his day, was commonly classed with Napoleon and Christ as a preeminent world-transforming personality—the 'messiah of a new age.'"[11] What *Wagnerism* is, however, is not so simple to describe. For some, Wagner was a reaffirmation of Romanticism—for better or worse (Max Nordau called Wagner "the last mushroom on the dunghill of romanticism" and "a bleating echo of the far-away past"[12]). For others, Wagner was, as the composer himself proclaimed, writing the music of the future. Some recognized a validation of religion in Wagner's mix of pagan, Christian, Hindu, and Buddhist themes. Some saw Wagner's work as a commentary on the immediate social, political, or economic circumstances of the moment. Just as Cather is hard to define, and as opera broadly is, so is Wagner. "Nietzsche accused Wagner of dilettantism," notes Ross, "in fact, the composer's legacy is so multifarious that anyone who studies it is a dilettante by default."[13] Whatever Wagnerism *is,* it certainly is peerless in aspiration; its varied possible approaches are rival faces ascending the same soaring alp.

Philip Kennicott notes that Cather seemed to associate Wagner's "endless" melody and rangy chromaticism, so erotically suggestive, as representing a philosophical boundlessness that evokes a literal boundlessness, as in "A Wagner Matinée," when a Boston concert hall becomes a "place of infinite emotional possibility and renders the open space of Nebraska a place of claustrophobic confinement."[14] The idea that Wagner defeats claustrophobia makes sense in a Catherian context, given the Wagner in "The Garden Lodge," where Catherine Noble has lived a life of rigid discipline, only feeling—briefly, illusorily—free upon imagining she and her would-be lover in the Wälsungen love duet, and in *The Song of the Lark,* where Thea Kronborg insists on freeing herself from the confines of Moonstone to become a Wagnerian soprano. In these instances, it is not the drama of the opera—the performance in "A Wagner Matinée" isn't even staged—but rather the style of the music that facilitates the characters' revelations. This is not to claim, however, that she *only* used Wagner as an aural analogue. Cather also tended to use Wagner in sophisticated intertextual ways, as in "A Wagner Matinée," when Georgiana reflects upon various shortcomings of life via a tour of plots and themes suggested by Wagner's music (see chapter 4). And Cather also referenced Wagner as a cultural moment, a vehicle for connection and nostalgia. In "Uncle Valentine," the title character asks Aunt Charlotte, "I say, Charlotte, do you remember how we used to play the Ring to each other hours on end, long ago, when Damrosch first brought the German opera over? Why can't people stay young forever?"[15] Wagner isn't just romantic for his knights and dragons and love duets and endless melodies;

he's also romantic in that he helps remind those of Cather's generation of their own emotional youths. Wagner is versatile, and Cather recognizes this, using his music to evoke musically metaphorical freedom, archetypal stories, and a shared cultural heritage.

In her preface to Gertrude Hall's *The Wagnerian Romances,* Cather wrote, "I know of only two books in English on the Wagnerian operas that are at all worthy of their subject; Bernard Shaw's 'The Perfect Wagnerite' and 'The Wagnerian Romances' by Gertrude Hall." Sadly, this statement does little to clarify Cather's own attitude toward the composer. Hall and Shaw's books are very different, the former a fairly straightforward paraphrase of Wagner's dramas, the latter an interpretation of the *Ring* as a contemporary socialist political allegory. Both Shaw and Hall engage with the source material, but Hall does so in a fairly normal, sometimes Christianizing fashion, Shaw with typically Shavian spleen and wit.

Catherians have been typically reticent on Cather's preface to Hall, certainly in part due to how middle-of-the-road the book itself is, at odds with Cather's description of it. Cather wrote that "this book is good—so good as to be unique among its kind—because the writer has the rare gift of being able to reproduce the emotional effect of the Wagner operas upon the printed page; to suggest the setting, the scenic environment, the dramatic action, the personality of the characters [. . .] the character of the music itself."[16] Cather notes that she'd encountered the book originally on a sojourn to the Southwest—Cather had traveled to the Southwest in 1912, and the book had been first published in 1907—reading first Hall's rendition of *Parsifal,* then *Meistersinger,* and then, presumably, the rest. Cather claims that she'd "paid Miss Hall the highest compliment one writer can pay another" by stealing her method in reproducing Wagner's impact on the page for one of Cather's own novels.

Hall's book is certainly not without its missteps. For example, her chapter on *Die Walküre* describes Sieglinde falling in love with Siegmund and fleeing her husband, Hunding: "The new sentiment of love," writes Hall, "so completely possessing her places her former union in the light of unspeakable pollution, and she adjures the 'noble one' to depart from the accursed who brings him such a dowry of shame." Greeting card fortunes are made of such lovers' banter. Farther down the same page, Siegmund cradles the unconscious Sieglinde, and "having ascertained that she has not ceased to breathe, almost glad perhaps for her of this respite from self-torment, he lets her gently down on to the ground, and seats himself so as to make an easy resting-place for her head."[17] Such tenderness! Of course, it's no noble sport to cherry pick a book's flaws, and there's much to recommend Hall as a story-book formulation of the Wagner dramas. Whereas audiences have frequently puzzled over what, exactly, is so heroic about Siegfried in *Götterdämmerung*—the man leaves his beloved, threatens strangers, allows himself to be drugged, facilitates his wife's rape, marries the sister of the rapist, and gets stabbed ignominiously in the back—when reading Hall's rendering of the same, it begins to make sense. For Hall, Siegfried is a hero swept along by history, behaving admirably within his capacity and within the expectations for behavior of the time and place. Hall, like many of her generation, fawns over Wagner's rendering of the Nibelung/Volsung sagas, but where many of her contemporaries were simply starry-eyed, Hall has a knack for channeling her admiration into page-turning stories and frequently graceful, occasionally stilted prose.

Certainly, Hall was not interested only in migrating Wagner's libretti into English prose. Her characters *act;* they catch each other's eyes, touch each other's hands, reach out and gesture. They sit in the light of the full moon. Settings come to life: "the great door of the hall, silently, without apparent reason, swings wide open, like a great curious eye"[18] and "we see [Erda] appear, as before, rising in the gloom of a rocky hollow up to half her height."[19] In her preface, Cather praises such effects. "Opera," she wrote, "is a hybrid art,—partly literary to begin with. It happens that in the Wagnerian music-drama the literary part of the work is not trivial, as it is so often in operas, but is truly the mate of the music."[20] Hall, she feels, effectively replicates the literary part of the opera without sacrificing or neglecting the full impact of sound and sight. Hall had high aspirations for her rendering of Wagner. Her take on *Rheingold* begins, "In the beginning was the Gold." Noting that the ring from which the *Ring* cycle gets its name could only be fashioned from that gold by one who has renounced love, Hall notes that "for these things no reason is given: they were, like the Word."[21] No less than the great asynoptic, mystical Gospel of John works as a parallel for the founding premise of the *Ring.*

If commentators like Shaw might have pshaw-ed such a reading, favoring instead the gold as a parallel to the greed of the Klondike gold frenzy, many have read more celestial parallels in the *Ring.* Paul Schofield's *The Redeemer Reborn,* which posits *Parsifal* as a fifth opera of the *Ring* in which characters from the tetralogy have been reincarnated into the Grail narrative, notes the importance of Greek tragedy to Wagner's vision. *Tragedy* comes from a Greek phrase meaning "goat song" (τραγος + ωδη), an apparent reference to an ancient fertility rite in which a group of trained performers would play out a drama in which Dionysus, or some representation, would be torn apart and distributed among the fields (these rituals had originated with a goat sacrifice to Dionysus, hence the term).[22] The drama, ending inevitably in literal or figurative death, eventually incorporated aspects of Dionysus rather than one figure, and later epic heroes to represent those various aspects. In what Nietzsche would call the "birth of tragedy" was this "union of the Dionysian arts of music with the Apollonian art of epic poetry," essentially a forerunner of the operatic tradition. But, Schofield notes, "the dichotomy of Apollo and Dionysus is far more complex than that of poetry and music alone. Apollo and Dionysus represent reason versus intuition, intellect versus sensuality, form versus formlessness, control versus abandon, and [. . .] the principle of individuation versus that of absorption into the collective."[23] This, for Schofield, is Wagner's ultimate aim—characters such as Siegfried and Wotan bringing about their own demise through their pursuit of individual success. Not necessarily greed or arrogance, merely the idea that their excellence will separate them from others. Equilibrium occurs only when such characters realize the moral shortcomings of individuality and relent to absorption into a greater whole. Or as Hall wraps up *Götterdämmerung:*

> So Wotan finds his rest [after retreating to the flames of Walhalla in resignation], and the ill consequences at last end of his unjust act—with the reparation of the injustice, the return of the gold to the Rhine. [. . .] When Wotan in pride of being committed it [. . .] how could he have divined that by this pin-point he set inexorable machinery moving which should bring about his confusion, forcing him in its progress to so many injustices more, injustices which his soul would loathe, which would blight his best beloved, which would by far be his greatest punishment! . . . The Trilogy is moral as a tract.[24]

While not a one-for-one framework for assessing *The Song of the Lark,* certainly Thea's persistent individuation, her need to ascend to levels of artistic fulfillment that eventually leave her isolated, manifests as the "many disappointments in [her] profession," the "bitter contempts" and the need to "hate the cheap thing" as much as one loves the good. Thea is, in this sense, a tragic figure. It makes sense, looking at the *Ring* as the tragedy of individuality, that Cather opted to end the novel not with Thea herself but with Aunt Tillie and the residents of Moonstone. As Cather wrote to Dorothy Canfield Fisher, "the last chapters were written not so much for Thea as for Moonstone and Dr. Archie. She had to make good to them"—essentially, Thea's promise was ultimately not to herself but to her community.[25]

Bernard Shaw's take on the *Ring* was predictably less mystical. Shaw, in his preface to the first edition of *The Perfect Wagnerite* insists that we've all got it wrong, that the "English and American gentleman-amateurs, who are always political mugwumps, and hardly ever associate with revolutionists"[26] completely fail to see the political relevance of the Cycle, namely that Siegfried represents a mid-1800s revolutionary anarchism in line with the 1848 upheavals of which Wagner was a part (as a result of which he suffered exile from Saxony), and that the "twilight of the gods" represents the demise of established capitalistic/royalistic/theistic institutions that have oppressed the worker. When Wotan and Loge visit Alberich and Mime in their mine among the enslaved dwarves in *Das Rheingold,* "the gloomy place," according to Shaw, doesn't need to be a mine, but could be "a match-factory, with yellow phosphorus, phossy jaw, a large dividend, and plenty of clergymen shareholders. Or it might be a white-lead factory, or a chemical works, or a pottery, or a railway shunting yard, or a tailoring shop, or a little gin-sodden laundry, or a bakehouse, or a big shop, or any other of the places where human life and welfare are daily sacrificed in order that some greedy foolish creature may be able to hymn exultantly to his Plutonic idol."[27] Shaw takes a breath, briefly describes the hammering of the dwarves, then discusses the Tarnhelm, the magical helmet that allows its wearer to transform into anything. In the *Ring* it is used to become things like dragons and toads. But for Shaw it "makes a man invisible as a shareholder, and changes him into various shapes, such as a pious Christian, a subscriber to hospitals, a benefactor of the poor, a model husband and father, a shrewd, practical, independent Englishman, and what not, when he's really just a pitiful parasite on the commonwealth, consuming a great deal, and producing nothing, feeling nothing, knowing nothing, believing nothing, and doing nothing."[28] The entire cycle, for Shaw, is meant to illustrate "sordid capitalist systems," which originated with medieval systems by which the "Christian laborer was drained by the knightly spendthrift, and the spendthrift was drained by the Jewish usurer," who was in turn drained by the Church and State as a matter of Christian duty.[29] Shaw protests his protesters, those who would say that he was reading too much of his own biases into the dramas, by pointing out Wagner's political activism and anticapitalist beliefs that extended to the mediocritizing effects of commercial interests on music, making capitalism and pure art incompatible.

Among the political screeching, Shaw presents a lively description of the dramas themselves, full of jibes at characters and plot turns, almost as a heckler in a small-town Orpheum. But there's certainly no dodging the immediate politics of his reading of the *Ring*, so it's curious that Cather would align Shaw with Hall as the only two worthwhile books on Wagner in her experience. They are so thoroughly different in manner and aim. Cather had reviewed *The Perfect Wagnerite* for the *Pittsburgh Leader* in 1899, beginning her review by noting that Shaw was "unconventional" and a "whimsical iconoclast" before observing that the most unconventional thing he could do would be to write a "thoroughly conventional book." This book, she decided, was such a one. "At any rate," she wrote, "he has done so, and his essays on the Nibelung Ring may safely be introduced into musical libraries, or quoted in musical lectures, and parts of his book, at least, may even be read with impunity by young ladies cramming for their first opera season." She wrote this in 1899 in Pittsburgh—one of the de facto capitals of capitalism at the peak of the Gilded Age—about a book so resolutely and angrily anticapitalist that it went through four editions by becoming a textbook on anticapitalist thought in the arts. Cather wrote that Shaw "does Wagner the honor to take him quite seriously" and that his "splenetic personal prejudices are kept becomingly in the background."[30] Cather doesn't make a single mention of the very overt politics that permeate the text. Almost certainly, Cather did not actually read *The Perfect Wagnerite* when reviewing it (if the review is ironic, it is so well-disguised as to make the irony useless), and apparently hadn't revisited it before writing the preface to Hall. Though Cather's politics remain somewhat murky, Joan Acocella sensibly claims that "in her politics Cather was indeed conservative. She hated Franklin D. Roosevelt and the New Deal and big government. [. . .] she also hated political art"—which would, in the 1930s and after have the dual effect of having Cather dismissed out-of-hand by Leftists while arbitrarily championed by the Right.[31] Of course, politics is more complicated than any single moment or movement, and from her youth on, Cather operated outside the expected norms of society. Some of her early fiction such as "The Clemency of the Court" and "Behind the Singer Tower" certainly evoke progressive themes. Cather was an individualist, conservative or liberal depending on the matter at hand. Regardless, the politics of Shaw's book can't be overlooked, but they might be reframed.

Philip Kennicott claims that Shaw's commentary isn't necessarily only political or economic, but can also be read as an "almost Catheresque" form of "meritocratic class struggle," which might make sense for a text like *One of Ours*, which focuses on a character whose worth's unknown until he finds a venue to make his merit shown.[32] The new trends in agriculture that had shut out Claude Wheeler from meaningful farm life could be seen as a manifestation of forces that can determine destiny unfairly. It takes some mental gymnastics to get there, however, because Cather seldom dwelled on such socioeconomic machinations. Other than "Clemency" and "Singer," class struggle is rarely a clear theme in her writing. Jim becomes a successful lawyer while Ántonia a poor farmwife; neither is oppressed or oppressor. Bartley Alexander is never chastised for being upper-class. Bishop Latour would certainly be in the crosshairs of any dutiful Jacobin, but he's never demonized. For the most part, Cather either stays silent on class struggle or openly resents (as in her essay "Escapism") any requirement that an author wrangle with class struggle in fiction. It seems unlikely that Cather would have been drawn to Shaw's book specifically because of the politics of his interpretation.

Kennicott, however, also points out that Cather, in her preface to Hall, had written that she had tried to write "the feeling of an operatic scene . . . in the course of the novel," meaning, potentially, the *whole course* of the novel, which invites, perhaps audaciously, incorporating the feeling of an opera through *an inter-related series of novels*. Compare, then, the *Ring* and Cather's plains tetralogy, each with four sprawling, complex narratives, spanning facets of their individual mythologies. *O Pioneers!*, like *Das Rheingold*, is a story of origin and transition between the old gods of nature and the ascendency of humankind. Where *Rheingold* has its plodding, laboring giants Fasolt and Fafner, *Pioneers* has Oscar and Lou. Alexandra, like Wotan, is a wise ruler whose new order has yet to be fully confirmed. *The Song of the Lark* features a dynamic, defiant heroine who sacrifices happiness to achieve artistic purity in a manner not entirely dissimilar from Brünnhilde in *Die Walküre*. *My Ántonia*—admittedly the square peg in this continuum—focuses on a bold, ungoverned youth (Ántonia as Siegfried), exploring a new world. Like *Siegfried*, it is highly archetypal, drawing on "horrible unconscious memories" of a primordial past;[33] and, like *Siegfried*, it concludes with the promise of further human generations having established themselves in a new land. And in *One of Ours* an old way of life—the pioneer life—is fading. New ways have come about to interrupt the established habits, leaving the protagonist unsure of his place in the world. As with Siegfried's fate in *Götterdämmerung*, the hero learns Truth only in the moment of his death. While it's probably too much to say that this is what Cather consciously intended, it's certainly not a stretch to claim that her deep familiarity with Wagner's *Ring* might have influenced the trajectory of these four novels. Beginning in 1923 with *A Lost Lady*, Cather's novels become notably more intimate, less focused on the sweep of history, less universal in scope. It's around that time, also, that Cather begins to emphasize opera less in her writings.

Cather lauded both Shaw and Hall in 1925 (and she'd praised Shaw's book in her 1899 review), but those are not the only texts to influence Cather's attitude toward Wagner. For thirty years after the mid-1880s, Wagner heralded a deutschophilic boomlet in America. As Dizikes notes, "the admiration for [Wagner's operas], and for German music in general, was part of a growing admiration for other aspects of German culture—German science, German philosophy, German economic power, German military might."[34] More or less coincidentally, Wagner's American adventure happened alongside a major influx of Germans to the United States. Until World War I, German culture was fashionable broadly, so much so that insights on German culture like Shaw and Hall's books could entice a general readership. Among other prominent authors were Jessie Weston (whose best-known contribution to American letters would be Eliot's Waste Land motif borrowed from her *From Ritual to Romance* [1920]), who published *The Legends of the Wagner Drama* (1896), a study of the mythological bases for Wagner's plots, and H. R. Haweis's *My Musical Memories* (1884). As Weston was a popular intellectual of the period, Cather was probably familiar with her work, and she certainly knew Haweis, as he is mentioned twice in *The Song of the Lark*. The first of those references pertains to Thea acquiring the book; she'd been given it for free from the local druggist, who couldn't sell it. This detail doesn't serve to make the book less special, but more special. The people of Moonstone come and go, completely incognizant of the potential for musical greatness in their midst—but Thea sees it. The second reference to the book is upon Thea's great musical awakening in Chicago. After hearing Dvořák's "New World" symphony, the orchestra plays a selection from *Rheingold*, the story to which Thea vaguely recalls from Haweis. It is the first time she hears "that troubled music, ever-darkening, ever-brightening, which was to flow through so many years of her life."[35] Haweis had prepared her for Wagner and for her destiny.

Haweis was an English clergyman and writer and a flamboyant personality. *My Musical Memories* is part memoir of his learning to play the violin (he published much on the violin and was considered an authority) and part paean to Wagner, whom he saw as the perfection of a completed musical tradition. "You cannot invent metre after the Greeks," he wrote, "or the modern drama after Shakespeare, or coloring and perspective after the Italians: there is a point at which an art ceases to grow and stands full-blown like a flower."[36] Essentially all human art forms have reached the limits of new technique; methods of art have been exhausted, but not perfected, which is where Wagner enters. "To concentrate into one dazzling focus all the arts, and having sounded and developed the expressional depth, and determined the peculiar function of each, to combine them at length into one perfect and indivisible whole"—that is what Wagner accomplished. Not invention, but arrangement and style. Haweis gushes about the "divine microcosm" of Wagner's mind, he who mastered Greek, Latin, mythology, and ancient history as a youth, who learned English in order to read Shakespeare, "weighed several schools of philosophy, studied and dismissed the contending theologies, absorbed Schiller and worshipped Goethe," all as a schoolboy.[37] By the age of eleven, Wagner had been writing in imitation of Shakespeare. As a young composer, he reconciled Aeschylus, Sophocles, and Shakespeare and bound them to Beethoven. He revitalized Christianity (recall that Haweis was an Anglican clergyman) by shining it through the prism of paganism to point toward a purer understanding of the divine. And so on.

While Haweis was overeager as a fan of Wagner, many of his 1884 pronouncements reflected the status quo then and later as to Wagner's chief effects. While decrying Italian opera as springing from the "indolent desire of the luxurious Italian nobles": "The object of grand musical drama is, in fact, to present a true picture of human feeling with the utmost fulness [sic] and intensity, freed from every conventional expression by the happy union of all the arts, giving to each only what it is able to deal with—but thus dealing with everything, leaving nothing to the imagination. The Wagnerian drama completely exhausts this situation."[38] Of course, Wagner as "unconventional" was doomed to fade, just as every successful radical is quaint to generations hence. By the time Shaw wrote the preface for the fourth edition of *The Perfect Wagnerite* in 1922, he felt compelled to begin by pointing out that "musically Wagner is now more old-fashioned than Handel and Bach, Mozart and Beethoven." Wagner had been a victim of his own success, "his own fashion [. . .] worn to rags by young composers in the first efforts to draw the bow of Ulysses."[39] But the idea of leaving nothing out, the "happy union of all the arts" working in concert to reach the absolute limits of expressive possibility, holding back nothing—that is Wagner. Not an idle entertainment, but a death-crawl to the icy peaks of possibility, unapologetically seeking perfection.

And such is what drew Cather to Wagner. Sure, there is Cather's predisposition, as Richard Giannone claims, in favor of "music replete with story and scene," the sort of "dramatic coherency" that Wagner epitomized in his generation and that Cather craved.[40] There's also Wagner's immense versatility, so far-ranging and diverse, for which Cather shares a profound affinity: Just as Cather can be impossible to pin down, so can Wagner. Wagner is the medieval and the modern, radical and conservative, a deep spirituality and a trumpet blast for humanism. He can be read as contemporary political allegory and biblical concomitant. His eternal characters are doomed to temporaneity, and his mortals deliquesce into eternity. His stories operate on a cyclical samsara and a linear path of cause and effect. Cather can be difficult to pigeonhole politically, socially, sexually, artistically. She is a reader's reflecting pool. So can Wagner be. Beyond even that, though, Cather was drawn to opera because opera represented high ideals among an immense diversity of expression, and Wagner the highest ideals and the broadest spectrum of interpretive possibilities. While she made reference to a total of nine Wagner operas over the course of seven individual stories and novels, certainly the story most emblematic of Cather's Wagnerism is that of Thea Kronborg.

The Song of the Lark begins with Thea's youth in Moonstone, Colorado. Central to Thea's musical education is her mother. Though Mrs. Kronborg had studied piano and sang well as a child, she, like her sisters, lacked the mysterious element of *talent*. While Cather makes frequent reference to the idea of talent, she never limits it to a notion of innate ability. The inheritor of talent is never one who is simply born with the ability to perform. Rather, talent is an intuitive connection with a form of expression present only in those blessed to be hardwired with it, and it is an extreme connection that always is to be developed through extreme work. Talent is the rare ability to make good on practice. Throughout the novel, Cather separates those who are merely capable of managing a performative feat from those who have a distinct and innate drive to perfecting that feat, able to channel the medium in ways that others are not. When young, Thea doesn't particularly like being pushed into music; she complains about having to practice despite a mashed finger (leaving her to practice for a time with only her left hand) and practicing four hours each day during vacation. Cather is channeling Olive Fremstad's recollection of her father's strict practice requirements that Cather had reported in "Three American Singers"—Fremstad eventually grew to appreciate the push, as would Thea.

Thea takes lessons—twice a week in the summer, once in the winter—at the home of the Kohler family, who hosts the itinerant German music teacher Wunsch. Wunsch's provenance and training are never fully described. Indeed, no one seems to know his first name beyond the initial "A."[41] Though a moderately common surname, his name also is a pun; *Wunsch* is German for "wish," so "A. Wunsch" is "a wish." Wunsch has traveled around Europe and America, apparently, looking for an apt pupil, his one wish, which finally is granted in the person of Thea. Wunsch is a heavy drinker, which most in town assume is the only reason he's found himself in such a backwater as Moonstone. Moonstone is a town of music, with church recitals and music "floating over" from Mexican Town throughout the day, but without Wunsch, it is a thoroughly provincial and undisciplined cultural arena, which, as far as Wunsch is concerned, is representative of America at large: "He had taught in music schools in St. Louis and Kansas City," he remembers, "where the shallowness and complacency of the young misses had maddened him."[42] A traveling teacher and musician, Wunsch had "encountered bad manners and bad faith, had been the victim of sharpers of all kinds, was dogged by bad luck. He had played in orchestras that were never paid and wandering opera troupes which disbanded penniless." Despite his disappointments, however, he finds hope in Thea. "It was his pupil's power of application, her rugged will, that interested him," he muses. "He had lived for so long among people whose sole ambition was to get something for nothing that he had learned not to look for seriousness in anything. Now that he by chance encountered it, it recalled standards, ambitions, of a society long forgot." Wunsch offers his theory to Thea that "it is necessary to know if you know somethings" and that "somethings cannot be taught. If you not know in the beginning, you not know in the end. For a singer there must be something in the inside from the beginning."[43] Wunsch feels passionately about talent, to the extent that his English begins to break down with the intensity of his belief: "That is the beginnings of all things; *der Geist, die Phantasie*. It must be in the baby, when it makes its first cry"—there must be a natural passion for expression that can't be taught. "Oh, much you can learn!" he begins to shout, "*Aber nicht die Americanischen Fräulein*. They have nothing inside them." He begins to strike himself. "They are like the ones in the *Märchen* [fairy tales], a grinning face and hollow in the insides." But Thea, he knows, is not hollow on the inside, and to clarify his position, he begins to pound his chest; "*in der Brust, in der Brust*, it is," he shouts, "*und ohne dieses giebt es keine Kunst, giebt es keine Kunst!*" ["In the chest . . . and without this there is no art!"]. As Sarah Young notes, his chest-pounding tells us that not only his English has failed him, but his German as well; as a "mouthpiece of Romantic philosophy [. . .] he must return to an imprecise metaphor, which implies that the source of the artist's power is largely incomprehensible," something he trusts Thea to understand.[44]

To highlight the distinction between the typical American *Fräulein* and Thea, Cather describes a Christmas Eve concert in Moonstone in which Wunsch convinces Thea (who'd been put down for an instrumental perfor-mance though she'd hoped for vocal) to play a ballade of Carl Reinecke, whereas Lily Fisher, the "most stuck-up doll in the world" and picked for a vocal selec-tion, sings "Rock of Ages." Whereas Thea's "Ballade" "took ten minutes, which was five minutes too long" for the audience, Lily's hymn is a crowd pleaser. Thea had been cautioned against playing a more modern piece by her own mother, who'd encouraged her to play "Invitation to the Dance"—a Weber piece in which bass and treble parts playfully call and respond, eventually "dancing" together—or something similarly waltzy. But Wunsch insisted on Reinecke. "It is time already that they learn something," he said of the audience.[45] This experience is an important step for Thea, embittering her against popular tastes and cultural superficiality.

Wunsch's theories of art are uncompromising. His view is that Gluck's *Orfeo ed Euridice*, a magnificent but almost painfully serious work, is "the most beau-tiful opera ever made" and that only one performer, Pauline Viardot, is capable of playing the role of Orfeo properly (Orfeo is a part for either alto or castrato). When Thea asks if Viardot was beautiful, Wunsch forcefully responds "*aber gar nicht!*"—not at all! But "she have something in there, behind the eyes." She was born to perform. In the same conversation, Wunsch observes Thea grimace at a difficult passage of music. "You see something a little difficult, may-be," he chides, "and you make such a face like it was an enemy."[46] When Thea responds

that difficult things are enemies, Wunsch reprimands her. Challenges are bless-
ings, and the challenge of art—a challenge that keeps one from beauty—only
makes the beautiful thing more so upon reaching it. It is a lesson that Wunsch's
former pupils could not have comprehended, but he knows that Thea can.

Thea, later wandering among nearby sand dunes, thinks that "she did not
altogether understand what Wunsch was talking about; and yet, in a way she
knew. She knew, of course, that there was something about her that was different. But it was more like a friendly spirit than like anything that was a part
of herself." This friendly spirit comes and goes; sometimes when she seeks it
out she finds it, sometimes not. But when it was there, she felt "a kind of warm
sureness" that made everything "more interesting and beautiful."[47] Certainly,
this is what Cather had in mind when she titled the novel after the Breton
painting. A young woman in the process of revelation. Nothing external has
changed. There is no new knowledge. But she encounters a sensation of eu-
phoria and beauty that is transformative of herself and the world around her.
Thea, as Wunsch recognizes, is one of the very rare individuals capable of experiencing this. "Yes," thinks Wunsch, "she was like a flower full of sun, but not
the soft German flowers of his childhood. He had it now, the comparison he
had absently reached for before: she was like the yellow prickly-pear blossoms
that open there in the desert; thornier and sturdier than the maiden flowers he
remembered; not so sweet, but wonderful."[48]

In the heroine's journey, of course, the mentor must subside. Wunsch loses
control of his drinking, nearly dying from alcohol poisoning, suffering delirium
tremens in withdrawals and smashing up the Kohler home, where he'd been
recuperating. The community of Moonstone, already distrustful of Wunsch's
habits, forces him out. Before he goes, he takes his prized copy of the score to
Orfeo and inscribes it to Thea, then leaves town never to be heard from again.
Thea stagnates in Moonstone, but an inheritance from Ray Kennedy, a lifelong
friend who'd wanted to marry Thea when she got old enough but who died in a
railroad accident, leaves Thea financially capable of pursuing her piano studies
in Chicago. There, she takes lessons with Andor Harsanyi, a Hungarian pianist,
who quickly realizes that Thea's true musical destiny is in her voice rather than
her hands (incidentally, he realizes this upon hearing her sing from *Orfeo*), and
passes her off to Madison Bowers, Chicago's finest vocal coach, for whom Thea
serves as accompanist in exchange for coaching.

During her stay in Chicago, Thea undergoes a deep personal transformation, particularly upon first being exposed to the music of a full orchestra. Harsanyi had given her a ticket to an afternoon performance, which Thea attends alone—all of her transformative moments are solitary. The first "number" does little for her. She is more interested in watching the musicians than listening to what they play. She finds herself looking around the auditorium, wondering how so many men could have left their work mid-afternoon for a concert. But with the second piece, Dvořák's Symphony in e minor, "From the New World," "instant composure fell upon her, and with it came the power of concentration." In the music, Thea hears the "high tableland above Laramie," wagon trails, eagles, the first telegraph message, sand hills, and grasshoppers. "There was home in it, too," she thinks, "first memories, first mornings long ago; the amazement of a new soul in a new world."[49] Cather is doing something complex. Thea is waking to a life that is both familiar and fresh, a baptism in which the world she knows is still there, only having taken on a new layer of significance she'd never previously perceived. Though she'd always had an intuitive grasp of music, she now has the ability to channel the physical world through that emotional medium. In this state of raw enlightenment, she hears the next piece, the entry of the gods into Walhalla from the conclusion of *Rheingold*. That moment in the opera, as she knows from Haweis's book, features the gods crossing the rainbow bridge into their newly built fortress, a moment of transition and triumph. Thea, emotionally exposed from her revelation of the previous piece, is herself experiencing a transition.

After the concert, she walks out into a gray, cold evening. She is elbowed and pushed about by people on the sidewalk. She gets on the wrong streetcar and is tossed off by the conductor, landing in front of a saloon where a young man asks her "looking for a friend tonight?" Waiting for another car, an older man with watery eyes approaches her, "thrusting his face up near hers" and whispering some undisclosed remark. "Oh, let me *alone!*" Thea demands, and he disappears "like the Devil in a play."[50] This is the ugly world, away from the world of the beauty of art, the "ugly, sprawling streets" and the brutish people were now "lined up against her, they were there to take something from her." "Very well," she considers,

> they should never have it. They might trample her to death, but they should never have it. As long as she lived that ecstasy was going to be hers. She would live for it, work for it; die for it; but she was going to

have it, time after time, height after height. She could hear the crash of the orchestra again, and she rose on the brasses. She would have it, what the trumpets were singing! She would have it, have it,—it! Under the old cape she pressed her hands upon her heaving bosom, that was a little girl's no longer.[51]

Thea has escaped the Lily Fishers of Moonstone, but the city has its own assortment of devils and insipidities. Though still at the outset of her journey, Thea will have to go beyond even Chicago, beyond humanity itself. She is developing a part of her that is "selfless and exalted." "Selfless," here, of course, doesn't mean *generous* or *considerate*, but rather without material self, something transcendent. "Thea had a hard kind of cockiness, a determination to get ahead." "Let people try to stop her," she thinks, "but the difference was that *she was going to get them!*"

Thea is developing a disdain for normalcy and the routine expectations that others have in life, but she remains unsure. Despite a troubled relationship with her hometown, she knows that "the most important thing was that one should not pretend to be what one was not." Her awakening had come at the synesthetic experience of hearing her homeland in Dvořák; she would need to revisit that home to fully understand what that experience meant. As Cather commonly represents, there's a divide between what a town like Moonstone can mean for the artist. She'd fled it for the sake of her artistic development, but she is also developing a need for rootedness and reconciliation with her home country. She returns to Moonstone, and to her "it was over flat lands like this, stretching out to drink the sun, that the larks sang—and one's heart sang there, too. Thea was glad that this was her country, even if one did not learn to speak elegantly there. It was, somehow, an honest country, and there was a new song in that blue air which had never been sung in the world before. It was hard to tell about it, for it had nothing to do with words; it was like the light of the desert at noon, or the smell of the sagebrush after rain; intangible but powerful."[52] At home, she has Spanish Johnny and the residents of the Mexican side of town; she is intimidated by them, thinking that "she had never before sung for a really musical people."[53] They sing from Donizetti and Verdi with vitality as though they were singing folk songs. She has her siblings, who are "*of her kind,*" she thinks, and not of the small-minded Moonstonians at large, whose "ambition and sacred proprieties were meaningless to her." Her return to Moonstone makes her appreciate authenticity, but it also gives her a more ambitious outlook. In Moonstone, even her childhood mentor Dr. Archie seems small minded. He's invested in silver mines—"chasing the elusive metal"—and hopes to be rich someday. Thea hopes so, too. Concernedly, he asks whether she needs money. She gets by "in a little way," she says, "but it's silly to live at all for the little things. [. . .] Living's too much trouble unless one can get something big out of it."[54] Thea isn't actually interested in money, however. Though she seems to expect a fairly high level of creature comfort once her career is established, and though she ends the novel quite wealthy, her motivation is always toward artistic greatness, an aim money can progress or impede, as it does with Madison Bowers, who sells his talent for teaching to the untalented wives of wealthy men—"the more money he made, the more parsimonious he became."[55]

It is in Bowers's studio that Thea meets Fred Ottenburg, scion of a brewing empire, with a habit of using business as an excuse to pop over to Bavaria for opera. "He's what they call an imaginative business man," says Bowers, "goes over to Bayreuth and seems to do nothing but give parties and spend money, and brings back more good notions for the brewery than the fellows who sit tight dig out in five years."[56] He is a naturally energetic man for whom music is a natural form of expression, alongside sport and fine dining: "When he was in Germany, he scarcely knew where the soup ended and the symphony began."[57] He came by his love of music naturally, his mother, Katarina Fürst, having been a German-American socialite, "sentimental and heavily romantic" "and not untouched by scandal." She'd been part of a coterie of young women who'd followed Wagner around in his waning days, keeping her distance but relishing the occasional acknowledgment from the man. When he'd died, she'd shut herself in her bedroom for a week.[58]

Fred will become a sort of cheerleader and fan of Thea's, watching her ascent close-up. Eventually, they marry, though this fact is disclosed in a throwaway line in the epilogue, and their romance, such as it is, never becomes too important in the story. Harsanyi and Bowers give Thea an entrée into the wider artistic world—the world that Chicago can offer—but it is Fred who gives Thea a sense of a greatness international in scale. Not only does he bring her stories of the great European opera capitals, eventually encouraging Thea to go abroad to perfect her art, he continually and superciliously berates American provincialism. "We may have a musical public in this country some day," he says, "but as yet there are only the Germans and the Jews. All the other people go to hear

Jessie Darcey sing, 'O, Promise Me!'" And later: "You bet in Germany people know their librettos by heart! You Americans are so afraid of stooping to learn anything."[59] These are the initial steps to Thea's progress: natural superiority in her youth youth, moving to the city to discover her voice, her revelation at the afternoon concert, and her introduction to the widest possible world of operatic achievement through the well-connected Fred. But there were further steps she'd have to take alone.

Part III of the novel is titled "Stupid Faces." If Cather wasn't always great with titles, one might give her credit for the willful, brattish bravado of this one. It happens after Thea leaves Moonstone and begins with her return to Chicago. When she left Moonstone, she resolved to "go away to fight, and she was going away forever." She was sick of the small minds in her hometown. Then, abruptly, she's back in Bowers's studio, thinking "so many grinning, stupid faces!" She's looking at an "illustrated musical journal"—likely the *Musical Courier* or a fictional analogue of that publication—, throwing psychic spite at the faces in the ads. In Parts I and II, Thea had wearied of the people of small towns and the big city, and now "she was getting tired of the human countenance" altogether.[60] Many of Cather's books are melancholy. *The Professor's House* focuses on a man who's lived a life of purpose long enough to see that purpose exhausted—but his life plodding on. *My Mortal Enemy* is a soul-scarred tour of the fallen ideals of marriage. Like these, *The Song of the Lark* explores a harsh reality: The artist must be specialized and the great artist so specialized that she is unable to relate to others or to accept the mediocrity of the rest of humanity, who are, by definition, lesser than she in her chosen field. The artist lists to misanthropy. And so Thea must leave people to connect with a higher plane of artistic achievement.

Obviously in need of a break from other humans, Thea travels west, to the San Francisco Peaks north of Flagstaff to be a guest at a ranch owned by the Ottenburg family. (As Wyllis and Margaret Elliot had done in "Eric Hermannson's Soul" years before, so had Fred been sent west once to mature.) At this point, Thea thinks of herself as a failure. She had failed as a pianist under Harsanyi's tutelage, and, by her reckoning, hadn't made sufficient progress under Bowers. But wandering in the desert, her mind unclouded by people and expectations, her days unhurried by work, in "a place where she was out of the stream of meaningless activity and undirected effort," she resets her relationship to music.[61] Though she sings little, songs keep welling up in her like a spring; "They had something to do with fragrance and color and sound, but almost nothing to do with words," just intuition. "Music had never come to her in that sensuous form before," she thinks, "It had always been a thing to be struggled with, had always brought anxiety and exaltation and chagrin—never content and indolence." She likes the casual, gentle way she is encountering music. Where "she had always been a little drudge, hurrying from one task to another," "now her power to think seemed converted into a power of sustained sensation. She could become a mere receptacle for heat, or become a color, like the bright lizards that darted about on the hot stones outside her door; or she could become a continuous repetition of sound, like the cicadas."[62]

About a mile from the ranch is the entrance to Panther Canyon, a long fissure in the rock in which is situated an ancient, long-abandoned Indian cliff city. Thea enters an "abstracted state" in the canyon, with "certain feelings [. . .] transmitted to her, suggestions that were simple, insistent, and monotonous, [. . .] not expressible in words, but seemed rather to translate themselves into attitudes of body."[63] She becomes hyper-aware of the relationship between her body in the present moment as well as her place in the long span of history. She thinks of the Indian women of the cliff city, catching water in their decorated jars, the jars themselves sculptures, the water itself life. "What was any art," she ponders, "but an effort to make a sheath, a mould in which to imprison for a moment the shining, elusive element which is life itself,—life hurrying past us and running away, too strong to stop, too sweet to lose?" Life was finite; art was infinite. She had come to a theory of art that said that human compulsion toward that "one unaccountable thing in man," the compulsion toward perfected expression, was the only sense, the only glimpse one would have in this life into eternity. She had only so much time in life to touch the full vastness of the expanse of time and space through art. Thea has independently arrived at Poe's "poetic principle":

Inspired by an ecstatic prescience of the glories beyond the grave, we struggle, by multiform combinations among the things and thoughts of Time, to attain a portion of that Loveliness whose very elements, perhaps, appertain to eternity alone. And thus when by Poetry,—or when by Music, the most entrancing of the Poetic moods—we find ourselves melted into tears—we weep then [not] through excess of pleasure, but through a certain, petulant, impatient sorrow at our inability to grasp *now*, wholly, here on earth, at once and for ever, those divine and rapturous joys, of which *through* the poem, or *through* the music, we attain to but brief and indeterminate glimpses.[64]

Art is a path for a moment, however brief, to paradise. But, in her "abstracted state," Thea also comes to the conclusion that "there was certainly no kindly Providence that directed one's life," that she ended up in Panther Canyon and at her moment of revelation only by chance. But, having had this revelation, she sets a path for Germany to study, fearing otherwise that she'd become subject to the "comfortable, self-satisfied people" like those in Moonstone who were hostile "toward any serious effort," who did not perceive the scope and potential of art as she saw it. In days to come, she would imagine the consequences of not leaving to study, a life that followed in Wunsch's underperforming footsteps. She dreamed of herself in Moonstone, beating her students in hideous rages of disappointment, struggling at the piano rather than embracing her voice. She has a dream in which she's looking into a mirror, getting prettier as the mirror gets smaller—that is success measured by small-town standards. "No more of that!" she affirms. She had inherited a length of art reaching all the way back to the cliff dwellers, and they had lengthened her past. Now, "she had older and higher obligations."

The final part of the novel is titled simply "Kronborg." We are to understand that, like Fremstad and Farrar and Nordica, her name stands without need for explanation. It takes place ten years after she sails for Germany. Dr. Archie has become wealthy through his mining investments and visits New York to see Thea perform as Elsa in *Lohengrin.* Archie is vaguely aware of Thea's success, but is unprepared for the experience of seeing her now that she's neared the peak of her potential. Fred attempts to explain Thea's transformation by re-counting a performance in which she'd played Woglinde. It is a minor role in *Rheingold,* one of three Rheinmaidens whose job it is to exemplify the beauty of the Rhein, antagonize the dwarf Alberich, who steals the hoard of gold at the bottom of the Rhein, inadvertently catalyzing the general apocalypse of the *Ring* cycle, then disappear. But she'd stood out, a fact noticed by the conductor that evening—none other than Gustav Mahler. Fred had spoken with Mahler after that performance (opera-loving beer barons have easy access to such men). "Interesting voice you tried out this evening," Fred prompted. Mahler "stopped and smiled. 'Miss Kronborg, you mean? Yes, very. She seems to sing for the idea. Unusual in a young singer.' I'd never heard him admit before that a singer could have an idea. She not only had it, but she got it across." Fred had known the music since he was young, but Thea had made it "fresh," "vocalized for the first time." As he explains it, with Thea as one of the three, one didn't hear three Rheinmaidens, but rather "two pretty voices *and* the Rhine voice."[65] Taking on even minor Wagnerian roles, Thea marked herself as something new.

Archie attends the performance of *Lohengrin* as a relative opera neophyte. When the Herald announces the arrival of Elsa, Archie's nervousness takes over. He likens the experience to that of "buck-fever," "the paralyzing moment that comes upon a man when his first elk looks at him through the bushes, under its great antlers; the moment when a man's mind is so full of shooting that he forgets the gun in his hand until the buck nods adieu to him from a distant hill."[66] Archie is nervous before she appears, not nervous for Elsa, but for Thea. To him, the one performing Elsa is the girl who used to hang about his office in Moonstone reading books and asking questions, the one he treated for a fever when she was near death as a little girl. Certainly, that person had no place on the stage of the Met. Then Thea appears. "Yes, unquestionably it was she," he realizes. "Her eyes were downcast, but the head, the cheeks, the chin—there could be no mistake; she advanced slowly, as if she were walking in her sleep. Some one spoke to her; she only inclined her head. He spoke again, and she bowed her head still lower." He cannot hear her as Elsa slowly enters her voice into the scene. Thea is perfectly one with the music, her voice, offering prayer, ethereal. Without realizing it, Archie is no longer nervous for her, but swept up into the scene with Elsa the focal point, he "was sitting quietly in a darkened house, not listening to but dreaming upon a river of silver sound. [. . .] As a lad he used to believe that the faces of people who died were like that in the next world; the same faces, but shining with the light of a new understanding. [. . .] She merely reminded him of Thea; this was not the girl herself." The woman on stage is something new, someone he'd never known, who had "somehow devoured his little friend as the wolf ate up Red Ridinghood." He thinks of how distant he'd felt to Thea when she'd gone to Germany, but that distance meant nothing now; "the ocean he could cross, but there was something here he could not cross."[67] Archie is a physician, a man whose profession is tied to material well-being. He's a successful investor, comfortable. But since her conversion in Panther Canyon, her commitment to "older and higher obligations," Thea is focused on things beyond material comfort. She has transcended the things Archie knows to attain something higher that Archie can sense but not define.

Though Archie has an intuitive sense of Thea's abilities, he's still unsure of his ability to assess opera relative to the Met habitués like Fred. He asks Fred whether Thea is "all right." "My dear Archie," Fred replies, "that's the high voice we dream of; so pure and yet so virile and human. That combination hardly ever happens with sopranos." He goes on to explain that what Thea has "can't be acquired" but is a "color" that has to be inborn. He recognizes that part of Archie's anxiety has to do with the possibility of Thea faltering on stage, but he reassures that "it can't go wrong in interpretation, because it has in it the thing that makes all interpretation. That's why you feel so sure of her. After you've listened to her for an hour or so, you aren't afraid of anything. All the little dreads you have with other artists vanish. You lean back and you say to yourself, 'No, *that* voice will never betray.'" Thea is able, like no other, to channel the *idea* upon which a character is based. "She simplified a character down to the musical idea it's built on," says Fred, "and makes everything conform to that":

> The people who chatter about her being a great actress don't seem to get the notion of where *she* gets the notion. It all goes back to her original endowment, her tremendous musical talent. Instead of inventing a lot of business and expedients to suggest character, she knows the thing at the root, and lets the musical pattern take care of her. The score pours her into all those lovely postures, makes the light and shadow go over her face, lifts her and drops her. She lies on it, the way she used to lie on the Rhine music.[68]

For Thea, Fred, and Cather, the music and drama are a unified whole, a total work of art that requires an artist ready to sacrifice herself completely to reach its full manifestation.

Even so, Thea doubts. The morning after her performance as Elsa, she wakes dreading the sensation of being "stale and disappointed after a great effort." She thinks of the "futility of such endeavor, and of the absurdity of trying too hard." She feels comfortable giving "eighty degrees" worth of effort, but ninety is too much: "The legend was that in those upper reaches you might be divine; but you were much likelier to be ridiculous." What "ridiculous" means in this instance is open to interpretation. On its face, it means that one might ascend to the plane of one's incompetence, failing by trying too hard to be great; alternatively, it might mean it's ridiculous to give too much effort knowing that no audience could deserve her giving her all. Her career has been built on the rigors of extreme work ethic. When studying in Berlin, "the other girls were mortally afraid of her. She has a pretty rough hand with women, dull ones, and she could be rude, too! The girls used to call her *die Wölfin.*"[69] She, as artist, is prepared to put everything she has into her work, but she questions why "people go to the opera, anyway,—serious people," she says in frustration. "I suppose they get something, or think they do."[70] Later, even Fred will confide to Thea that, though he is "grateful" to her for her drive and discipline, he doesn't understand it, and, in fact, isn't "much interested in how anybody sings anything."[71] Those closest to her are Dr. Archie and Fred. Archie is too provincial and materialistic to appreciate her, and Fred, her future husband and a genuine opera enthusiast, admits that his interest in the technique of opera has waned. "When you needed enthusiasm from the outside," he says, "I was able to give it to you. Now you must let me withdraw." Thea is simply too consistently intense in her pursuit of greatness and has worn thin Fred's ability to be supportive. And beyond Fred and Archie are the masses that come to the opera, the people who *think*, in Thea's estimation, that they get something out of it. She recalls the popularity of a woman who'd recently sang Ortrud in *Lohengrin* who is "stupid as an owl and coarse as a pig" and yet is "quite as popular as Necker [a character in the story who likely represents either Lilli Lehmann or Lillian Nordica], who's a great artist. How can I get much satisfaction out of the enthusiasm of a house that likes her atrociously bad performance at the same time that it pretends to like mine? If they like her, they ought to hiss me off the stage."[72] But even if Thea can't offer a rational justification for her work, she still compulsively strives for greatness.

Having been chosen for the role of Sieglinde in *Die Walküre*, Thea is with Fred one day when he begins to play the piano accompaniment for "*Du bist der Lenz*," Sieglinde's profession of love for Siegmund. Thea violently jerks his hands away from the keys. The performance is still a week out. Something could happen to take her out of the performance. The cast could be changed. With days to go, Thea can't bear to face the music that could make her career. She refers to the music as "inaccessibly beautiful," something she apparently worries she's not able to pull off. She says that the system of rehearsals is "well enough for phlegmatic singers; it only drains me." The anxiety of needing to be perfect wears her in a way that it doesn't others. "I have to work hard to do my worst," she says, "let alone my best. I wish you could hear me sing well, once." Of course, she's in a room with Fred and Archie, both of whom are friendly and both of whom have heard her sing well many times. But that is Thea: her best on one day is still her worst measured against a hypothetical best in the ether. And those two are entirely unqualified to know the difference between a 99.5 percent perfect soprano and a 99.6 percent perfect soprano—but to Thea that 0.1 percent is glaringly obvious. Worth noting is that Fred began to play "*Du bist der Lenz*"—the same piece that Caroline Noble had played with Raymond d'Esquerré in "The Garden Lodge." In that story, the piece represents a perfect happiness that can never be. Here, Cather is using the same piece to represent art of impossible perfection. But one can never concede that that perfection *might* be possible. To do so would be de-motivating. "There are many disappointments in my profession, and bitter, bitter contempts!" Thea declares. "If you love the good thing vitally, enough to give up for it all that one must give up for it, then you must hate the cheap thing just as hard. I tell you, there is such a thing as creative hate! A contempt that drives you through fire, makes you risk everything and lose everything, makes you a long sight better than you ever knew you could be."[73]

Despite her anxiety, nothing comes between Thea and her first Sieglinde. And she doesn't give the eighty degrees for fear of looking ridiculous: "The voice gave out all that was best in it. Like the spring, indeed, it blossomed into memories and prophecies, it recounted and it foretold. [. . .] Fervently she rose into the hardier feeling of action and daring, the pride in hero-strength and hero-blood, until a splendid burst, tall and shining like a Victory." In this scene where Sieglinde gives the hero's sword, Nothung, to Siegmund, "her impatience for the sword swelled with her anticipation of his act, and throwing her arms above her head, she fairly tore a sword out of the empty air for him, before Nothung had left the tree. *In höchster Trunkenheit*, indeed, she burst out with the flaming cry of their kinship: 'If you are Siegmund, I am Sieglinde!' Laughing, singing, bounding, exulting,—with their passion and their sword,—the *Volsungs* ran out into the spring night." Thea has embraced her full expressive capacity, leaving nothing either musical or dramatic out—by the end of the passage, Cather no longer describes her as Thea, with Thea's voice, but rather as a Volsung, a daughter of Wotan.

Andor Harsanyi is in the audience that night. "At last," he says, "somebody with *enough!* Enough voice and talent and beauty, enough physical power. And such a noble, noble style!" Introduced to Fred, Harsanyi declares that Thea will sing Isolde and "all the great rôles, I should think." A journalist in the box with them, writing of Thea's "explosive force" and "projecting power," asks Harsanyi what he thinks is Thea's secret. "Her secret?" he replies. "It is every artist's secret [. . .]—passion. That is all. It is an open secret, and perfectly safe. Like heroism, it is inimitable in cheap materials." Harsanyi's take on the matter is certainly quoteworthy, but Cather gives her readers another:

> Artistic growth is, more than it is anything else, a refining of the sense of truthfulness. The stupid believe that to be truthful is easy; only the artist, the great artist, knows how difficult it is. That afternoon, nothing new came to Thea Kronborg, no enlightenment, no inspiration. She merely came into full possession of things she had been refining and perfecting for so long. Her inhibitions chanced to be fewer than usual, and, within herself, she entered into the inheritance that she herself had laid up, into the fullness of the faith she had kept before she knew its name or its meaning.[74]

Thea has experienced a truth, but not a literal truth, and it is nothing suddenly given but the aggregate of a lifetime of focused training, allowed by refining away spiritual detritus, the moment appearing when she is unburdened by inhibitions and given over to the music, to an ideal she'd believed in before she knew what to call it. As Isolde ascends to pure bliss "in the billowy surge, / in the gush of sound, / gusting spirit of the universe— / to drown— / to sink— / unconscious— / highest desire," so Thea is caught up into a transcendent realm that only she knows. Harsanyi, Fred, and others see this and sense her experience, but will never themselves attain it. The reward for her decades of tireless focus in the expectation of never relating again fully to another human, Thea enters into an "inheritance" she had set up for herself in blind expectation of the rewards of perfection.

But Cather never reveals those rewards. She couldn't, and that's the point. Whatever Thea gained from her quest—beyond a thousand-dollar-per-night fee and her name on boards and bills worldwide, which never seemed to be her real motivation—is left unexplored and undescribed. The novel ends with an epilogue in Moonstone, told through the perspective of Aunt Tillie. Before that, in the final chapter of "Kronborg," Cather describes Thea's performance through the eyes of Archie and Fred, then Harsanyi—but the reader by then is too far removed from Thea. We've seen her as a sick child in Moonstone, a frustrated adolescent, a defiant young artist. Then, midnovel, Thea goes to Germany and we see her less. Then, upon the reappearance of Dr. Archie, we're given a brief, backstage glimpse at Thea, but she's an altogether different person than the youth we'd known, different in temperament and in capability. Then we see her on stage, from hundreds of feet away, and we talk about her—amongst ourselves and to journalists who want to know more about her—but no longer to the artist herself. The novel proper (before the epilogue) ends with Thea emerging from a stage exit onto the street, bowing graciously to the crowd before mounting into her cab and disappearing. Nearby is "the only man in the crowd who had removed his hat when she emerged, and who stood with it crushed up in his hand." He is a man "she would have known" if she'd seen him, "changed as he was" with his hair now gray and his face worn. "She passed so near that he could have touched her, and he did not put on his hat until her taxi had snorted away," whereupon he walks down Broadway smiling. Spanish Johnny, who'd played folk songs on the mandolin alongside *Trovatore* and the *Lucia* sextette, was in New York playing with a Mexican band in a circus and had attended Thea's performance. Whereas Archie, Fred, and Harsanyi all struggle to articulate Thea's accomplishment in words, enjoying their proximity to the singer, Johnny stands his ground and smiles "a smile which embraced all the stream of life that passed him." A great musician himself, he knows there's nothing to say, and "if the singer, going home exhausted in her cab, was wondering what was the good of it all, that smile, could she have seen it, would have answered her. It is the only commensurate answer."[75]

CHAPTER 8

❧

OPERA INCOGNITA
Later Novels

She loved her own little town, but it was a heart-breaking love, like
loving the dead who cannot answer back.
—*Lucy Gayheart*

ather wrote less about opera after the 1910s. There are several possible explanations for this. Her early enthusiasm for opera was no doubt driven in part by the fact that it represented a break from rural Nebraska. There were occasional traveling troupes in Red Cloud, operatic celebrities sporadically in Lincoln, the Met in its traveling form in Chicago and Pittsburgh, and the Met itself in New York. At each stop, opera gets better as the sum of the locale's cultural importance increases. Opera was a way for Cather to assure herself that she was moving in the right direction, so it makes sense that it would be more prominent early in her creative career when she was still establishing herself. By the mid-1910s, also, her career as cultural critic was growing farther behind her. The half million words of commentary she'd published before leaving Nebraska—much of it theatrical criticism—was half a lifetime ago. She continued producing theatrical criticism, including writings about opera, during her stint in Pittsburgh, but her work as a teacher, editor, and creative writer gradually pushed that work aside. Opera increasingly became an entertainment rather than a source of critical engagement and intellectual growth. By the 1910s, Cather had attended dozens (probably hundreds) of individual opera performances. She'd made reference to twenty operas in her fiction prior to *O Pioneers!* and at least as many in her critical works by that time. By her early forties, when she began to succeed as a novelist, no doubt opera was beginning to seem like something from her youth, not part of who she then was. Certainly, after the sustained focus on opera and its philosophical meaning in *The Song of the Lark*—her longest novel, at nearly twice the length of *My Ántonia*—she might have simply been burned out on the subject. And finally, something fundamental seemed to change for Cather in the early 1920s, around that moment in 1922 when, as she wrote in "Not under Forty," "the world broke in two" between the forward-looking Moderns and "yesterday's seven thousand years."[1] A confluence of factors caused Cather to perceive such a break. Entering firmly into middle age at that point, she visited Red Cloud twice in as many years, the second time to celebrate her parents' fiftieth wedding anniversary. She had been by this time acclaimed multiple times as a novelist, but the most recent of her accolades at that point, the Pulitzer Prize for *One of Ours*, thrust her into a controversial limelight in which her high-minded romanticizing of the soldier's triumph-in-death left her afoul of the upstart Lost Generation. She was acutely aware that her role in the cultural landscape had changed from boundary-breaker to traditionalist. After this point, her writing becomes more character-oriented and reflective. She thinks of marriage in an unflattering long view, as in *A Lost Lady*, *The Professor's House*, and *My Mortal Enemy*. She meditates on outliving one's usefulness in *The Professor's House*. She reaches into the past with *Death Comes for the Archbishop*, *Shadows on the Rock*, and *Sapphira and the Slave Girl*. Whereas her youth had been rhapsodies on art—"There is no God but one God and Art is his revealer"—her later adulthood was "Art is too terribly human to be very 'great.'" The American composer Sidney Homer, hearing the *Ring* for the first time as a music student, wrote that "life would never be the same again, the commonplace was banished from our several lives forever! Music went beyond, where words could not go. The music—the music was truth itself, the unveiling of fundamentals, a revelation of the primitive impulses and sources of all things."[2] Cather might have written such a thing in the 1890s, but certainly not in the 1920s or after. Opera, *the* ambition of all art, was really the product of a deeply flawed and underwhelming humanity.

In *One of Ours*, Cather makes only a brief reference to opera—and then not really to opera, but to a violin piece recorded by Lt. Gerhardt, the "Meditation" from Massenet's *Thaïs*. Opera isn't referenced at all in her subsequent novels *A Lost Lady*, *Shadows on the Rock*, and *Sapphira and the Slave Girl*. In the prologue to *Death Comes for the Archbishop*, a group of clergymen are discussing art and politics and make reference to a "new opera by young Verdi, which was being sung in Venice."[3] Bellini's *Norma* has a brief but memorable mention in *My Mortal Enemy*. *The Professor's House* references Cimarosa's *Il Matrimonio Segreto* and Thomas's *Mignon*, both as important intertextual references, though Cather dwells on neither. *Lucy Gayheart* mentions ten operas, but only in the context of singers whose focus is on art songs rather than musical drama—opera is only an incident of vocalism generally. In sum, Cather's writing about opera in the second half of her career is sparing, but that's not to say those references aren't frequently meaningful or that ideas *about* opera or *from* opera don't continue to influence what she wrote.

One of Ours follows Claude Wheeler, a young man from a farming family in the first generation after the settlers. He is the heir of Alexandra's prosperity, but he wants something more than a life of relative comfort on a well-established farm. Eventually enlisting in the army in World War I, Claude sees combat in France, his travels and experiences greatly expand his worldview, and in his participation in an effort larger than himself, he finds some measure of meaning and content. The brief reference to *Thaïs* isn't wholly arbitrary. Lt. David Gerhardt, the friend of protagonist Claude Wheeler who leads Claude into an understanding of the wider world, was based on the violinist David Hochstein, whom Cather had met on three occasions and who, like Gerhardt, died in World War I. Hochstein had left a deep impression; in a private audience made possible by Jan Hambourg, he'd played Schubert's "Death and the Maiden" and "Trout" quintets, and, according to Cather, "had the *stimmung* of that particular composition ['Trout'] on that occasion more than any of the other players." She found him to be a "very thoughtful young man," who had many things to say but who kept his opinions and ideas largely to himself. She recounted that he wasn't entirely pro-Ally at the outset of the war, having been trained in Germany, where he developed a profound appreciation for German culture. He was a nephew of Emma Goldman and a socialist—in short, thoroughly an outsider in the context of the American military of the First World War.[4] *Thaïs* is an opera about a cenobitic monk, Athanaël, morally torn by lust for Thaïs; living in an ascetic monastic community, Athanaël is likewise an outsider. The reference to *Thaïs* is subtle and clever. In the novel, Claude finds that his military unit has been relaxing to a record that happens to be Gerhardt performing the Meditation; a few paragraphs before, Captain Owens of the corps of engineers, whom Gerhardt detests, thinks that "there was something out of the ordinary" about the erstwhile violinist.[5] Cather might have included any piece from the violin repertoire, but she chose one drawn from an opera about a man out of place.

While *Thaïs* is the only explicit reference to opera in the novel, Philip Kennicott has written that the "deeply pessimistic" novel is a reflection of Cather's ambivalence regarding Wagner in the context of a war against the Germans. He notes that the novel has elements of *Parsifal* in that Claude is "a holy fool, uncomprehending, inarticulate, only vaguely aware of his role as a redemptive hero" and that Cather had considered naming the last section of the novel "The Blameless Fool by Pity Enlightened," after the prophecy that anoints Parsifal as the hero of the opera.[6] (She called it "Bidding the Eagles of the West Fly On," instead—again, Cather struggled with titles.) But Parsifal is a redemptive hero, and, in Kennicott's estimation, Claude is not. Instead, he sees *One of Ours* as a reflection of the "strange and pessimistic twist" that Wagner presents in *Götterdämmerung*, the last of the *Ring* operas, in which "the vigorous young hero is literally knifed in the back and the Gods who once controlled the world will their own destruction."[7] Such an interpretation is willfully incognizant of Cather's attitude toward the book, however. She clearly viewed Claude as a young man out of place in the new agricultural paradigm and prosperity of the plains, someone who needed a calling in life and found it in the war; those looking for remunerative value in his death, that Claude's demise needs to result in some concrete benefit, ignore that Claude died a hero to himself, not for any objective quid pro quo. Cather had based Claude on her cousin G. P. Cather, who died in the war and with whom she claimed a "Siegmund and Sieglinde bond."[8] In *Walküre*, those two Volsungs are not only twins and lovers, thus physically attuned, but spiritually attuned, as well. Cather probably never thought of herself as "uncomprehending" and "inarticulate," and she doesn't represent Claude as such so much as she does "frustrated" and "searching." When Cather set out to write her Volsung-cousin's story, "life became a series of assignations, of stolen interviews with Claude. He met me when I walked in the park; in the middle of a symphony concert he was suddenly at my shoulder. I always had tea alone [. . .] for I never knew when he would appear and sit opposite me." Claude *is* a Parsifal figure, not cannon fodder, but one eager to find a place in life. In the opera, Parsifal arrives at the grail castle, Monsalvat, having slain a beautiful swan. He is proud of this fact, claiming he can shoot any creature from the sky—but he is chastised by Gurnemanz, elder grail knight, and Parsifal is instantly remorseful for killing for sport and bringing violence onto the holy grounds of the Grail. Seeking expiation, Parsifal takes up the challenge of finding a cure for the wounded grail king, Amfortas, and navigates various challenges to do so, ultimately redeeming himself, Amfortas, and the general accursedness that had plagued the grail knights. He and Claude both begin as unschooled and rootless, but they both find purpose and succeed in justifying themselves—that one lives and one dies is beside the point. Though Cather pursued a rather pessimistic trend throughout the 1920s, *One of Ours,* particularly in its Parsifalian overtones, isn't representative of that trend.

Later novels, however, are pessimistic. Godfrey St. Peter, titular professor of *The Professor's House,* should be a happy man, but is not. He spent his youth split between the Great Plains and Versailles—adventure and civilization. He fell in love and married, and his marriage has endured untroubled, now with two happily married adult daughters. St. Peter has succeeded wildly in his chosen profession, historian, his nine-volume work on Spanish explorers in North America garnering international acclaim and a measure of wealth that has allowed him to buy a nice new house for his and his wife's twilight years (though he prefers remaining nested in the house they'd rented previously). The university at which he teaches is not prestigious, but it provides what he needs professionally, and he seems to enjoy a substantial measure of freedom and respect there. And yet he's ill at ease. Though he is only in middle age, his life's work is completed and he has no new project. Financially set, he prefers the simpler home in which he raised his daughters and wrote his books rather than the modern home that reflects his success. His wife is warm, but their marriage is passionless. And St. Peter is fixated on Tom Outland, a former student of his, the likes of whom St. Peter will never see again. The novel is predicated on these apparent contradictions, the hollowness of conquest.

In the first part of the novel, St. Peter reflects upon meeting Outland, then a young man in his twenties, just up from the Southwest, hoping to enroll in St. Peter's university. Having read St. Peter's books and respected the view of the Southwest they represent, he wants to study at the same institution. And though Outland is enthused by history, highly proficient in Latin, and seems generally to be a humanities-bound student, his academic passion turns out to be engineering. In postgraduate work, he designs an airplane engine, the patent for which turns out to be worth a fortune that he will never enjoy—he is killed in the War. Instead, the fortune goes to St. Peter's daughter Rosamund, to whom Outland is engaged, and her new husband Louis Marsellus, who use the money to build a Norwegian manor house on the lake. The second part of the novel tells Outland's story in his own voice, following his time in New Mexico, his discovery of an abandoned cliff dweller city, his frustrated attempts to get Washington bureaucrats to help him preserve and protect the ruins, and his betrayal by a friend who sells the relics from the city while Outland's away. Hence, the professor's "house" is actually at least four houses: the house in which St. Peter raised his family, the new house he's bought his wife, the house Outland's fortune has bought his daughter, and the ancient homes nestled in the cliff side. The singular "house" of the title is an apparent mystery, but Cather hints at its solution in the way she references opera in the novel.

The novel mentions two operas by name. One is Cimarosa's *Il Matrimonio Segreto,* an opera buffa centering on a rich man's secretary having to conceal his marriage to one of the rich man's daughters, hilarity ensuing. Godfrey St. Peter is humming an unspecified "favorite air" from the opera as he prepares for a family dinner. At the dinner, Marsellus remarks upon a turquoise stone set in a silver bracelet that Rosie had worn the night they met. The turquoise, as noted elsewhere in the novel, had been a gift from Outland. As with the *Thaïs* reference in *One of Ours,* the Cimarosa reference is an operatic in-joke, reminding us of Rosie's "secret marriage" to Tom Outland, which lives on in St. Peter's imagination, in Rosie's jewelry, and in the house that Tom's patent is allowing to be built. It might also signify, as John Flannigan notes, "the professor's awareness of his and his family's unfortunate resemblances to some rather absurd opera characters."[9]

The other opera in the novel is more substantially intertextual. St. Peter had spent much of his youth in Versailles and "always had an *abonnement* at the Opéra Comique" in Paris, where he saw Ambroise Thomas's *Mignon* several times.[10] In the novel, Rosie and Louis gift St. Peter tickets to *Mignon* during a visit to Chicago, allowing him to revisit his youth. The plot of *Mignon* is very similar to *The Bohemian Girl,* which Cather had referenced a few times earlier in her career, and for similarly intertextual purposes. The opera, taken from an episode in Goethe's *Wilhelm Meisters Lehrjahr,* involves a wealthy young man, Wilhelm, who encounters a group of gypsy entertainers in a small German village. One of the gypsies, a young girl, is clearly being held against her will and forced to dance for money. Wilhelm has an opportunity to talk to her. He asks her her name, but she can only reply "*Ils m'appellent Mignon, je n'ai pas d'autre nom*" ("I'm called Mignon, I have no other name"). He asks about her parents and where she's from, but she can't answer, instead telling him of a land she vaguely remembers from her youth, a place as much a fantasy as a real location.

Feeling sympathy for her, he purchases her freedom from the gypsy band, and she travels with him to a baron's castle where they will see Philine, Wilhelm's love interest, play Titania in a performance of *A Midsummer Night's Dream.* Mignon, in love with Wilhelm and jealous of his ardor for Philine, expresses a desire to see the castle burned to the ground. One of their companions, an old, semidemented musician named Lothario, hears this desire and obliges. Wilhelm rescues Mignon from the fire. In the final act, Wilhelm and company have taken Mignon to Italy, where they are residing at another castle as she recuperates from the trauma of the previous act. Wilhelm, seeing Mignon's speedy recovery, offers to buy the castle for her, but it turns out that Lothario is the rightful owner of the castle and Mignon is his long-lost daughter. Lothario's wife—Mignon's mother—had died after the girl had been kidnapped in her infancy, and he had gone mad with grief. However, seeing her in her home setting restores his memory and sanity. Wilhelm falls in love with Mignon, and the two live happily in her castle.

At the core of the opera's narrative is Mignon's recollection of a time happier and more splendid than she'd ever known since, a time and place rising to the level of fantasy. While we learn by the end of the opera that the memories were based in the reality of her actual infancy, she seems to have come to believe that the memories are too perfect to have been real. "Do you know the country," she asks Wilhelm, "where the orange flowers bloom? The land of golden fruit and crimson roses [. . .] a land of eternal spring." Men made of marble call to her and dance with her in the courtyard by moonlight. There is a perfectly clear lake bordered by a happy shore. There are birds and bees and, important for this comparison, a house waiting for her. Given the itineracy with which Mignon has lived, the stability of a permanent physical home is the most important element of the scene. But, importantly, it's an element that only exists in a more perfect and bygone time, a time and place too perfect to be real. It is only through a process of suffering and education that she is able to reclaim her home in reality.

Likewise for Godfrey St. Peter, who had been eight when his parents sold the family farm along one of the Great Lakes and carried him and his siblings "out to the wheat lands of central Kansas." The transition had nearly killed St. Peter: "Never could he forget the few moments on the train when that sudden, innocent blue across the sand dunes was dying for ever from his sight. It was like sinking for the third time. No later anguish, and he had had his share, went so deep or seemed so final. Even in his long, happy student years with the Thierault family in France, that stretch of blue water was the one thing he was home-sick for."[11] Like Mignon in her earliest memories of her home, St. Peter never outgrew the need to return to his origins. Though Cather focuses on St. Peter's career, family, and his relationship with Outland, his foundational experiences should not be overlooked; just as he carried his memories of the "innocent blue" of Lake Michigan with him to the prairie and to France, his need to feel a sense of homeplace persists to the present action of the novel, even to its enigmatic conclusion.

The novel's ending has puzzled readers. After the middle section, "Tom Outland's Story," the novel returns to St. Peter. He has declined to accompany his family on a European vacation, and while working in the attic office of his old rent house, he naps through a storm, during which wind blows out the pilot light of his heater and closes the window, filling the room with gas. The professor comes to in a haze, vaguely realizing his peril. He had been suffering an existential crisis. His career was behind him. His star pupil long dead. His wife and daughters had moved on to lives largely independent from his own. He finds peace in not raising up to save himself in the gas cloud and drifts off to sleep, reasoning that passively allowing himself to die doesn't amount to suicide. He later awakens, having been rescued by the housekeeper. In the end of the book, he considers that "his temporary release from consciousness seemed to have been beneficial. He had let something go."[12] What that *something* is never clarified. It's possible that he let go of his youth and drive, accepted that he'd lived out his best years already and had nothing to look forward to. Many readers seem to interpret the moment as a bit of antiheroic stoicism, a self-pitying, laissez-faire approach to fate. Carmen Skaggs writes that St. Peter "feels trapped and manipulated by his life as a husband and a father," which she contrasts with *Mignon,* which "concludes with the joyous anticipation of Mignon and Wilheim's [sic] marriage." Conversely, "*The Professor's House* offers the bleak vision of a middle-aged man who anticipates his death and longs to 'fall out' of 'all domestic and social relations, out of his place in the human family' [. . .]. Rather than seeking restoration with his family, he longs for a life of solitude. Ironically, the fanciful escape at the opera grounds St. Peter in the reality of his past, solidifying his isolation in the present."[13] Such a reading sees the repeated references to *Mignon* as an ironic contrast—Mignon's fancy-house made real and full versus St. Peter's refuge, the house in which he wrote his books and raised his kids, becoming hollow. This is an assessment bolstered by Cather's own assessment of the book as a "grim little tale." Certainly, the novel has grimness to go around, such as St. Peter's various interpersonal alienations or Outland's various disappointments and needless death. But the conclusion of the novel isn't necessarily the grim part, and *Mignon* might actually make the book more hopeful than it at first seems.

Though Mignon's character and experience might provide a contrast to those of St. Peter, they also could suggest the novel's underlying continuity: the theme of *finding home*. Mignon was kidnapped as a child and batted about the world while dreaming of a home that might only exist in the imagination, then that home turned out real. Tom Outland was an orphan and seemed destined for a life of minor jobs on the railway before he found a series of homes: the tutelage of Father Duchene, the domesticated Blue Mesa with Roddy Doyle and Henry Atkins, Hamilton with St. Peter and Rosalind, and, centrally, the Cliff City to which he feels a deep affinity. St. Peter's background is somewhat hazy, but it's evident that his earliest childhood was spent on Lake Michigan; at eight he was uprooted to Kansas; some time thereafter, presumably through his French-Canadian ancestral connections, he moved to France, where he lived with the Thierault family (to whom he refers as a "foster" family) for schooling before eventually returning to Lake Michigan. His youth isn't as orphanish as Mignon's or Tom's, but it's certainly rootless and itinerant, colored by a desire to get back to a fundamental homeplace. Somewhere along the way, however, St. Peter's career took over. He became focused on his scholarship and on his generally unhappy life in the classroom and in academic institutional governance. He became so fixated on his research that he openly referred to his books as his children, and he published his books to mounting acclamation. Most of the novel takes place with this reality in the background; St. Peter's life was his work, and now his work is realized, but his life persists. The ensuing existential crisis leads to his unhappiness for most of the book, but ensuing his near-death experience is the realization that only his career has been exhausted. He is now free to reconnect with *home*—both the physical community on Lake Michigan and the family relationships that had semisoured during his work life. He realizes that facing death had been "beneficial." He had "let something go [. . .] something very precious, that he could not consciously have relinquished"; he recognizes that his work had been too much a part of him; compulsively he could not have let it go, but having come so close to letting everything go, he has recalibrated. His family might not notice "that he was not the same man they had said good-bye to," when they return, but "at least, he felt the ground under his feet." Like Mignon, the novel ends with the professor returning to reality. Not a internal subjective reality like Mignon's fantasy castle or his own Spanish adventurers, but to the reality of home and family. In fact, if we look at the novel's earlier preoccupation with the Cimarosa opera—an originally ridiculous opera buffa that loses its buffa elements in a haze of Modernist anxiety—then a turn toward *Mignon* and the stable home life it represents might even render the novel unexpectedly optimistic.

Such subtle operatic references become the norm in Cather's later novels when she mentions opera at all. Giannone notes that her transition "from the dramatic and symphonic to the more intimate, lyrical forms, from the elaborate to the simple," is a move "familiar to lovers of music."[14] It is the move from heady youth to aged sagacity, or boiling blood to vein-borne sludge. Youthful Cather saw "the emotional and intentional plane of life" as "infinitely higher than the intellectual: It is the source of every great purpose, of every exalted aim." To reach it, one "must travel the old path to paradise, which leads down through hell."[15] Greatness is emotional and can be achieved only through suffering. As Slote wrote, "the world was haunted by a divinity, there were forces on the earth and in heaven greater and more mysterious than man could interpret. She chose action and power; emotion, sympathy, and life."[16] The world "is lessened by our failure to aspire and in 'these days of pigmies' no one seemed to be attempting greatness in literature, the 'Wagnerian flashes and thunders and tempests of Carlyle and the lofty repose and magnificent tranquility of Emerson.'"[17] (Slote adroitly points out that even Emerson's "repose" and "tranquility" are supercharged with "lofty" and "magnificent"—even states of rest had intensity for a young Cather.)

An aging Cather, however, refined the scope of her vision. It's possible to see her pivot to those more "intimate, lyrical forms"—be they musical, literary, or social—as a sort of resignation, an embrace of defeat, much as Godfrey St. Peter tends to be interpreted and as *My Mortal Enemy*—the grimness of which is indisputable—comes to terms with disappointment. Cather tried to move mountains in her first four plains novels. They might have been about Alexandra, Thea, Ántonia, and Claude, but the physical landscapes and the ideas they represented were indisputably grand. Cather's novels of the mid-1920s focus on personal turning points. Giannone notes that novels like *A Lost Lady*,

The Professor's House, and *My Mortal Enemy* all "treat failure and go so far as to honor it. Willa Cather's sense of defeat makes the hero a spiritual stranger in a transitional world; and while the *isolato* is certainly not new in her work, he is now a principal figure and a model of integrity where he was once minor and pathetic."[18] Previously she'd written of "separation as the means to individuality, to freedom, and to community of men. Now the hero converts isolation into a personal knowledge which bears no relation to the new, corrupt manner around him." It's a transition strangely in line with the *Ring.* In the latter, two operas feature Wotan, god-chief, ruling with confidence at first, then wavering after a series of missteps, only a few of which are his own fault. By the second half of the cycle, Wotan has become the Wanderer, moving about earth in disguise, watching the drama he's set in motion play out as he passively awaits his fate. That the *Ring* spends that first half establishing Siegfried's origin only to have the brash hero—a veritable icon of youthful vigor—ignominiously slaughtered at the end only serves to double the notion that life is, if long enough, a process from passion to passivity. Cather's heroes from Alexandra to Claude are all determined to bend life to their will; Marian Forrester, Godfrey St. Peter, and Myra Henshawe all discover the hollow after-effects of getting what one wants, awaiting death with some measure of complacent resignation.

When opera appears in these later novels, its presence is subtle. In the *Thaïs* and *Mignon* references in *One of Ours* and *The Professor's House,* they are almost like road signs to remind you what highway you're on, little clues to character and motivation. But Cather's use of opera was beginning to change. In *My Mortal Enemy,* the narrator, Nellie Birdseye, attends a New Year's Eve party in New York with her glamorous aunt Myra Henshawe at which the actor Helena Modjeska is present and has brought along an opera singer friend of hers. "Emelia," says Modjeska, "I think you must sing something. Something old . . . yes, from *Norma.*"[19] Someone goes to the piano and begins the accompaniment to "*Casta diva,*" "which begins so like the quivering of moonbeams on the water. It was the first air on our old music-box at home, but I had never heard it sung—and I have never heard it sung so beautifully since." Nellie heavily associates the music with the image of her aunt "crouching" next to the singer with her head in both hands, overcome with emotion. Nellie "thought of that aria as being mysteriously related to something in her nature that one rarely saw, but nearly always felt; a compelling, passionate, overmastering something for which I had no name." Though Myra is simply listening, wholly inactive, to the music, her response suggests a reservoir of emotional fortitude deeper than anyone else in the room. "When I wanted to recall powerfully that hidden richness in her," Nellie thinks, "I had only to close my eyes and sing to myself: '*Casta diva, casta diva!*'" Cather again reminds us of the ubiquity of opera—Nellie recognizes the air from her family music box in Parthia, Illinois. The aria itself, from the first act of Vincenzo Bellini's *Norma*, is sung by a druid priestess in Roman-occupied Gaul who has conceived two children by the Roman proconsul Pollione, thus breaking her sacred chastity vow. The opera plays out as a love triangle between Norma, Pollione, and Adalgisa, another priestess, with Norma eventually executed by fire for her transgressions and Pollione, who had rejected her previously but now overcome by her honor and courage, joining her in the flames. As always, Cather could have picked any number of operatic texts for that moment. Modjeska describes the aria as "something old"; *Norma* premiered in 1831, so it was old, but it was also out of fashion, having not been performed at the Met since 1892 (the first part of the novel, in which this scene appears, is set shortly before Modjeska's death in 1909). It is memory upon memory: the ancient subject to the old opera to the music box to the New Year's Eve party, and on for as long as Nellie remembers her aunt. Some have seen an intertextual approach to this moment similar to how Cather had used opera elsewhere. For example, Richard Giannone makes a thorough but somewhat attenuated case for Norma's strain between the forces of sacred and profane love mimicking Myra's crypto-Catholicism strained by her husband's nonbelief.[20] However, it is a stretch to view Myra's emotional reaction to the music coming from a transposition of herself and the ill-fated druidess. Rather, Myra is a woman beginning to realize the depth of her unhappiness and the long-term inevitability of that unhappiness. It is the *emotion* of the music, rather than the drama of its source text, that overcomes her. Cather's use of opera is still important, but it's no longer intertextual; Cather is moving away from opera as a way to import dramatic meaning from one story to another. Instead, she is beginning to see opera as musical rather than dramatic expression—*prima la musica e poi le parole.*

This trend is certainly evident in *Lucy Gayheart*, Cather's penultimate novel and the second, after *The Song of the Lark*, to focus on the development of a singer. It is, in fact, a sort of truncated revisiting of *The Song of the Lark*, but one that shows that Cather had herself developed musically in key ways. A talented young woman (this time Lucy Gayheart) from a small plains town (this time

Haverford) travels to Chicago to study music. As in *The Song of the Lark,* she develops personally and artistically and even has an artistic epiphany related to Wagner. The cultural life of the city is contrasted with that of the small town. Some nexus between art and romance is tangentially addressed, though such is much more to the fore for Lucy than for Thea. There are a few key differences, however. Most importantly, Lucy drowns. Thea lives, as best as we can tell, happily ever after, at least within the scope of how a perfectionist like Thea might do so. So the novels' final outcomes are entirely dissimilar. Where Thea went after her music "like a terrier after rats," even as a child, Lucy is "talented, but too careless and light-hearted to take herself very seriously." Thea saw opera as a path to transcendent perfection. Lucy "thought of music as a natural form of pleasure, and as a means of earning money." Finally, *The Song of the Lark* is a novel about opera; in *Lucy Gayheart,* Cather replaces opera with art song.

The distinction between opera and song is more than one of scale. As the composer Daron Hagen, who has composed both art songs and operas, compared them, "an opera is a mural; an art song is an exquisite miniature, requiring the tiniest of brush strokes."[21] If that seems like a slight against opera, it isn't. Rather it's simply the recognition that even a modest opera performance is a multiparty affair engaging a spectrum of artistic elements. Consider the sort of performance that often took place in the Red Cloud Opera House (the sort that Cather describes at one point in *Lucy Gayheart*): There could be a conductor who doubled as a piano player (there might be no orchestra), and with him might be a half a dozen performers, who doubled up in roles and also served as costumers and stage technicians. But even in that extremely streamlined affair, the audience was observing multiple singers, some potentially playing multiple characters; there would be scenery and props; the pianist/conductor would have used a range of theatrical piano techniques to evoke a variety of orchestral instruments; and the words would have demanded attention both in their poetic technique and in their dramatic revelation. The art song, that "exquisite miniature" with its tiny brush strokes, is a singer and an accompanist. The performance is poetry blended into melody, harmony, and rhythm. It is far more exposed and intimate, both because it is smaller and because it is music with poetry, not music with drama. Moving from opera in *The Song of the Lark* to *Lieder* in *Lucy Gayheart* is a meaningful shift from Thea, godlike, commanding the full force of artistic revelation, to Lucy as accompanist learning to move as one with her singer, Clement Sebastian. It indicates that Cather was more committed to her refined *démeublé*ism, less given to ecstatic proclamations about that "one unaccountable thing" in humankind. As Giannone describes it, *Gesamtkunstwerk* is no longer Cather's aim, but rather something "narrower and more personal": "In the *Lied* she finds the fusion of language and music—meaning heightened by melody—which she sought to achieve in her own work in her own way. In its melodic line the *Lied* has the classical simplicity that Cather came to prefer."[22]

Cather makes this transition more or less explicit when Lucy attends a recital given by Clement of Schubert's *Die Winterreise* (*The Winter Journey*), the song cycle most associated with the character and the novel as a whole. Lucy hears the cycle as an integral whole for the first time, "feeling that this was not an interpretation, this was the thing itself, with one man and one nature behind every song."[23] It is not an interpretation any more than it is perception; rather, the songs are independent existences, things-in-themselves, and by bringing them to life, Lucy experiencing them just as Clement and others experience them, they all become part of a reality beyond representation. Nothing could be more intimate. Opera is a carnival; song is a candlelit dinner. Clement's singing "was not dramatic, in any way she knew. Sebastian did not identify himself with this melancholy youth; he presented him as if he were a memory, not to be brought too near into the present. One felt a long distance between the singer and the scenes he was recalling, a long perspective."[24] Dramatizing a narrative is a way of explaining it. Such presupposes a gulf to be crossed. It requires Dr. Archie to experience something akin to "buck-fever" to fully communicate its meaning. But a sequence of art songs, as Cather describes their effect here, is emotional transportation without the need for dress-up and stage effects. She is both divorcing the artificiality of opera and conceding that artistic truth is more a matter of restraint than one of abandon.

As with her operatic references, Cather associating *Lucy Gayheart* with *Die Winterreise* is meaningful. The long sequence of twenty-four songs set to poems by Wilhelm Müller follows the wanderings of a desolate figure over an unspecified length of time. We do not know who the wanderer is or what has precipitated his peripateticism, only that "he seems to grow older and increasingly tired. His travels exist in a void; with each new song, life seems to have less meaning. As the cycle winds toward its close, the traveler draws nearer to death" with ominous signs like "the cemetery that symbolizes an inn, [. . .] the forbidding suns whose setting forecasts light departing from life; and, finally, the mysterious organ-grinder, whose presence might symbolize death itself."[25] Like a Poe vignette, the sequence is eerie, unsettling largely because it lacks a clear direction and narrative line. Schubert, first presenting the songs to his friends, invited them to hear, in his words, "a cycle of horrible songs." No doubt Schubert had his own mortality in mind; he died of a long-since-contracted venereal disease only a year later at the age of thirty-one. And no doubt Cather had mortality in mind, as well, both her own (she was in her sixties by the novel's publication) and her character's (*Lucy Gayheart* is the only novel other than *Alexander's Bridge* and *One of Ours* to feature the untimely death of its protagonist). Beyond the obvious theme of death, however, *Winterreise* is a journey through a land without warmth, physically and metaphorically.

Before leaving for Chicago, Lucy rides in a sleigh with Harry Gordon, hometown hero and suitor. He has rigged the sleigh with bells to appeal to her—"very musical bells," Cather notes—but the effect of this is that she wants no conversation, merely quiet to contemplate the night sky and to consider her future:

> In the darkening sky she had seen the first star come out; it brought her heart into her throat. That point of silver light spoke to her like a signal, released another kind of life and feeling which did not belong here. It overpowered her. With a mere thought she had reached that star and it had answered, recognition had flashed between. Something knew, then, in the unknowing waste: something had always known, forever! That joy of saluting what is far above one was an eternal thing, not merely something that had happened to her ignorance and her foolish heart.
>
> The flash of understanding lasted but a moment. Then everything was confused again.[26]

Lucy briefly comes into contact with some celestial truth, something beyond her and Haverford, something suggestive of what-will-be, then that clarity dissipates and her own plans return to confusion. Where Alexandra and Thea never had a moment's doubt, Lucy is not a creature of destiny, and her life will swing between poles of uncertainty. She moves from Haverford and Harry, to Chicago and Clement, then back to Haverford; Clement dies, Harry spurns her, and she dies. This sequence happens over a series of two winters, one in which she moves to

Chicago and has a musical and personal awakening, one in which she returns to Haverford and sees that awakening come to nothing. As Giannone writes, "the invigorating wintry cold of Chicago carried Lucy's spirits on lifts of wind, but the psychological frigidity of the small town stings the girl and forcers her to bundle up into psychic withdrawal. Unfortunately the cold does not anaesthetize."[27] Lucy, through her exposure to the wider world in Chicago—where "the air trembled like a tuning-fork with unimaginable possibilities"[28]—and through her relationship with Clement, is alienated from the small town. Like the speaker in *Winterreise,* she has become an aimless wanderer, and, upon Clement's death, one operating in a vague and unsettlingly dreary landscape.

The shift to *Lieder,* however, isn't absolute. Cather doesn't completely abandon opera in the novel. In fact, *Lucy Gayheart* actually mentions more opera titles than any other single work of Cather's other than *The Song of the Lark.* Even so, the specific operas referenced and the way in which they are used only serves to suggest her departure from the form. Before Lucy leaves Haverford, Harry offers to visit her in Chicago and take her to the opera every night for a week. Opera, in this sense, is a pastime and a social plaything, not taken seriously, akin to Nelly Deane saying that she's "going to live in Chicago, and take singing lessons, and go to operas, and do all those nice things." When Harry does visit, they go to *Traviata*—that which Cather had called both "clap-trap" and "heartbreaking" in *Ántonia,* something emotional but juvenile—and *Lohengrin.* Lucy has some measure of awakening with the Wagner opera, but it's mostly an awakening to how little she likes Harry: "Before the first act was half over she was longing to be alone; this wasn't the kind of opera to be hearing with Harry. She found herself leaning away from him as far as possible. The music kept bringing back things she used to feel in Sebastian's studio; belief in an invisible, inviolable world."[29] Harry, with whom she'd earlier squabbled over the validity of nonrepresentative art on a museum trip and who had already outed himself as a troglodyte, has nothing more meaningful to say than "that tenor's fine, now isn't he?" Lucy, with tears "still shining" in her eyes, whispers, "yes, he believes in it." Though Harry was "behaving so well," she was "beginning to feel hostile toward him." Patronizingly, he finds her being deeply affected by the opera was "that sort of thing [he would have found] ridiculous in a man, but in a girl it was rather attractive." But the difference between Lucy's and Harry's reactions to the performance isn't a division of man and woman any more than city and country; as with so many of Cather's artists, some few are simply more deeply endowed with emotional understanding than others. The fact that they are attending *Lohengrin,* an opera about a knight who is, by the narrative, literally God's gift to women, only serves to underscore how far short Harry measures.

The other opera titles referenced in the story seem to be mentioned only in passing and generally represent either a stretched definition of the term *opera* (e.g., three references to the Mendelssohn oratorio *Elijah*), an opera aria treated as a stand-alone song (*"Vision fugitive"* from Massenet's *Hériodiade*), or light opera. "That Gilbert and Sullivan stuff," says Mr. Gayheart, "I can't see much in it. [. . .] If you want something light and amusing, now, there is *Die Fledermaus.* Or *La Belle Hélène.* You never heard it, Lucy? I was crazy about that opera when I was a boy. *The Bohemian Girl* is a little old-fashioned, maybe, but it's very nice."[30] While the aria from *Hériodiade,* a passionate declaration of love, probably is meant to indicate some emerging eroticism between Clement and Lucy—he puts it on the rack for her to play as a contrast to "Largo al factotum"—the references to light opera is a catalog of easy entertainment: Arthur Sullivan, Johann Strauss, Jacques Offenbach. It is a way of dismissing opera. Having set the scene thus, Gayheart accompanies his daughter to the Haverford Opera House (Cather makes a point that "the theatre in every little Western town was then called an opera house"), where they attend a performance of *The Bohemian Girl.* One attuned to Cather's use of opera in her work should immediately see this for what it is: a return to youth, to that earnest place where she could reference tinny music about a gypsy-kidnapped princess to explain emotion on the prairie. Putting Lucy in the Haverford Opera House, where she'd had her own commencement exercises just four years earlier, where folding chairs had just been installed in the place of straight-back wooden ones, accompanied by her father, is a way of Cather revisiting the Red Cloud Opera House with the appraising eye of experience, especially given that Lucy had just returned from Chicago, now equipped herself to judge her hometown.

The conductor of the traveling troupe doubles as the pianist. The chorus is "fair" and the "tenor had his good points." It is "a little road company," as Cather characterizes it, one of the dozens fading in and out of obscurity in small towns like Hanover, Red Cloud, and Moonstone, a fraternity of Wunsches. But it's to be expected that much of our greatest art happens out of the broad public eye; there's simply too much talent in the world, too much ambition, for all the best performers to appear only on the best stages. The Gayhearts are treated to a soprano, "fair skinned [. . .], slender and graceful, but far from young," who captivates them. Though Lucy has by now been exposed to performers at the highest level, she is still impressed. Despite the fact that "her voice was worn, to be sure, like her face, and there was not much physical sweetness left in it [. . .] there was another kind of sweetness; a sympathy, a tolerant understanding. She gave the old songs, even the most hackneyed, their full value." She treats the aria "I dreamt that I dwelt in marble halls" as a special piece, articulating delicately where the rhythm is—now in Cather's estimation—"too regular" and gives "freshness to the foolish old words because she phrased intelligently; she was tender with their sentimentality, as if they were pressed flowers which might fall apart if roughly handled." This passage suggests not only Lucy's return to an emotional homeplace, but Cather's as well, this time from a position of greater musical understanding. Lucy is enjoying outdated, frivolous opera, but is making astute judgments about the manner in which it is performed, noting especially, as John Flannigan has observed, the rhythmic competence of the singer who avoids the traps of simple, "too regular" accompaniments. Lucy has been exposed to sophisticated music by this point, as had Cather, music more sophisticated than Balfe. But her true appreciation of music arrives only when she's able to dissolve the bounds of "high" and "low" art to see sophistication in simple perfection.[31]

Lucy wonders why she bothers to sing "this humdrum music to humdrum people." Her talent could not possibly be appreciated by the average Haverford theatergoer. And yet she sings not for the audience, not even for herself, but for the art: "This poor little singer had lost everything: youth, good looks, position, the high notes of her voice. And yet she sang so well! Lucy wanted to be up there on the stage with her, helping her to do it. A wild kind of excitement flared up in her. She felt she must run away tonight, by any train, back to a world that strove after excellence—the world out of which this woman must have fallen."[32] Lucy goes through a series of epiphanies in the novel: the enigmatic starlight, the infatuation with Clement, the realization that Harry is "humdrum," and now the idea that art is a thing itself, existing freely of human expression and worthy of performance not for the performer's profit or the audience's accolades, but for the living expression in its own right. That this unnamed soprano sings to humdrum people doesn't matter; Thea railed against the inability of even the most sophisticated audiences to fully understand. In this moment, Lucy realizes that beauty is its own justification. It is the tenderness of how *The Bohemian Girl* is treated in this scene that contrasts with the absence of opera in Book III, making Harry's denouement silent beyond the mere absence of sound.

Lucy Gayheart is a good novel in its own right, but it's also unnerving for someone who knows Cather's work well. It's so obviously an attempt to reconnect with the blastwrought confidence of her "Wagnerian flashes and thunders and tempests" of art. It is a stabilizing of the uncompromising upwardness of Thea Kronborg without Thea's tunnel vision. There was Alexandra's triumph, followed by Thea's, then the various pioneer women's stories around Ántonia's world, then Claude's battlefield death believing, however erringly, in the moral validity of his quest. But these heroes precede Marian Forrester smiling through a flailing marriage, Godfrey St. Peter bidding a fruitful career farewell, Myra Henshawe scowling at her husband from her deathbed. Cather followed these with two historical novels set in New Mexico and Canada, clearly needing a break from the bleakness of her overcontemplated experienced reality. And then, in her second-to-last novel, an apparent attempt to get back to the passion under the white mulberry tree, the emotional gut-kicks of *Traviata* in a Lincoln playhouse, the grand ascendancy of the Wagnerian soprano moving into a realm of superhuman expression appreciable only by angels' ears. But in *Lucy*, opera, the means by which Cather had achieved those high aims in the 1910s, is replaced by *Lieder*, delicate and personal, and that novel never attains the rush of its forebears. Lucy, like Cather herself, "is no longer a despairing little creature standing in the icy wind and lifting beseeching eyes. [. . .] She is no longer near. [. . .] She has receded to the far horizon line, along with all the fine things of youth, which do not change."[33] Those fine things of youth don't change, but they don't move on with us, either. In her later career Cather cautiously set aside the operatic tendencies of her youth, the things she still understood, but no longer felt.

CONCLUSION

Men travel faster now, but I do not know if they go to better things.
—*Death Comes for the Archbishop*

J n an obscure corner of literary history rests Truman Capote's last work, written a day before his death at age fifty-nine. It is a reminiscence of the time he met Willa Cather.[1]

Capote would have been in his late teenage years, working as a "very young journalist" as he describes his position in the Cather essay, though really he was an office boy for the *New Yorker*. He had been spending time at the New York Society Library, researching for a "historical book" about his Confederate ancestors, where he'd often noticed a "blue-eyed lady," with a "wholesome and countrified" face, perpetually clad in tweed suits and a "beautiful sable coat which she almost never took off," and adorned by a "handsome turquoise necklace." Having left the library simultaneously one day, the two of them agreed to have tea—Capote ended up with a double martini—to wait out a bout of bad weather. Having neglected formal introductions, they began to discuss literature. After the young Capote rattled off his favorite world authors—Flaubert, Turgenev, Proust, etc.—she asked whether there were any American authors he enjoyed. Of course, he loved Willa Cather, citing *My Ántonia*, *Death Comes for the Archbishop*, *A Lost Lady*, and *My Mortal Enemy* as favorites.

"I ought to tell you," said his companion, "I wrote those books."

"Of course she was Willa Cather!" he remembered thinking. "Those flawless sky-like eyes. The bobbed hair; the square face with the firm chin. [. . .] I swallowed my double martini in one gulp." Eventually they walked on, as far as her residence at 570 Park Avenue. She invited him to dinner the following Thursday, requesting he bring some of his writing. He did so, and the unfinished remembrance ends with Capote at Cather's home, meeting Edith Lewis, commenting on the "masses" of flowers all around the apartment and the fact that "beautifully bound books line[d] all walls of the living room." What happened at dinner is lost to posterity. The encounter occurred around five years before Cather's death, at least a few years before Capote attained any level of literary notoriety, and there's no record of the two ever communicating again, though Capote, years later, referred to Cather as "one of my first intellectual friends" (Capote was known for exaggerating the depth of an acquaintance).

Regardless, years later, in 1984, on the eve of his death, Cather was on Capote's mind. He remembered her as she tends to be remembered: wholesome, broad-faced, and countrified. A prairie gal with a Western accent. Approaching her apartment before the dinner party, Capote recollected, he "was still amazed to think that Willa Cather wore sable coats and occupied a Park Avenue apartment. (I had always imagined her as living on a quiet street in Red Cloud, Nebraska.)" That is the Cather that persists in popular memory, a sturdy girl in a forever-field.

But Cather lived in Nebraska for only thirteen years. She lived in New York City for forty. While two-thirds of her novels take place in part on the prairie, one-third does not at all, and only two of her novels are *thoroughly* frontier in orientation. Among her collected and uncollected short fiction, the plains represent a minority setting, and her voluminous cultural criticism and commentary seldom mentions Nebraska or its adjacent states. Open to any random page in Cather's oeuvre and it's statistically unlikely to take place on the Great Plains. As early as 1896, she was referring to Red Cloud as "Siberia," and when her writings address the small-town prairie world, they typically do so with at least a measure of ambivalence, often hostility. Certainly Cather's most visible contribution to American letters is having made the rural Midwest a palatable setting for literary art. But that by no means is an accurate appraisal of her total body of work, and focusing on Cather as a rural author risks overlooking a large body of beautiful and important writing. Cather is no more just a plains writer than Hemingway is a guy who only wrote about fishing. And yet Nebraska has stuck to Cather the way that Mississippi—much more justifiably—has stuck to Faulkner.

Cather's style remained fairly consistent during her career. As Merrill Maguire Skaggs noted, "after mentioning line, balance, smoothness, and rhythm, one feels the words which can apply [to Cather's style] are exhausted"; "Cather's fictions arrive in the hard absoluteness of a very simple polished stone form;

each work appears to provoke scarcely more comment than, 'What a beautiful sculpture.'"[2] Due to her apparent straightforwardness of sentence-level style (though one should be careful not to underestimate her verbal, syntactic, and perspectival complexity), Cather is sometimes seen as a workmanlike author with a narrow range. But no other author has a portfolio as diverse in subject matter as "Coming, Aphrodite!," *O Pioneers!*, and *Shadows on the Rock*. No other author was as equally comfortable stepping into male and female perspectives, young and old, urban and rural. No other author's private life (barring notable antisocials like Salinger—Cather was very socially oriented) was so guarded, now so speculative.

Cather's work is complex in both geography and subject. When Bernice Slote wrote that Cather's being eventually labeled a "classicist, a Jamesian sophisticate, and the reserved stylist of the novel démeublé" was "one of the great jokes of literary criticism" because Cather, even at fifty, was still a primitive, she's only partly right. Cather never lost her frontier bona fides, but she adopted so much more into her literary method, selective in detail like James, cognizant of the long stretch of culture and appreciative of refined simplicity like a classicist, all while bearing on the deep understanding of the brute beauty of nature that one has when one grows up on the edge of one's own civilization, a primitive outlook Cather often successfully carried over into her understanding of urban and suburban life. She wrote often of the prairie in its negative comparison to the city; she wrote often of the callousness and insincerity of the city relative to the prairie. She wrote of the stoic purity of the desert and the lively sophistication of the coastal hub. She is perhaps the only major author to split her characters evenly between types: as many bushwhackers as tea drinkers, as many children as old folks, as many men as women, as many defiant wills as resigned pessimisms. But what binds the many threads of Cather's identity as author is her compulsion toward art as a universal among the human experience. Overwhelmingly, art meant music. And at least as often as not, music meant opera.

Opera itself is a victim of typecasting, so often portrayed as a performing art in which attendance itself is presumed performative, a space for people to go to prove they can—financially or intellectually. But the history of opera doesn't bear that out. It began as an intimate form for wealthy Italian intellectuals, but quickly became an internationally popular phenomenon built on popular tastes. In its nineteenth-century heyday, opera was a pop culture common denominator, including in the United States. Venues for musical theater numbered in the thousands stateside in the late nineteenth century; dozens of opera companies worked steadily, traveling the coasts and heartland, performing grand and light opera, some growing wealthy for their efforts; music racks on pianos across the country featured piano reductions of Rossini, Verdi, and Wagner. For Cather, the Midwestern opera experience was formative, giving her an entrée into global culture, while starting her at a point of exceeding modesty so that from Red Cloud it was easy to look up to Lincoln and from there to Chicago, on to New York, and on to the undefinable limits of human expressive potential. Opera gave her a spectrum of Art upon which she could build her kingdom in her early, exploratory years, scaffold up to mastery, and look back on as a youthful exuberance. Opera was a pinnacle in her work through the 1910s, seen as a distant peak behind her in her middle career, and a comfortable reminder of youthful aspiration in her later years. In a 1929 letter, Cather reflected that

> when I go about among little Nebraska towns (and the little towns, not the big cities, are the people), the thing I miss most is the opera house. No number of filling stations or moving picture theatres can console me for the loss of the opera house. To be sure, the opera house was dark for most of the year, but that made its events only more exciting. Half a dozen times during each winter—in the larger towns much oftener—a traveling stock company settled down at the local hotel and thrilled and entertained us for a week.[3]

Those little road companies, however, didn't entertain her only for a week. They stayed with her, propelling her to grander performances and grander aspirations for her own work. They were frontier entertainments, but part of something more. John Dizikes described the culture that opera made possible in the both small towns "lifeline to the great world beyond the plains or the mountains, a part of the tradition which stretched from San Cassiano to San Francisco."[4] Cather's early introduction to opera helped give her a sense of artistic possibility and the aspiration to pursue it.

ACKNOWLEDGMENTS

Many thanks to the following for their contributions, direct and indirect, to this project: the Faculty Research and Lecture Committee of Union College, Barbourville, Kentucky, for its support in the earliest phase of my research on Willa Cather's relationship to opera; everyone at Louisiana State University Press and in particular James Long; John Flannigan, whose insightful suggestions have made this a more accurate, complete, and useful book; Stephanie Gibson, whose editing and encouragement moved this project from stalled to complete in record time; and my family, Presley, Erin, Katie, Mom, and Dad—without my compulsive need to impress you, I'd probably never get anything done.

APPENDIX 1

A List of Operas and Oratorios Mentioned
in Fiction by Willa Cather

Composer	Title	Cather's Work
Michael William Balfe	*The Bohemian Girl*	"The Bohemian Girl"
		Lucy Gayheart
Vincenzo Bellini	*Norma*	*My Ántonia*
		My Mortal Enemy
Hector Berlioz	*Le Damnation de Faust*	"The Prodigies"
Domenico Cimarosa	*Il Matrimonio Segreto*	*The Professor's House*
Claude Debussy	*Pelléas and Mélisande*	"Double Birthday"
Gaetano Donizetti	*Lucia di Lammermoor*	*The Song of the Lark*
Friedrich von Flotow	*Martha*	*My Ántonia*
		"Paul's Case"
Christoph Willibald Gluck	*Orfeo ed Euridice*	"148 Charles Street"
		The Song of the Lark
Charles Gounod	*Faust*	"A Gold Slipper"
		"Paul's Case"
		O, Pioneers!
	Romeo et Juliette	"The Prodigies"
George Frideric Handel	*Messiah*	*The Song of the Lark*
	Queen Esther	"The Joy of Nelly Deane"
Joseph Haydn	*The Creation*	*The Song of the Lark*
Edward Jakobowski	*Erminie*	*The Song of the Lark*
Reginald de Koven	*Robin Hood*	*My Ántonia*
		The Song of the Lark
Ruggero Leoncavallo	*I Pagliacci*	"Coming, Aphrodite!"
		"Paul's Case"

Composer	Title	Cather's Work
Pietro Mascagni	*Cavalleria Rusticana*	"Eric Hermannson's Soul"
Jules Massenet	*Hériodiade*	*Lucy Gayheart*
	Manon	"The Diamond Mine"
		The Song of the Lark
	Thaïs	*One of Ours*
Felix Mendelssohn	*Elijah*	*Lucy Gayheart*
Giacomo Meyerbeer	*Les Huguenots*	"A Wagner Matinée"
Wolfgang Amadeus Mozart	*Don Giovanni*	"The Diamond Mine"
Modeste Mussorgsky	*Boris Godunov*	"A Chance Meeting"
Jacques Offenbach	*La Belle Hélène*	*Lucy Gayheart*
	Les Contes d'Hoffmann	"Scandal"
Robert Planquette	*The Chimes of Normandy*	"Old Mrs. Harris"
Amilcare Ponchielli	*La Gioconda*	*The Song of the Lark*
Johann Strauss	*Die Fledermaus*	*Lucy Gayheart*
Arthur Sullivan	*H. M. S. Pinafore*	*Lucy Gayheart*
		"Two Friends"
	The Mikado	*Alexander's Bridge*
Ambroise Thomas	*Mignon*	*The Professor's House*
Guiseppe Verdi	*Aida*	*Lucy Gayheart*
	Otello	*Lucy Gayheart*
	La Traviata	*Lucy Gayheart*
		My Ántonia
	Il Trovatore	*Alexander's Bridge*
		The Song of the Lark
		"A Wagner Matinée"
	Rigoletto	*My Ántonia*
		"Old Mrs. Harris"
		"Paul's Case"
Richard Wagner	*Das Rheingold*	"A Death in the Desert"
		"The Diamond Mine"
		"The Garden Lodge"
		The Song of the Lark
	Der Fliegende Holländer	"A Wagner Matinée"
	Götterdammerung	*The Song of the Lark*

Composer	Title	Cather's Work
	Lohengrin	*The Song of the Lark*
		Lucy Gayheart
	Die Meistersinger von Nürnberg	"A Wagner Matinée"
		The Song of the Lark
	Parsifal	"The Garden Lodge"
	Tannhäuser	*The Song of the Lark*
		"A Wagner Matinée"
	Tristan und Isolde	"A Chance Meeting"
		"The Diamond Mine"
		The Song of the Lark
		"A Wagner Matinée"
	Die Walküre	"The Garden Lodge"
		The Song of the Lark
Carl Maria von Weber	*Euryanthe*	"A Wagner Matinée"

Note: Titles are provided in full and in their original languages, unless it is clear that Cather is referencing an opera translated into English. Opera titles mentioned in creative nonfiction are included, but those referenced in critical works are not.

APPENDIX 2

Operas and Oratorios in Cather's Work

"The Prodigies" (1897): *Le Damnation de Faust* (Berlioz), *Romeo et Juliette* (Gounod)

"Eric Hermannson's Soul" (1900): *Cavalleria Rusticana* (Mascagni)

"A Death in the Desert" (1903): *Das Rheingold* (Wagner)

"A Wagner Matinée" (1904): *Les Huguenots* (Meyerbeer), *Il Trovatore* (Verdi), *Der Fliegende Holländer* (Wagner), *Die Meistersinger von Nürnberg* (Wagner), *Siegfried* (Wagner), *Tannhäuser* (Wagner), *Tristan und Isolde* (Wagner), *Euryanthe* (Weber)

"The Garden Lodge" (1905): *Parsifal* (Wagner), *Das Rheingold* (Wagner) *Die Walküre* (Wagner)

"Paul's Case" (1905): *Martha* (Flotow), *Faust* (Gounod), *I Pagliacci* (Leoncavallo), *Rigoletto* (Verdi)

"The Joy of Nelly Deane" (1911): *Queen Esther* (Handel)

Alexander's Bridge (1911): *The Mikado* (Sullivan), *Il Trovatore* (Verdi)

"The Bohemian Girl" (1912): *The Bohemian Girl* (Balfe),

O Pioneers! (1912): *Faust* (Gounod)

The Song of the Lark (1915): *Lucia di Lammermoor* (Donizetti), *Orfeo ed Euridice* (Gluck), *Messiah* (Handel), *The Creation* (Haydn), *Erminie* (Jakobowski), *Robin Hood* (de Koven), *Manon* (Massenet), *La Giocanda* (Ponchielli), *Il Trovatore* (Verdi), *Die Meistersinger von Nürnberg* (Wagner), *Das Rheingold* (Wagner), *Götterdammerung* (Wagner), *Lohengrin* (Wagner), *Tannhäuser* (Wagner), *Tristan und Isolde* (Wagner), *Die Walküre* (Wagner)

"The Diamond Mine" (1916): *Manon* (Massenet), *Don Giovanni* (Mozart), *Das Rheingold* (Wagner), *Tristan und Isolde* (Wagner)

"A Gold Slipper" (1917): *Faust* (Gounod)

My Ántonia (1918): *Norma* (Bellini), *Martha* (Flotow), *Robin Hood* (de Koven), *La Traviata* (Verdi), *Rigoletto* (Verdi)

"Scandal" (1919): *I Pagliacci* (Leoncavallo), *Les Contes d'Hoffmann* (Offenbach)

"Coming, Aphrodite!" (1920): *I Pagliacci* (Leoncavallo)

"148 Charles Street" (1922): *Orfeo ed Euridice* (Gluck)

"A Chance Meeting" (1922): *Boris Godunov* (Mussorgsky), *Tristan und Isolde* (Wagner)

One of Ours (1922): *Thaïs* (Massenet)

The Professor's House (1925): *Il Matrimonio Segreto* (Cimarosa), *Mignon* (Thomas)

My Mortal Enemy (1926): *Norma* (Bellini)

"Double Birthday" (1929): *Pelléas and Mélisande* (Debussy)

"Old Mrs. Harris" (1932): *The Chimes of Normandy* (Planquette), *Rigoletto* (Verdi)

"Two Friends" (1932): *H. M. S. Pinafore* (Sullivan)

Lucy Gayheart (1935): *The Bohemian Girl* (Balfe), *Hériodiade* (Massenet), *Elijah* (Mendelssohn), *La Belle Hélène* (Offenbach), *Die Fledermaus* (Strauss), *H. M. S. Pinafore* (Sullivan), *Aida* (Verdi), *Otello* (Verdi), *La Traviata* (Verdi), *Lohengrin* (Wagner)

NOTES

CHAPTER 1
Cather and Opera

Note to epigraph: Ann Satterthwaite, *Local Glories: Opera Houses on Main Street Where Art and Community Meet* (New York: Oxford University Press, 2016), 9. This text incorrectly identifies Cather as being twelve years old in 1888.

1. L. Brent Bohlke, ed., *Willa Cather in Person: Interviews, Speeches, and Letters* (Lincoln: University of Nebraska Press, 1990), 184.

2. Bohlke, *Willa Cather in Person,* 185.

3. Ann Satterthwaite, *Local Glories: Opera Houses on Main Street Where Art and Community Meet* (New York: Oxford University Press, 2016), 41.

4. Vincent Giroud, *French Opera: A Short History* (New Haven, CT: Yale University Press, 2010), 213.

5. "The Chimes of Normandy," *Internet Broadway Database.* Accessed October 9, 2019. https://www.ibdb.com/broadway-production/the-chimes-of-normandy-412125.

6. Donald Jay Grout and Hermine Weigel Williams, *A Short History of Opera,* 4th eed. (New York: Columbia University Press, 2003), 486.

7. Edith Lewis, *Willa Cather Living: A Personal Record* (Lincoln: University of Nebraska Press, 2000), 74.

8. Bernice Slote, ed. *The Kingdom of Art: Willa Cather's First Principles and Critical Statements, 1893–1896* (Lincoln: University of Nebraska Press, 1966), 31.

9. John H. Flannigan, "'Before Its Romanzas Have Become Street Music': Cather and Verdi's *Falstaff,* Chicago, 1895," *Cather Studies,* 9 (2011), 285; Slote, *Kingdom,* 33.

10. Willa Cather, *The Song of the Lark,* in *Willa Cather: Early Novels and Stories,* ed. Sharon O'Brien (New York: Library of America, 1987), 509.

11. Bohlke, *Willa Cather in Person,* 68–72.

12. James Woodress, *Willa Cather: A Literary Life* (Lincoln: University of Nebraska Press, 1987), 476.

13. Willa Cather, prefatory note to *Not Under Forty,* in *Willa Cather: Stories, Poems, & Other Writings,* ed. Sharon O'Brien (New York: Library of America, 1992), 812.

14. Woodress, *Willa Cather,* 250.

15. Slote, *Kingdom,* 135.

16. Willa Cather, *My Ántonia*, in *Willa Cather: Early Novels and Stories*, ed. Sharon O'Brien (New York: Library of America, 1987), 731.

17. Cather, *My Ántonia*, 741.

18. Cather, *My Ántonia*, 743.

19. Gary Schmidgall, *Shakespeare & Opera* (New York: Oxford University Press, 1990), xi.

20. "American Christmas," *Time Magazine* 78, no. 26 (December 29, 1961), 27.

21. Woodress, *Willa Cather*, 54. Alex Ross has uncovered much about Albert Gustav Balthasar Schindelmeisser. He was born in Pest in 1842—his father had been a clarinetist, composer, and conductor who often presented Wagner operas—and arrived in the United States in 1862. He taught music and modern languages at Lawrence University in Wisconsin before beginning an itinerary that took him through Kansas, Iowa, and Nebraska, where he ended up in Red Cloud in the mid-1880s. He is last recorded as a piano tuner in Nashville in 1898. Alex Ross, *Wagnerism: Art and Politics in the Shadow of Music* (New York: Farrar, 2020), 327–328.

22. Woodress, *Willa Cather*, 55.

23. Cather, *Song of the Lark*, 634.

24. Cather, *Song of the Lark*, 306.

25. Willa Cather, "Uncle Valentine," in *Willa Cather: Stories, Poems, & Other Writings*, ed. Sharon O'Brien (New York: Library of America, 1992), 242.

26. William M. Curtin, ed., *The World and the Parish*, vol. 1 (Lincoln: University of Nebraska Press, 1970), 52.

27. John H. Flannigan, "Cather's Evolving Ear: Music Reheard in the Late Fiction," *Cather Studies* 12 (2020), https://cather.unl.edu/scholarship/catherstudies/12/cs012.flannigan. Flannigan, "'Before Its Romanzas,'" 284.

28. Willa Cather, "A Wagner Matinée," in *Willa Cather: Stories, Poems, & Other Writings*, ed. Sharon O'Brien (New York: Library of America, 1992), 494.

29. Philip Kennicott, introduction to *Music in Willa Cather's Fiction*, by Richard Giannone (Lincoln: University of Nebraska Press, 2001), vii.

30. Kennicott, introduction, viii.

31. Woodress, *Willa Cather*, 73.

32. Cather's enormous journalistic output during her time in Lincoln and afterward remains to be fully cataloged, and likely never will be given how much of it was published anonymously and pseudonymously. Even so, *Willa Cather: A Bibliography* includes an extensive list of her articles and reviews; this list has been reproduced online in the Cather archive. Joan Crane, *Willa Cather: A Bibliography* (Lincoln: University of Nebraska Press, 1982), 255–311. https://cather.unl.edu/writings/journalism/bibliography.

33. Woodress, *Willa Cather*, 102.

34. Garry Wills, *Verdi's Shakespeare: Men of the Theater* (New York: Penguin, 2012), 103.

35. Cather, "Uncle Valentine," 235.

36. Willa Cather, "Coming, Aphrodite!," in *Willa Cather: Stories, Poems, & Other Writings*, ed. Sharon O'Brien (New York: Library of America, 1992), 362.

37. Willa Cather, "The Diamond Mine," in *Willa Cather: Stories, Poems, & Other Writings*, ed. Sharon O'Brien (New York: Library of America, 1992), 414.

38. Cather, *Song of the Lark*, 474.

39. Lewis, *Willa Cather Living*, 89.

40. Willa Cather, "Three American Singers: Louise Homer, Geraldine Farrar, Olive Fremstad," *McClure's Magazine* 42 (December 1913): 33–48. See also Jonathan Goldberg's chapter "Cather Diva" in *Willa Cather & Others* (Durham, NC: Duke University Press, 2001).

41. Cather, "Three American Singers," 35.

42. Cather, "Three American Singers," 36.

43. Cather, "Three American Singers," 38.

44. Cather, "Three American Singers," 44.

45. Cather, "Three American Singers," 46.

46. Cather, "Three American Singers," 44.

47. Willa Cather to Elizabeth Shepley Sargent, April 22, 1913, in *The Selected Letters of Willa Cather*, ed. Andrew Jewell and Janis Stout (New York: Knopf, 2013), 177.

48. Cather, "Three American Singers," 42.

49. Richard Giannone, *Music in Willa Cather's Fiction* (Lincoln: University of Nebraska Press, 2001), 6.

50. Catherine Clément, *Opera, or the Undoing of Women* (Minneapolis: University of Minnesota Press, 1999), 12, 17. The libretto is chronically overlooked. In what Patrick J. Smith calls "The Pathetic Fallacy of Opera," people tend to think of opera as a creation of the composer "for two reasons," the first of which is that it's easier to write "Verdi" than to look up which of his librettists is attached to a particular work and the other because very little is known about librettists and much about composers. Patrick J. Smith, *The Tenth Muse: A Historical Study of the Opera Libretto* (New York: Knopf, 1970), xviii.

51. Cather, *Song of the Lark*, 517.

52. Cather, "Three American Singers," 47.

53. Wallace Dace, *Opera as Dramatic Poetry* (New York: Vantage, 1993), ix.

54. Willa Cather to Elizabeth Shepley Sargent, New York City, February 24, 1914, in *Selected Letters*, 187.

55. Willa Cather to Carrie Miner Sherwood, New York City, March 13, 1918, in *Selected Letters*, 192. This passage itself is worth a book.

56. Willa Cather to Elizabeth Shepley Sargent, Pittsburgh, June 23, 1914, in *Selected Letters*, 192.

57. Willa Cather to Elizabeth Shepley Sargent, Pittsburgh, December 7, 1915, in *Selected Letters*, 212. Willa Cather to Ferris Greenslet, Pittsburgh, November 17, 1915, in *Selected Letters*, 210.

58. Giannone, *Music in Willa Cather's Fiction*, 213.

59. Flannigan, "Before Its Romanzas," 285.

60. Willa Cather, "A Chance Meeting," in *Willa Cather: Stories, Poems, & Other Writings,* ed. Sharon O'Brien (New York: Library of America, 1992), 824.

61. Cather, "A Chance Meeting," 825.

62. Slote, *Kingdom,* 34.

63. Willa Cather, "The Novel Démeublé," in *Willa Cather: Stories, Poems, & Other Writings,* ed. Sharon O'Brien (New York: Library of America, 1992), 835.

64. Willa Cather, "The Bohemian Girl," in *Willa Cather: Stories, Poems, & Other Writings,* ed. Sharon O'Brien (New York: Library of America, 1992), 119.

65. Cather, "Uncle Valentine," 229.

66. Slote, *Kingdom,* 132.

67. Cather, *My Ántonia,* 912.

68. Flannigan, "Before Its Romanzas," 283.

69. Bohlke, *Cather in Person,* 169.

70. Giannone, *Music in Willa Cather's Fiction,* 6.

71. Willa Cather, "Escapism," in *Willa Cather: Stories, Poems, & Other Writings,* ed. Sharon O'Brien (New York: Library of America, 1992), 968.

CHAPTER 2

Wagner and Church Choirs: Opera in America in Cather's Time

Note to epigraph: John Dizikes, *Opera in America: A Cultural History* (New Haven, CT: Yale University Press, 1993), 58.

1. Carmen Trammell Skaggs, *Overtones of Opera in American Literature from Whitman to Wharton* (Baton Rouge: Louisiana State University Press, 2010), 1.

2. Charles Burney, "The New Technique for Marrying Words and Music," in *The Faber Book of Opera,* ed. Tom Sutcliffe (London: Faber, 2000), 79.

3. Skaggs, *Overtones of Opera,* 1.

4. Elise K. Kirk, *American Opera* (Urbana: University of Illinois Press, 2001), 1.

5. Kirk, *American Opera,* 38.

6. Dizikes, *Opera in America,* 3.

7. Kirk, *American Opera,* 12.

8. Dizikes, *Opera in America,* 42.

9. Dizikes, *Opera in America,* 9.

10. Dizikes, *Opera in America,* 26.

11. Dizikes, *Opera in America,* 58.

12. Dizikes, *Opera in America,* 59.

13. Quoted in Dizikes, *Opera in America,* 269.

14. Dizikes, *Opera in America*, 269–270.

15. John H. Flannigan, "Words and Music Made Flesh in Cather's 'Eric Hermannson's Soul,'" *Studies in Short Fiction* 32, no. 2 (1995): 213.

16. Marilyn Arnold, *Willa Cather's Short Fiction* (Athens: Ohio University Press, 1984), 21.

17. Woodress, *Willa Cather*, 250.

18. Woodress, *Willa Cather*, 294–295.

19. Willa Cather, "The Joy of Nelly Deane," in *Willa Cather: Stories, Poems, & Other Writings*, ed. Sharon O'Brien (New York: Library of America, 1992), 76.

20. Cather, "The Joy of Nelly Deane," 80.

21. Cather, "Three American Singers," 48.

22. Willa Cather, *O Pioneers!*, in *Willa Cather: Early Novels and Stories*, ed. Sharon O'Brien (New York: Library of America, 1987), 262.

23. Cather, *My Ántonia*, 824.

24. Cather, *Song of the Lark*, 496–497.

25. Willa Cather to Dorothy Canfield Fisher, March 15, 1916, in *Selected Letters*, 218.

26. Bohlke, *Willa Cather in Person*, 123–124.

27. Willa Cather, "My First Novels (There Were Two)," in *Willa Cather: Stories, Poems, & Other Writings*, ed. Sharon O'Brien (New York: Library of America, 1992), 964.

28. Bohlke, *Willa Cather in Person*, 42.

29. Bohlke, *Willa Cather in Person*, 68–70.

30. Slote, *Kingdom*, 134.

31. Willa Cather, *Lucy Gayheart*, in *Willa Cather: Later Novels*, ed. Sharon O'Brien (New York: Library of America, 1990), 746–747.

32. Willa Cather to Will Owen Jones, March 6, 1904, in *Selected Letters*, 80.

33. Bohlke, *Willa Cather in Person*, 185.

34. Cornelia Andrews DuBois, "Operatic Pioneers: The Story of the Andrews Family," *Minnesota History*, 33, no. 8 (1953), 325.

35. Dizikes, *Opera in America*, 263.

36. Dizikes, *Opera in America*, 258.

37. Dizikes, *Opera in America*, 260.

38. Dizikes, *Opera in America*, 260.

39. Kirk, *American Opera*, 39, 103.

40. Charles Affron and Mirella Jona Affron, *Grand Opera: The Story of the Met* (Berkeley: University of California Press, 2014), 147.

41. Satterthwaite, *Local Glories*, 35.

42. Dizikes, *Opera in America*, 259.

43. Affron, *Grand Opera*, 33.

44. Woodress, *Willa Cather*, 65–66.

45. Kirk, *American Opera*, 126–127.

46. Woodress, *Willa Cather,* 129.

47. Woodress, *Willa Cather,* 129–130.

48. Lewis, *Willa Cather Living,* 46.

49. Skaggs, *Overtones of Opera,* 4.

50. Dizikes, *Opera in America,* 239.

51. Dizikes, *Opera in America,* 243.

52. Kirk, *American Opera,* 121–122.

53. Jed Rasula, "Wagnerism: A Telephone from the Beyond," *Georgia Review* 65, no. 2 (2011): 404.

54. Kirk, *American Opera,* 124. Cosima's objection might have been merely strategic, as Wagnerian knickknackery had been the norm at Bayreuth for years. During the 1876 festival that featured the first full *Ring,* "shops were full of tacky merchandise, with Wagner's face emblazoned on beer mugs, pipe bowls, cigar boxes, and sundry toiletries." The Reuter Wagner Museum in Eisenach has a collection that includes "Wagner figurines, Wagner pipes, Bayreuth paperweights, Wagner candlestick holders, Wagner plates and mugs, Siegfried slippers, and Rheingold *sekt.*" Restaurants of the period were known to serve Siegfried Schnitzel, Wotan Ham à la Walhall, and Nibelung Dumplings. Ross, *Wagnerism,* 47, 135, 203.

55. Dizikes, *Opera in America,* 231.

56. Affron, *Grand Opera,* 25.

57. Dizikes, *Opera in America,* 232.

58. Lewis, *Willa Cather Living,* 74.

CHAPTER 3

Rustic Chivalry: Opera in Cather's Early Fiction

Note to epigraph: Slote, *Kingdom,* 49.

1. Bohlke, *Willa Cather in Person,* 140.

2. Mildred Bennett, *The World of Willa Cather* (Lincoln: University of Nebraska Press, 1989), 178.

3. Bohlke, *Willa Cather in Person,* 142.

4. Bohlke, *Willa Cather in Person,* 141.

5. *Selected Letters,* 13.

6. Slote, *Kingdom,* 142.

7. Willa Cather, "The Fear That Walks by Noonday," *The Sombrero* (1895), 225. https:// cather.unl.edu/writings/shortfiction/ss025. All subsequent references to Cather's uncollected short fiction originate from the short fiction listings of the Cather archive at https://cather. unl.edu/writings/shortfiction.

8. Willa Cather, "An Open Letter to Nordica," in *The World and the Parish: Willa Cather's*

Articles and Reviews, 1893–1902, ed. William M. Curtin (Lincoln: University of Nebraska Press, 1970), 643.

9. Cather, "An Open Letter to Nordica, 645.

10. Willa Cather, "Three Operas," in *The World and the Parish: Willa Cather's Articles and Reviews, 1893–1902*, ed. William M. Curtin (Lincoln: University of Nebraska Press, 1970), 656.

11. Slote, *Kingdom*, 116.

12. "It was probably submitted on Willa Cather's behalf by her English instructor, Herbert Bates, a young New Englander and a Harvard graduate. [. . .] In her mature years Willa Cather believed that Bates had stimulated her to publish stories in the magazines before she had the command of her craft; but the encouragement he gave her, if it may have been somewhat uncritical, helped a great deal more than it hurt." E. K. Brown, *Willa Cather: A Critical Biography* (New York: Knopf, 1953), 57.

13. Willa Cather, "Peter," in *Willa Cather: Stories, Poems, & Other Writings*, ed. Sharon O'Brien (New York: Library of America, 1992), 5.

14. Bennett, *World of Willa Cather*, 32.

15. This quote is expediently expurgated. Cather didn't write "child" but "n****r boy" in this passage. I've trimmed the quote not so much to protect Cather's reputation—her racial problematics have yet to be, but should be, fully explored in scholarship—but so as not to distract from the main point of this paragraph.

16. Giannone, *Music in Willa Cather's Fiction*, 25.

17. Kennicott, introduction to *Music in Willa Cather's Fiction*, ix.

18. Willa Cather, "Eric Hermannson's Soul," in *Willa Cather: Stories, Poems, & Other Writings*, ed. Sharon O'Brien (New York: Library of America, 1992), 23.

19. Cather, "Eric Hermannson's Soul," 24.

20. Cather, "Eric Hermannson's Soul," 26.

21. Cather, "Three Operas," in *World and the Parish*, 657.

22. Flannigan, "Words and Music Made Flesh," 212.

23. Cather, "Eric Hermannson's Soul," 44.

CHAPTER 4

Cather and Her Artists: Evolving Short Fiction

Note to epigraph: Willa Cather, *The Autobiography of S. S. McClure*, in *McClure's Magazine* 42 (January 1914), 108. https://cather.unl.edu/ writings/books/nf006_04.

1. Will Owen Jones, "More or Less Personal," *Nebraska State Journal* (Lincoln, NE), Feb. 24, 1904. Incidentally, the same issue of the *Journal* offered a sunny take on the Manchurian effort against the Russians in the Russo-Japanese War of 1904–1905.

2. Willa Cather to Will Owen Jones, March 6, 1904, in *The Selected Letters of Willa Cather*, ed. Andrew Jewell and Janis Stout (New York: Knopf, 2013), 80.

3. Woodress, *Willa Cather*, 178.

4. The Library of America edition of Cather's work features the *Youth and the Bright Medusa* versions of stories in Vol. I and *The Troll Garden* versions in Vol. II; my comparison texts come from these sources. When only one version is referenced, I will cite to *Youth and the Bright Medusa*. "A Wagner Matinée" in *Willa Cather: Stories, Poems, & Other Writings*, ed. Sharon O'Brien (New York: Library of America, 1992), 493. "A Wagner Matinée" in *Willa Cather: Early Novels and Stories*, ed. Sharon O'Brien (New York: Library of America, 1987), 107.

5. Woodress, *Willa Cather*, 309.

6. Woodress, *Willa Cather*, 312.

7. Cather, "Wagner," 490.

8. Cather, "Wagner," 491.

9. Giannone, *Music in Willa Cather's Fiction*, 44.

10. Cather, "Wagner," 493.

11. Cather, "Wagner," 495.

12. Cather, "Wagner," 496.

13. Cather, "Three American Singers," 36.

14. Cather, "Paul's Case," 472. For a complete list of emendations and substitutions between the editions, see the emendations section of the scholarly edition of *Youth and the Bright Medusa:* https://cather.unl.edu/writings/books/0021.

15. Cather, "Paul's Case," 475.

16. Cather, "Paul's Case," 478.

17. Cather, "Paul's Case," 483.

18. Bennett, *World of Willa Cather*, 112.

19. Willa Cather, "The Joy of Nelly Deane," in *Willa Cather: Stories, Poems, & Other Writings*, ed. Sharon O'Brien (New York: Library of America, 1992), 80.

20. Woodress, *Willa Cather*, 227.

21. Giannone, *Music in Willa Cather's Fiction*, 51–52. Cather had seen *The Bohemian Girl* in her teens, and five different companies performed it in Lincoln while she was in school there. Eleven companies mounted twelve productions of it in Pittsburgh during Cather's time in that city. John H. Flannigan, "*The Bohemian Girl* and *Lucy Gayheart:* Cather's Valediction to Opera," *Willa Cather Review* 62, no. 1 (2020): 42.

22. Richard Aldrich, introduction to Michael William Balfe, *The Bohemian Girl* (New York: Schirmer, 1902).

23. Willa Cather, "The Bohemian Girl," in *Willa Cather: Stories, Poems, & Other Writings*, ed. Sharon O'Brien (New York: Library of America, 1992), 126.

24. E. K. Brown, *Willa Cather: A Critical Biography* (New York: Knopf, 1953), 165.

25. Wayne Koestenbaum, *The Queen's Throat: Opera, Homosexuality, and the Mystery of Desire* (New York: Poseidon, 1993), 20, 26, 22, 24.

26. John H. Flannigan, "Domenico Cimarosa: A Possible Source for *The Professor's House*," *Willa Cather Pioneer Memorial Newsletter* 38, no. 4 (1994): 19. See also Mark Madigan's historical essay on the sources of the stories of *Youth and the Bright Medusa*. https://cather.unl.edu/writings/books/0021.

27. Willa Cather, "The Diamond Mine," in *Willa Cather: Stories, Poems, & Other Writings,* ed. Sharon O'Brien (New York: Library of America, 1992), 429.

28. Cather, "The Diamond Mine," 431.

29. Willa Cather, "A Gold Slipper," in *Willa Cather: Stories, Poems, & Other Writings*, ed. Sharon O'Brien (New York: Library of America, 1992), 435.

30. Woodress, *Willa Cather*, 282.

31. Giroud, *French Opera*, 239–240. "Garden, Mary," in *Metropolitan Opera Encyclopedia: A Comprehensive Guide to the World of Opera*, ed. David Hamilton (London: Thames & Hudson, 1987).

32. Cather, "Gold Slipper," 442.

33. Woodress, *Willa Cather*, 282.

34. Joan Acocella, *Willa Cather and the Politics of Criticism* (New York: Vintage, 2002), 2.

35. Willa Cather, "The Garden Lodge," in *Willa Cather: Early Novels and Stories*, ed. Sharon O'Brien (New York: Library of America, 1987), 50.

36. Cather, "The Garden Lodge," 56–57.

37. John H. Flannigan wonders whether Cather is "misremembering her Wagner and confusing Sieglinde's words with Siegmund's? Or is Caroline's hearing playing tricks on her, inverting the roles of the love duet [. . .] thus adding to the phantasmagoria of her dream?" This blending of gender, along with other Wagner references in the story, could indicate that Caroline is less fixated on d'Esquerré than she is on her own power, that she is possessed of an "idea that has the sexual potency of a man without its being embodied in a masculine figure." On any account, it diminishes the sense that the story is about "Caroline's entrapment in a conventional love triangle." "Issues of Gender and Lesbian Love: Goblins in 'The Garden Lodge,'" *Cather Studies* 2 (1993): 34.

38. Cather, "Garden Lodge," 78.

39. Woodress, *Willa Cather*, 315.

40. Woodress, *Willa Cather*, 312–313.

41. Willa Cather, "Coming, Aphrodite!" in *Willa Cather: Stories, Poems, & Other Writings*, ed. Sharon O'Brien (New York: Library of America, 1992), 362.

42. Affron, *Grand Opera*, 47.

43. Cather, "Coming, Aphrodite!," 366.

44. Cather, "Coming, Aphrodite!," 389.

45. Cather, "Coming, Aphrodite!," 387.

CHAPTER 5.
Entr'acte: *Alexander's Bridge*

Note to epigraph: Willa Cather, Preface to *Alexander's Bridge*, in *Willa Cather: Stories, Poems, & Other Writings*, ed. Sharon O'Brien (New York: Library of America, 1992), 942.

1. Willa Cather, "Behind the Singer Tower," *Collier's* (May 18, 1912), 16. https://cather.unl.edu/writings/shortfiction/ss045.

2. Woodress, *Willa Cather*, 216.

3. Sharon O'Brien, *Willa Cather: The Emerging Voice* (New York: Oxford University Press, 1987), 384.

4. Willa Cather, "My First Novels (There Were Two)," in *Willa Cather: Stories, Poems, & Other Writings*, ed. Sharon O'Brien (New York: Library of America, 1992), 963.

5. Henry W. Simon, *100 Great Operas and Their Stories* (New York: Doubleday, 1960), 5.

6. Willa Cather, *Alexander's Bridge*, in *Willa Cather: Stories, Poems, & Other Writings*, ed. Sharon O'Brien (New York: Library of America, 1992), 285.

7. Cather, *Alexander's Bridge*, 282.

8. Cather, *My Ántonia*, 912.

9. Cather, *Alexander's Bridge*, 284.

10. See, generally, Loretta Wasserman, "*Alexander's Bridge:* The 'Other' First Novel," *Cather Studies* 4 (1999).

11. Cather, *Alexander's Bridge*, 299.

12. Cather, *Alexander's Bridge*, 337.

13. Cather, *Alexander's Bridge*, 344.

14. Cather, *Alexander's Bridge*, 328.

15. Cather, "A Wagner Matinée," in *Willa Cather: Stories, Poems, & Other Writings*, ed. Sharon O'Brien (New York: Library of America, 1992), 495.

16. Woodress, *Willa Cather*, 216.

CHAPTER 6
Prose Operas: *O Pioneers!* and *My Ántonia*

Note to epigraph: Cather, *O Pioneers!*, 156.

1. Mary Jane Humphrey, "'The White Mulberry Tree' as Opera," *Cather Studies* 3 (1996): 55.

2. Humphrey, "The White Mulberry Tree," 54.

3. See, e.g., Charles M. Smith, "*Eric Hermannson's Soul:* Comparing and Contrasting Two Musical Adaptations of the Willa Cather Short Story," (PhD diss., University of Nebraska, 2006).

4. Cather, *O Pioneers!*, 135.

5. Woodress, *Willa Cather,* 229.

6. Cather, *O Pioneers!,* 139.

7. Giannone, *Music in Willa Cather's Fiction,* 79.

8. Cather, *O Pioneers!,* 197.

9. Cather, *O Pioneers!,* 196.

10. Cather, *O Pioneers!,* 238.

11. Cather, *O Pioneers!,* 263.

12. Cather, *My Ántonia,* 718.

13. Cather, *My Ántonia,* 737.

14. Jane Smiley, introduction to *My Ántonia* (New York: Vintage, 2018), xi.

15. Cather, *My Ántonia,* 824.

16. Reginald DeKoven, *Robin Hood* (New York: Burr, 1896), 21.

17. Cather, *My Ántonia,* 894.

18. Willa Cather to Ferris Greenslet, March 7, 1918, in *The Selected Letters of Willa Cather,* ed. Andrew Jewell and Janis Stout (New York: Knopf, 2013), 252.

19. Carolyn Abbate and Roger Parker, *A History of Opera* (New York: Norton, 2015), 379.

20. Cather, *My Ántonia,* 881–884.

CHAPTER 7

Bitter Contempt: *The Song of the Lark* and Cather's Wagnerism

Note to epigraph: George Bernard Shaw, *The Perfect Wagnerite* (New York: Dover, 2015), 35.

1. Willa Cather, preface to the 1937 Autograph Edition of *The Song of the Lark,* in *Willa Cather: Early Novels and Stories,* ed. Sharon O'Brien (New York: Library of America, 1987), 1328.

2. Flannigan, "Before Its Romanzas," 285.

3. Brown, *Willa Cather,* 189.

4. Woodress, *Willa Cather,* 272.

5. Hermione Lee, *Willa Cather: Double Lives* (New York: Vintage, 2017), 118.

6. Willa Cather to Dorothy Canfield Fisher, October 22, 1925, in *The Selected Letters of Willa Cather,* ed. Andrew Jewell and Janis Stout (New York: Knopf, 2013), 375.

7. Woodress, *Willa Cather,* 260–261.

8. Cather, preface to *Song of the Lark,* 1328.

9. Dizikes, *Opera in America,* 277.

10. Ross, *Wagnerism,* 323, 325.

11. Rasula, "Wagnerism," 400.

12. Qtd. in Rasula, "Wagnerism," 408.

13. Ross, *Wagnerism,* 15.

14. Philip Kennicott, "Wagner, Place, and the Growth of Pessimism in the Fiction of Willa Cather," *Cather Studies* 5 (2003): 191–192.

15. Cather, "Uncle Valentine," 235.

16. Willa Cather, preface to Gertrude Hall's "The Wagnerian Romances," in *Willa Cather: Early Novels and Stories,* ed. Sharon O'Brien (New York: Library of America, 1987), 951.

17. Gertrude Hall, *The Wagnerian Romances* (New York: Knopf, 1942), 90.

18. Hall, *The Wagnerian Romances,* 82.

19. Hall, *The Wagnerian Romances,* 134.

20. Cather, preface to "The Wagnerian R,omances," 952.

21. Hall, *The Wagnerian Romances,* 37.

22. Paul Schofield, *The Redeemer Reborn: Parsifal as the Fifth Opera of Wagner's Ring* (New York: Amadeus, 2007), 50.

23. Schofield, *Redeemer Reborn,* 53.

24. Hall, *The Wagnerian Romances,* 190.

25. Willa Cather to Dorothy Canfield Fisher, New York City, March 15, 1916, in *Selected Letters,* 218.

26. Shaw, *Perfect Wagnerite,* xix.

27. Shaw, *Perfect Wagnerite,* 17.

28. Shaw, *Perfect Wagnerite,* 17–18.

29. Shaw, *Perfect Wagnerite,* 20.

30. Willa Cather, "The Perfect Wagnerite," in *The World and the Parish: Willa Cather's Articles and Reviews, 1893–1902,* ed. William M. Curtin (Lincoln: University of Nebraska Press, 1970), 617–618.

31. Acocella, *Politics of Interpretation,* 26.

32. Kennicott, "Wagner, Place, and the Growth of Pessimism," 194.

33. Cather, *My Ántonia,* 742.

34. Dizikes, *Opera in America,* 244.

35. Cather, *Song of the Lark,* 468.

36. H. R. Haweis, *My Musical Memories* (New York: Funk & Wagnalls, 1884), 144.

37. Haweis, *My Musical Memories,* 146–147.

38. Haweis, *My Musical Memories,* 155.

39. Shaw, *Perfect Wagnerite,* vii.

40. Giannone, *Music in Willa Cather's Fiction,* 11.

41. Oddly, Hermione Lee cites his name as "Fritz" Wunsch, but that prenom has no other attestation. It is probably a confusion with Fritz Kohler, one of Wunsch's drinking buddies. *Willa Cather,* 125.

42. Cather, *Song of the Lark,* 319.

43. Cather, *Song of the Lark,* 362.

44. Cather, *Song of the Lark,* 363. Sarah L. Young, "The Singer as Artist: Willa Cather,

Olive Fremstad, and the Artist's Voice," *Cather Studies* 12 (2020), https://cather.unl.edu/scholarship/catherstudies/12/cs012.young.

45. Cather, *Song of the Lark,* 347.

46. Cather, *Song of the Lark,* 356.

47. Cather, *Song of the Lark,* 363.

48. Cather, *Song of the Lark,* 379.

49. Cather, *Song of the Lark,* 468.

50. Cather, *Song of the Lark,* 469.

51. Cather, *Song of the Lark,* 470.

52. Cather, *Song of the Lark,* 484.

53. Cather, *Song of the Lark,* 495.

54. Cather, *Song of the Lark,* 504.

55. Cather, *Song of the Lark,* 511.

56. Cather, *Song of the Lark,* 523.

57. Cather, *Song of the Lark,* 537.

58. Cather, *Song of the Lark,* 536.

59. Cather, *Song of the Lark,* 530, 627.

60. Cather, *Song of the Lark,* 509.

61. Cather, *Song of the Lark,* 548.

62. Cather, *Song of the Lark,*

63. Cather, *Song of the Lark,* 550.

64. Edgar Allan Poe, "The Poetic Principle," in *Edgar Allan Poe: Poetry, Tales, and Selected Essays* (New York: Library of America, 1984), 1437.

65. Cather, *Song of the Lark,* 626.

66. Cather, *Song of the Lark,* 638–639.

67. Cather, *Song of the Lark,* 640. The idea of Thea as a wolf that ate Red Ridinghood is highly evocative of the "vocal transvestism" posited by John H. Flannigan and Elizabeth Wood, the idea that the vocal range produced by one's throat allows for "transgressive and transvestite possibilities of the contralto voice" facilitating "progress toward sexual awareness and professional success." While the distinctly physical component of Thea's progress is beyond the scope of this discussion, it's worth noting that other commentators have made observations about the external importance of Thea's face to illustrate her internal dimensions. John H. Flannigan, "Thea Kronborg's Vocal Transvestism: Willa Cather and the 'Voz Contralto,'" *Modern Fiction Studies* 40, no. 4 (1994): 738; Elizabeth Wood, "Sapphonics," in *Queering the Pitch: The New Gay and Lesbian Musicology,* ed. Philip Brett, Elizabeth Wood, and Gary C. Thomas (New York: Routledge, 2006), 33–34.

68. Cather, *Song of the Lark,* 649.

69. Cather, *Song of the Lark,* 672.

70. Cather, *Song of the Lark,* 674.

71. Cather, *Song of the Lark*, 686.

72. Cather, *Song of the Lark*, 681.

73. Cather, *Song of the Lark*, 680.

74. Cather, *Song of the Lark*, 697.

75. Cather, *Song of the Lark*, 698–699.

CHAPTER 8.

Opera Incognita: Later Novels

Note to epigraph: Cather, *Lucy Gayheart*, 722.

1. Willa Cather, prefatory note to *Not under Forty*, in *Willa Cather: Stories, Poems, & Other Writings*, ed. Sharon O'Brien (New York: Library of America, 1992), 812.

2. Dizikes, *Opera in America*, 243.

3. Possibly *Ernani*, which premiered in Venice in 1844. The priests also discuss "the Lombard war," presumably the first Italian War of Independence, which took place 1848–1849. Willa Cather, *Death Comes for the Archbishop*, in *Willa Cather: Later Novels*, ed. Sharon O'Brien (New York: Library of America, 1990), 284.

4. Bohlke, *Cather in Person*, 52–53.

5. Willa Cather, *One of Ours*, in *Willa Cather: Early Novels and Stories*, ed. Sharon O'Brien (New York: Library of America, 1987), 1227.

6. Kennicott, "Wagner, Place, and the Growth of Pessimism," 195.

7. Kennicott, "Wagner, Place, and the Growth of Pessimism," 197.

8. Willa Cather to Dorothy Canfield Fisher, New York City, April 7, 1922, in *Selected Letters*, 318.

9. Willa Cather, *The Professor's House*, in *Willa Cather: Later Novels*, ed. Sharon O'Brien (New York: Library of America, 1990), 151. Flannigan, "Domenico Cimarosa," 19.

10. Cather, *The Professor's House*, 161.

11. Cather, *The Professor's House*, 115.

12. Cather, *The Professor's House*, 271.

13. Carmen Skaggs, "The Transporting Power of Opera: *Mignon* in Willa Cather's *The Professor's House*," *The Explicator* 71, no. 2 (2013), 134.

14. Giannone, *Music in Willa Cather's Fiction*, 213.

15. Willa Cather, "Shakespeare and Hamlet," *Nebraska State Journal* (Lincoln, NE), November 1, 1891, 16, https://cather.unl.edu/writings/nonfiction/nf064.

16. Slote, *Kingdom*, 33.

17. Slote, *Kingdom*, 34.

18. Giannone, *Music in Willa Cather's Fiction*, 126.

19. Willa Cather, *My Mortal Enemy*, in *Willa Cather: Stories, Poems, & Other Writings*, ed.

Sharon O'Brien (New York: Library of America, 1992), 555.

20. Giannone, *Music in Willa Cather's Fiction,* 182.

21. Qtd. in Carol Kimball, *Art Song: Linking Poetry and Music* (Milwaukee, WI: Hal Leonard, 2013), 18.

22. Giannone, *Music in Willa Cather's Fiction,* 214.

23. Cather, *Lucy Gayheart,* 665.

24. Cather, *Lucy Gayheart.*

25. Carol Kimball, *Song: A Guide to Art Song Style and Literature* (Milwaukee, WI: Hal Leonard, 2005), 67.

26. Cather, *Lucy Gayheart,* 650.

27. Giannone, *Music in Willa Cather's Fiction,* 227.

28. Cather, *Lucy Gayheart,* 657.

29. Cather, *Lucy Gayheart,* 703–704.

30. Cather, *Lucy Gayheart,* 745.

31. Flannigan, "Cather's Evolving Ear." Flannigan also notes the vaguely apocalyptic fact that this scene is set shortly after the première of Puccini's *Turandot,* the emphatic punctuation of pre-Modern opera. Flannigan, "*The Bohemian Girl,*" 44.

32. Cather, *Lucy Gayheart,* 746–747.

33. Cather, *Lucy Gayheart,* 770.

Conclusion

Note to epigraph: Cather, *Death Comes for the Archbishop,* 454.

1. Truman Capote, "Willa, Truman. Truman, Willa," *vanityfair.com, Vanity Fair,* November 2006, https://www.vanityfair.com/news/2006/11/capote-200611.

2. Qtd. in Jo Ann Middleton, *Willa Cather's Modernism: A Study of Style and Technique* (Rutherford, NJ: Fairleigh Dickinson University Press, 1990), 21.

3. Bohlke, *Cather in Person,* 184.

4. Dizikes, *Opera in America,* 269.

BIBLIOGRAPHY

Primary Texts

For the sake of consistency and ease of access, all of Cather's collected primary texts, unless otherwise indicated, are referenced from the following Library of America volumes of Cather's work:

O'Brien, Sharon, ed. *Willa Cather: Stories, Poems, and Other Writings.* New York: Library of America, 1992.

———. *Willa Cather: Early Novels and Stories.* New York: Library of America, 1987.

———. *Willa Cather: Later Novels.* New York: Library of America, 1990.

Unless otherwise indicated, references to Cather's uncollected short fiction come from the short fiction section of the University of Nebraska Cather Archive online:

"Index to Short Fiction." *Willa Cather Archive.* University of Nebraska. Updated 2020. https://cather.unl.edu/writings/shortfiction.

Other Texts

Abbate, Carolyn, and Roger Parker. *A History of Opera.* New York: Norton, 2015.

Acocella, Joan. *Willa Cather and the Politics of Criticism.* New York: Vintage, 2002.

Affron, Charles, and Mirella Jona Affron. *Grand Opera: The Story of the Met.* Berkeley: University of California Press, 2014.

Arnold, Marilyn. *Willa Cather's Short Fiction.* Athens: Ohio University Press, 1984.

Bennett, Mildred. *The World of Willa Cather.* Lincoln: University of Nebraska Press, 1989.

Bohlke, L. Brent, ed., *Willa Cather in Person: Interviews, Speeches, and Letters.* Lincoln: University of Nebraska Press, 1990.

Brown, E. K. *Willa Cather: A Critical Biography.* New York: Knopf, 1953.

Burney, Charles. "The New Technique for Marrying Words and Music." In *The Faber Book of Opera,* edited by Tom Sutcliffe. London: Faber, 2000.

Capote, Truman. "Willa, Truman. Truman, Willa." *Vanity Fair.* November 2006. https://www.vanityfair.com/news/2006/11/capote-200611.

Cather, Willa. "Three American Singers: Louise Homer, Geraldine Farrar, Olive Fremstad." *McClure's Magazine* 42 (December 1913): 33–48.

"The Chimes of Normandy." *Internet Broadway Database.* Accessed October 9,
2019. https://www.ibdb.com/broadway-production/the-chimes-of-norman-
dy-412125.

Clément, Catherine. *Opera, or the Undoing of Women.* Minneapolis: University of
Minnesota Press, 1999.

Crane, Joan. *Willa Cather: A Bibliography.* Lincoln: University of Nebraska Press,
1982.

Curtin, William M., ed. *The World and the Parish,* 2 vols. Lincoln: University of Nebraska Press, 1970.

Dace, Wallace. *Opera as Dramatic Poetry.* New York: Vantage, 1993.

Dizikes, John. *Opera in America: A Cultural History.* New Haven, CT: Yale University
Press, 1993.

DuBois, Cornelia Andrews. "Operatic Pioneers: The Story of the Andrews Family."
Minnesota History 33, no. 8 (1953): 317–325.

Flannigan, John H. "'Before Its Romanzas Have Become Street Music': Cather and
Verdi's *Falstaff,* Chicago, 1895." *Cather Studies* 9 (2011): 266–288.

———. "*The Bohemian Girl* and *Lucy Gayheart:* Cather's Valediction to Opera." *Willa Cather Review* 62, no. 1 (2020): 40–46.

———. "Cather's Evolving Ear: Music Reheard in the Late Fiction." *Cather Studies*
12 (2020). https://cather.unl.edu/scholarship/catherstudies/12/cs012.flannigan.

———. "Domenico Cimarosa: A Possible Source for *The Professor's House.*" *Willa
Cather Pioneer Memorial Newsletter* 38, no. 4 (1994): 19–20.

———. "Issues of Lesbian Love and Gender: Goblins in 'The Garden Lodge.'" *Cather
Studies* 2 (1993): 23–40.

———. "Thea Kronborg's Vocal Transvestism: Willa Cather and the 'Voz Contralto.'"
Modern Fiction Studies 40, no. 4 (1994): 737–763.

———. "Words and Music Made Flesh in Willa Cather's 'Eric Hermannson's Soul.'"
Studies in Short Fiction 32 (1995): 209–216.

Giannone, Richard. *Music in Willa Cather's Fiction.* Lincoln: University of Nebraska
Press, 2001.

Giroud, Vincent. *French Opera: A Short History.* New Haven, CT: Yale University
Press, 2010.

Goldberg, Jonathan. *Willa Cather and Others.* Durham, NC: Duke University Press,
2001.

Grout, Donald Jay, and Hermine Weigel Williams. *A Short History of Opera,* 4th ed.
New York: Columbia University Press, 2003.

Hall, Gertrude. *The Wagnerian Romances.* New York: Knopf, 1942.

Hamilton, David, ed. *Metropolitan Opera Encyclopedia: A Comprehensive Guide to the World of Opera.* London: Thames & Hudson, 1987.

Haweis, H. R. *My Musical Memories.* (New York: Funk & Wagnalls, 1884.

Humphrey, Mary Jane. "'The White Mulberry Tree' as Opera." *Cather Studies* 3 (1996): 51–66.

Jewell, Andrew, and Janis Stout, eds. *The Selected Letters of Willa Cather.* New York: Knopf, 2013.

Jones, Will Owen. "More or Less Personal." *Nebraska State Journal* (Lincoln, NE), February 24, 1904.

Kennicott, Philip. Introduction to *Music in Willa Cather's Fiction,* by Richard Giannone. Lincoln: University of Nebraska Press, 2001.

———. "Wagner, Place, and the Growth of Pessimism in the Fiction of Willa Cather." *Cather Studies* 5 (2003): 190–198.

Kimball, Carol. *Art Song: Linking Poetry and Music.* Milwaukee, WI: Hal Leonard, 2013.

———. *Song: A Guide to Art Song Style and Literature.* Milwaukee, WI: Hal Leonard, 2005.

Kirk, Elise K. *American Opera.* Urbana: University of Illinois Press, 2001.

Koestenbaum, Wayne. *The Queen's Throat: Opera, Homosexuality, and the Mystery of Desire.* New York: Poseidon, 1993.

Lee, Hermione. *Willa Cather: Double Lives.* New York: Vintage, 2017.

Lewis, Edith. *Willa Cather Living: A Personal Record.* Lincoln: University of Nebraska Press, 2000.

Middleton, Jo Ann. *Willa Cather's Modernism: A Study of Style and Technique.* Rutherford, NJ: Fairleigh Dickinson University Press, 1990.

O'Brien, Sharon. *Willa Cather: The Emerging Voice.* New York: Oxford, 1987.

Poe, Edgar Allan. "The Poetic Principle." In *Edgar Allan Poe: Poetry, Tales, and Selected Essays.* 1431–1454. New York: Library of America, 1984.

Rasula, Jed. "Wagnerism: A Telephone from the Beyond." *Georgia Review* 65, no. 2 (2011): 399–430.

Ross, Alex. *Wagnerism: Art and Politics in the Shadow of Music.* New York: Farrar, 2020.

Satterthwaite, Ann. *Local Glories: Opera Houses on Main Street Where Art and Community Meet.* New York: Oxford University Press, 2016.

Schmidgall, Gary. *Shakespeare and Opera.* New York: Oxford University Press, 1990.

Schofield, Paul. *The Redeemer Reborn: Parsifal as the Fifth Opera of Wagner's Ring.* New York: Amadeus, 2007.

Shaw, George Bernard. *The Perfect Wagnerite.* New York: Dover, 2015.

Simon, Henry W. *100 Great Operas and Their Stories.* New York: Doubleday, 1960.

Skaggs, Carmen Trammell. *Overtones of Opera in American Literature from Whitman to Wharton.* Baton Rouge: Louisiana State University Press, 2001.

———. "The Transporting Power of Opera: *Mignon* in Willa Cather's *The Professor's House." The Explicator* 71, no. 2 (2013): 131–134.

Slote, Bernice, ed. *The Kingdom of Art: Willa Cather's First Principles and Critical Statements, 1893–1896.* Lincoln: University of Nebraska Press, 1966.

Smith, Charles M. *"Eric Hermannson's Soul:* Comparing and Contrasting Two Musical Adaptations of the Willa Cather Short Story." PhD diss., University of Nebraska, 2006.

Smith, Patrick J. *The Tenth Muse.* New York: Knopf, 1970.

Wasserman, Loretta. *"Alexander's Bridge:* The 'Other' First Novel." *Cather Studies* 4 (1999).

Wills, Garry. *Verdi's Shakespeare: Men of the Theater.* New York: Penguin, 2012.

Wood, Elizabeth. "Sapphonics." In *Queering the Pitch: The New Gay and Lesbian Musicology,* ed. Philip Brett, Elizabeth Wood, and Gary C. Thomas. New York: Routledge, 2006: 27–63.

Woodress, James. *Willa Cather: A Literary Life.* Lincoln: University of Nebraska Press, 1987.

Young, Sarah L. "The Singer as Artist: Willa Cather, Olive Fremstad, and the Artist's Voice." *Cather Studies* 12 (2020). https://cather.unl.edu/scholarship/cather-studies/12/cs012.young.

INDEX

INDEX

www.ingramcontent.com/pod-product-compliance
Lightning Source LLC
Chambersburg PA
CBHW030306100426
42812CB00002B/582